Walter Montagu Kerr, J. D. Cooper

The Far Interior - A Narrative of Travel and Adventure...

Vol. 1, Second Edition

Walter Montagu Kerr, J. D. Cooper

The Far Interior - A Narrative of Travel and Adventure...
Vol. 1, Second Edition

ISBN/EAN: 9783337279042

Printed in Europe, USA, Canada, Australia, Japan

Cover: Foto ©Andreas Hilbeck / pixelio.de

More available books at **www.hansebooks.com**

THE FAR INTERIOR:

A NARRATIVE

OF

TRAVEL AND ADVENTURE

FROM

THE CAPE OF GOOD HOPE ACROSS THE ZAMBESI

TO THE

LAKE REGIONS OF CENTRAL AFRICA

BY

WALTER MONTAGU KERR, C.E., F.R.G.S.

WITH NUMEROUS ILLUSTRATIONS ENGRAVED BY
MR. J. D. COOPER AND OTHERS

IN TWO VOLUMES.—Vol. I.

SECOND EDITION.

LONDON
SAMPSON LOW, MARSTON, SEARLE & RIVINGTON
CROWN BUILDINGS, 188, FLEET STREET
1887

(The right of Translation is reserved.)

TO

The Earl of Dunraven, K.P.,

WHOSE INSPIRING COUNSEL AND KIND ENCOURAGEMENT STRENGTHENED

THE DESIRE FOR THOSE TRAVELS, OF WHICH THE

FOLLOWING PAGES ARE A RECORD,

THIS BOOK

𝔍𝔰 𝔞𝔣𝔣𝔢𝔠𝔱𝔦𝔬𝔫𝔞𝔱𝔢𝔩𝔶 𝔇𝔢𝔡𝔦𝔠𝔞𝔱𝔢𝔡,

BY HIS KINSMAN AND FRIEND,

THE AUTHOR.

PREFACE.

THESE volumes do not contain the story of an expedition in the accepted meaning of that term: in other words, they do not relate the intentions, progress, and achievements of an organised and fully-equipped company entering and traversing unknown territory. Records of such expeditions, more particularly in connection with African investigation, are numerous; but in the case of the present narrative I hope for a hearing because my journey was undertaken and accomplished *alone*; I was unaided, and had no companionship of white men, neither had I a corps of regularly enlisted carriers.

When, at Chibinga, I was abandoned by the few so far faithful Kaffirs, who had accompanied me northwards from Matabeli-land, I was left to depend upon personal resources— to seek food and guides from the various wild tribes whom I encountered.

From that circumstance I imagine that the recital of my experiences should present a very clear reflection of the natural life of some of the races in south-east equatorial Africa. What I mean by this is, that regularly organised bodies of men, total strangers to the communities they meet with, are often kept at a distance from the people through natural suspicion or prejudice. Being alone, and taking guides merely from tribe to tribe, I was looked upon generally as a sort of curiosity, although it must be remarked that through this very solitariness several dangerous emergencies arose, which might have terminated fatally. Passing as I did from tribe to tribe, I lived during a large stretch of my travels as the Kaffirs lived, mingling freely among them, certainly not from choice, but from stern necessity. Opportunities therefore for observing closely the modes and conditions of native life were unusually good; and if in these pages I have been successful in describing clearly my varied experiences, I hope the result in book form will be considered both a readable as well as a useful contribution to geographical knowledge, especially in its relation to the peoples of Africa. Should my readers be of opinion that I have painted a faithful and tolerably vivid picture, not wearisome to the eye, I shall feel that this self-imposed mission has not been fruitless. With regard to Africa and the Africans, I am convinced that any white man following in my footsteps will not be less kindly received on account of my having preceded him.

It is my fortune to have been the first white to traverse, throughout, the great extent of territory stretching between Cape Colony and the Lake regions of Central Africa. I crossed the Zambesi at Tette, and skirting the Makanga country, passed through Angoni-land, and ultimately reached Lake Nyassa, only to find that the mission station of Livingstonia, which had been the bright goal of my long journey and the centre of my hopes of relief (for by that time I was in a wretched condition), was deserted!

South of the Zambesi I passed through various hitherto unknown lands, and alighted upon the tribe called Makori-kori, now described for the first time.

My rescue at Livingstonia, by the steamer of the African Lakes Company, on board which I found Lieutenant Giraud, the gallant leader of the French Exploring Expedition, may be spoken of as being the climax of a series of happy deliverances without which the journey would have been frustrated on several occasions, even at a very early period of its course. Desertions by followers, scarcity of provisions, and, in later stages, the want of articles for the purposes of barter, landed me frequently in apparently desperate plights, from which by almost miraculous coincidences of fortune I was lifted at the last moment, when my purpose seemed to have been finally balked, and even Hope was well-nigh dead.

When I left Livingstonia, I canoed down the Shiré river, passing through a war between the Mazinjiri and Portuguese.

It is much to be regretted that all, or nearly all the natural history and botanical specimens which I collected were lost, or had to be abandoned. Rapidity of movement precluded close investigation in these and other branches of science. I took, however, every opportunity I could take of making as many geographical observations as possible. These are embodied in the present work, and in the map which accompanies it.

Hunting incidents were numerous, all along the line of travel; and most of the mammalia and birds which I encountered in the chase are mentioned in the narrative. But I have thought it advisable not to dilate too much upon sporting experiences, choosing rather to confine such descriptions to accounts of some of the principal adventures. In omitting some of this matter, I am partly influenced by the knowledge that numerous admirable books on the aspects of the hunter's life are already in existence. With regard to Southern Africa, I know of none better than the work of my friend Mr. Selous, who is frequently mentioned in the following pages, namely, "A Hunter's Wanderings in Africa."

A word or two must be said respecting the gold regions. One of the results of this journey is that those regions, lying between Matabeli-land and Tette, on the Zambesi, have been located as accurately as circumstances would allow. Thus future travellers and prospectors may find some useful hints in the information now supplied. A very sanguine man would doubtless see in those gold regions the future uprising of vigorous trade, and the subsequent and consequent wealth of Eastern Africa. While I sincerely think that this is a consummation devoutly to be wished, I have been careful to speak of things just as I found them, without colour and without gloom. But I have been taught the lesson of caution with regard to these matters in an old and tried school, namely, the golden lands of the far west of America, where fortune and failure in mining go like the strokes of a pendulum. To any one experiencing the buffeting of that roughly practical school, the romantic side of gold-seeking and the idle dreams of fairy lands of hidden treasure must of necessity have lost their charms.

Connected with the preparation of this account of my travels and experiences, I have to acknowledge a deep debt of gratitude to my friend Mr. William Stephen, for his generous and painstaking assistance in the work of literary revision.

To my publishers I express thanks for the attention they have paid to the book, and the interest they have taken in its progress.

I think the names of most of those who aided me at different points, when I was beginning and when I was ending this journey, are mentioned in the body of the book; but I must again thank, with most grateful feelings, all those hospitable and kind-hearted people who assisted me *en route*. Whether they are white or black, their kindness is not likely to be forgotten. The list of names is copious, and in it that of Mr. Thomas, of Shilo, bears a prominent place, so that it was with the deepest regret that I recently heard of the mystery which now surrounds his fate. Soon after my departure Mr. Thomas started on a hunting expedition to the north, accompanied by a large following of Matabeli hunters. Nearly all the following became frightened on reaching the river, and refused to cross. Mr. Thomas therefore sent them home. On returning they reported that they had left Mr. Thomas on the Zambesi suffering from fever. Not a word has been heard of him since that time.

This opportunity must also be taken to mention the excellent work done by Mr. Rowland Ward, of Piccadilly, the well-known naturalist, who has prepared various hunting trophies for me with admirable effect.

One word more. The remark I have made respecting the fact of my speaking of the gold regions just as I found them, must apply to the whole range of subjects in these two volumes. I know that in some instances I have not shown that enthusiasm towards projects for opening up Africa as has been displayed by other travellers; but then it was not my lot to come across any peculiar encouragement such as would have enabled me to speak with hope and with confidence of success in that direction. I would not write words of absolute despair regarding the prospects of the lands through which I passed, but I have endeavoured to draw all my conclusions without the sway of prejudice.

I will therefore withhold any definite judgment as to the value of this portion of Africa to the countries of Christendom, leaving my readers to draw their own conclusions from the descriptions and thoughts contained in the following pages, and always advising them to bear in mind the words of our famous Laureate—

"Cleave ever to the sunnier side of doubt."

W. MONTAGU KERR.

South Kensington, *July* 1886.

CONTENTS OF VOL. I.

CHAPTER I.

DARTMOUTH TO THE DIAMOND FIELDS.

Hopes of "Golden Africa"—Influence of old writers—My early dreams of travel—On board the *Drummond Castle*—Madeira—Curiosities of the wine trade—Madeira as a health resort—St. Helena—Africa at last!—Cape Town—Telegraphing to the interior—News of the hunters—Mr. Selous—Happy days at Wynberg—Objections to my plan—Dr. Holub's expedition—An odd and dangerous landing—A tremendous explosion—Description of Port Elizabeth—Northward ho!—"Bad luck to the man that dhrove it!"—Colesberg railway terminus—145 miles in a Cape cart—Arrival at Kimberley—The Diamond Fields—The mining fever—Hard times—Kimberley Mine—Description of mining and mining gear—Restrictions on diamond trade—Kaffir workers—A contested election 1–16

CHAPTER II.

THROUGH THE NEW PROTECTORATE.

Nearing a station—Klerksdorp—Unexpected meeting with Selous—His opinions of my project—The humours of Lo-bengula—The danger of shooting "sea-cow"—Hunters in trouble—Gold-seeking Americans—Equipping for the veldt—Kimberley again—"Cape Smoke"—Coach passengers—Starting for the veldt—Uncertainty of the future—Lichtenburg—Absence of hard cash—Odd trading—Jacobsdaal—Zeerust—Boer troubles—Small-pox and fumigation—A hasty departure—Linokana in Bechuana-land—Kaffir taxes—Linokana attacked by the Boers—Hermansberg Missionary Society—Moghose's station—Measures for the prevention of small-pox—Excessive power of a landdrost or chief magistrate—Religious zeal of the Boers—King Secheli—Dilapidated royalty—Hunting memories—"Camels, by Jove!"—Khama's Town—Shoshong or Bamangwato—Another "Lord of

Boundless Dominions"—An awkward squad—Trade of Shoshong—Dread of Matabeli—Giraffe hunting—War preparations—Khama's wife—Little Kanyemba—A queer medicine chest—A worthless land—Irrigation impossible—The Shashi river—Matabeli-land 17–39

CHAPTER III.

IN LO-BENGULA'S COUNTRY.

The Tati Gold Fields—Dinner with the Jesuit fathers—A reckless traveller—The mines and their working—First appearance of Korana John—Game gradually disappearing—A disastrous flash of lightning—Among the Matabeli—Symptoms of horse-sickness—Lost in the veldt—A shot at a pauw—Unexpected aid—Return to the waggons—" Lo-ben is friendly "—An escort sent—Matabeli gardens—Scene at Magubuduani—Approaching Buluwayo—The "New Valhalla"—The country full of fever—An improvised hospital—Poor Whitaker!—The King in his kraal—Reception by Lo-ben—The Queens of the Matabeli—In the royal harem—Meeting a Yorkshireman—Interior of a queen's hut—Beef and beer with a vengeance!—" The King can do no wrong "—" Go well, Son of the Sea"—Poetical expressions of the Matabeli—Description of Buluwayo—Inxwālā, the great dance—Royal bloodshed—Matabeli morality—Selous attacked by fever—The Comte de Lapanose—Farewell to Selous—Lo-ben's origin—The King explains the country's customs—His final permission—Description of my party—A bad start—" Why, man, he's drunk!"—Breakdown of the cart—Start with waggon and oxen—John's penitence—Shiloh—Massacre of Captain Paterson's party—An apostle of work—Inyati mission station—Last outpost of the London Missionary Society—Kind friends—Farewell to the last white man 40–76

CHAPTER IV.

THE "BIG GAME" COUNTRY.

Stocking the larder—My "C. L. K." rifle—A zebra hunt—"Gijima, gijima!"—Hollow bullets—An unpleasant ducking—The mountains between the Zambesi, Sabia and Limpopo—Difficulty in lion hunting—Humours of ox-driving—The Sepaque river—Out of the track—Clearing under difficulties—Elephant spoor—Fruitless pursuit—Umvuli river—A catalogue of miseries—Story of Windvogel's victim—John and the wolf—Lion incidents—A dangerous ford—An elephant hunt—The honey-bird's note of warning—Thrilling moments—A good day's work—Kaffir gluttony—Game and honey—Selous' deserted camp of 1883—Taroman missing 77–95

CHAPTER V.

INTO MASHONA-LAND.

Food supplies—John's concertina—Stirring dreams—Protection at night—John has an eye to the future—We leave Taroman behind—His revenge—The prairie on fire—A close escape—Matabeli raids—Sudden appearance of Mashona hunters—Chibero's—Description of a Mashona stronghold—Matabeli war tactics—Desolating results—Advantages of silence—Chibero is stubborn—The carrier difficulty—Stupid advice—Little Unyamwenda—One of Nature's dungeons—Native trading—Recruiting volunteers—" Villum" or Chirumutu—Writing unknown—Harassing bargains—" I melt de fat of de olifant, Master "—That exasperating fellow Taroman—Harte-beest hunting—Mashona mode of hunting—Netting game—General appearance of the Mashona—Mashona girls—Weapons—The assegai—A persecuted race—Diet—Cattle—A dilatory start—The waggon abandoned—" Tussa, tussa ! "—Baggage for the journey—The body-guard—Taroman incensed—Helplessness of the whites among the blacks—The company start on foot for the north   96–124

CHAPTER VI.

MASHONA-LAND.

A funny ceremony—Working on superstition—Hypocritical Taroman—An immense prairie fire—Meditations on the journey—Cold dews—The slumbering camp—Unyamwenda, the chief—A tough-skinned fellow—Desertions—Bundles of wisdom—Old Sebaii appears—The charred plain—The Zururu river—John's success in hunting—Gorging the crowd—Furious quarrels over meat—The best way to manage natives—Sterile rocks of Mashona-land—Making a skerm—Mashona music—Karemba's repute as a performer—Native dancing—Pleasure in primitive life—" Ah, master, I never see people like here ! "—Craving for limbo and beads—The Umvukwe and Rusaka mountains—Etsatse river—A troublesome goat—Curious hut—Prospecting for gold—Mashona ablutions—Honest natives—Unexpected appearance of Mchesa, the Vulcan of Mashona-land—Pursued by grass fires—Blacksmithing in the wildernesses—A primitive forge—Ironstone of the country—Troubles in camp—A night scene—Clannishness—Threat to kill Sagwam—Quarrels in camp—A doubtful expedition 125-166

CHAPTER VII.

FROM THE WAYNGE RIVER TO THE UMVUKWE MOUNTAINS.

Sebaii the orator—Appearance of the country—The Ruia river—"Igova, Muliliti"—The solemnity of snuffing—Fortunate shooting—"Ten thousand devils, John and Sagwam dead!"—The treacherous Unyamwenda—An early start—Effects of a sudden appearance—John in despair—Astonishing the disturbers—Lucky help—Necessity for quick progress—Visit to Muliliti, the chief—His home circle—The 'cute old dodger Sandani—Feet torments—Marshy country—New carriers and a new guide—A marrow-bone feast—Endurance of natives on the march—Signs of lions—The Umzengezi river—Discouraging news—Humours of roll-call—Splendid view from the Umvukwe mountains—Solitude 167-195

CHAPTER VIII.

CHUZU'S.

Soothing of the followers—Names of trees—The Karue river—Warnings of danger—Rocks alive with people—The Makorikori people—Fear to approach the white man—Alarm in the camp—"Geeve it um, master, geeve it um!"—Surrounded by armed warriors—Forebodings of danger—Chuzu, the chief—An unsatisfactory interview—Demands for powder—"Master, master, the people are coming to kill us!"—The bag of sovereigns—Anxious moments—"You are M'zungo"—Tricks of intimidation—The party is threatened with massacre—An old woman's friendly warning—Ominous signs—Our midnight retreat—An awkward bridge—Out of the difficulty—The disappointing check—"Ho, for northern Matabeli-land!"—Shall I return? 196-213

CHAPTER IX.

RECONNOITRING.

"Ah, master! I tink of me leetle wife"—Negotiating with Sandani—He tells of Negomo—Chibero dread and mistrust—The valley of the Etsatse—The Grumapudzi river—An uninviting country—Gold finding possible—A friendly welcome—"Gughle, gughle seree!"—Curing a fit—My first present—Frightening the white man—Native drums—Gold—Products of the country—Mode of life—Chibabura presents me with an ox—Friendly people—Assegai practice—A successful shot—Cobbling shoes—Appearance of the people—Adornments of the women and men—Absence of gold ornaments—Smoking customs—Entertainments—Weapons and implements—The "look-out"—A strange musician—Anxiety about John—Powder of native manufacture—Reflections on the retreat from Chuzu's—Startled by a baboon—Retrospect 214–235

CHAPTER X.

INYÓTA'S TRANQUIL LAND.

Camp fires in the distance—Reappearance of John—His miserable looks—Sandani is gratified—Camp before Inyota—Karemba's eccentricities—John's troubles—Kaffir ingratitude—The Bushman lost—A vain search—My terrified companion—The numerous wives of Sandani—The "oracle" sings the praises of the white man—Chibabura's reception—A palaver—Wonders of the mirror—Physicking the crowd—Settling Sandani's claims—The Rock of Wisdom—Chibabura's town—Native workmanship—Bark blankets—Pottery—A favoured land and people—Makorikori songs—Character of the people—Customs—Knowledge of agriculture—Contentment—Freedom from crime—Their life compared with civilized poverty—A peaceful scene—Oh, happy and favoured Inyota! 236–253

CHAPTER XI.

AMONG THE MAKORIKORI PEOPLE.

Tedious marching—Magombegombe mountains—John is "varee seek"—Our comical goat—Baboons—Lubola mountains—Zingabila—Mode of making bark blankets—M'jela, the chief—Kunyungwi still far off—Desertions—Method of securing an ox—Difficulty in getting boys—Presents from M'jela—Umfana's eating powers—The Dorah river—Camping places selected by natives—A lioness in the way—Lost chances of a shot—John's lion experiences—A fearful position—A wild forest scene—Hovering vultures—Adventure with a lioness—Native scramble for the lion's prey—Happy natives—The Mutua river—The Ruiana river—The Makomwe mountains—An amusing old fossil—Long fasting—Poor diet—The "dry goods bank" nearly

empty—"How many moons is dat since we leave Buluwayo?"
—Miseries of travel—Native houses—The "Three Brothers"—
The great basin of the Zambesi—Tropical forests . . . 254–277

CHAPTER XII.

ENTERING THE "FLY COUNTRY."

A descent into heat—Tea the best drink—Drinking generally—Rhinoceros—Symptoms of another strike—Intense heat—Msingua river—Suru—"Dar is the tsetse fly now, master!"—The "Fly Country" at last—An odd hue and cry—Mysterious words—Strange conduct of the guides—Unravelling the mystery 278–284

CHAPTER XIII.

CHIBINGA.

Skulls on gate-posts—Black but *not* comely—Meaning of Mzungo—A dubious reception—Karemba's *nonchalance*—Marching into the town—Confusion of tongues—Undesirable quarters—A waterless river—Hungry retainers—Absence of King Sakanii—Hunting, a last resource—The mother of the monarch—Rats swarming—A mutilating wolf—Inyota *versus* women—"Satan" is bibulous—Flies in myriads—Signs of disaffection—Negotiations with the "faithfuls"—Truculent Inyota—The monarch's mother commands my attendance—Curious reception—Hopes revived—Deplorable servility—Comparison with Mexican peone—The palmero punishment—"Us shall die from de hunger"—I start in search of the King—Bringing down a boar—Game on the route—The Mkumbura river—Spoor of wild animals—The busy tsetse—Description of the tsetse—A lion adventure—Fierceness of heat—The Umzengaizi river—Msenza—Meeting with Sakanii—Courteous greeting—Civilized comforts—The King's mode of travelling—His Portuguese connection—Returning to Chibinga—The King's bearers—Rapid progress—Prospects of relief—Noisy welcome to Chibinga 285–316

ILLUSTRATIONS.

Portrait of the Author	*Frontispiece*
A South African Trophy	page xviii.
Landing at Port Elizabeth	To face page 8
"Outspan"	" 26
Portrait of Mr. F. C. Selous	page 35
The Royal Kraal of Lobengela	To face page 56
"The Faithfuls"	page 68
Across the Umvuli	To face page 88
An Anxious Moment	" 92
Mode of Crossing Rivers	page 127
The Vulcan of Mashona-land	To face page 153
Midnight Retreat from Chuzu's	" 212
Making Bark Blankets	page 258
"With a low growl she stalked through the tall grass"	To face page 268
A Night Surprise—Mkumbura River	" 308

Map of a Journey from the Cape of Good Hope, across the Zambesi, to Lake Nyassa (*from a Survey by W. Montagu Kerr, C.E.*).

A SOUTH AFRICAN TROPHY.

THE FAR INTERIOR.

CHAPTER I.

DARTMOUTH TO THE DIAMOND FIELDS.

Hopes of "Golden Africa"—Influence of old writers—My early dreams of travel—On board the *Drummond Castle*—Madeira—Curiosities of the wine trade—Madeira as a health resort—St. Helena—Africa at last!—Cape Town—Telegraphing to the interior—News of the hunters—Mr. Selous—Happy days at Wynberg—Objections to my plan—Dr. Holub's expedition—An odd and dangerous landing—A tremendous explosion—Description of Port Elizabeth—Northward ho!—"Bad luck to the man that drove it!"—Colesberg railway terminus—145 miles in a Cape cart—Arrival at Kimberley—The Diamond Fields—The mining fever—Hard times—Kimberley Mine—Description of mining and mining gear—Restrictions on diamond trade—Kaffir workers—A contested election.

AMONG some fugitive writings of Thackeray's which have lately been embodied in a volume, most readers doubtless will have observed the following lines:—

> "Desolate Afric! thou art lovely yet!
> One heart yet beats which ne'er shall thee forget.
> What though thy maidens are a blackish brown,
> Does virtue dwell in whiter breasts alone?
> Oh no, oh no, oh no, oh no, oh no!
> It shall not, must not, cannot e'er be so.
> The day shall come when Albion's self shall feel
> Stern Afric's wrath, and writhe 'neath Afric's steel.
> I see the tribes the hill of glory mount,
> And sell their sugars on their own account;
> While round her throne the prostrate nations come,
> Sue for her rice and barter for her rum."

The great satirist here gives, in humorous heroics, a fair description of the hopes of Christendom with regard to the progress of "golden Africa." No land in modern times has attracted so much curious attention among the sons of civilisation. Missions have been maintained in the country at enormous cost, and worked in many instances with indomitable pluck. Pioneers of commerce have penetrated to its inmost recesses, and the same may be said of the great explorers who pushed on with the higher purpose of adding to the knowledge of mankind some new facts relating to hitherto unknown races and regions.

There is a peculiar charm in the idea of being able to help in developing the resources of a country, to raise it from prostration, and to lighten its darkness, so that finally it may attain a position similar to that which is occupied by ourselves. But I fancy that much of the fascination which clings to the story of mystery-enshrouded Africa is due to the power of the narratives related by its older explorers.

Personally, I know that by some influence of this kind, inscrutable perhaps, my fancy in the days of early boyhood was fired with the thought that at some time or another I would wander over virgin soil on the dark continent.

It was a dream—I had almost said the dream—of my youth, but years elapsed before the dream became a real life experience. In the interval it was my fortune to visit a good many lands, some of them savage even in civilisation, but I never lost sight of the early African vision. At length the long cherished wish was gratified, and my journey through the mysterious region has become a thing of the past.

And now I find myself asking the reader to accompany me along the line of my travels. I am to begin at once, telling the story in the good old fashion by noting the wonders that I saw and heard.

It was a bitterly cold December morning, in 1883, when I boarded the *Drummond Castle* moored at Dartmouth, and a few hours later I had my last glimpse of the lessening shores of old England.

At lovely Madeira—the pearl of the Atlantic—a short stay impresses every traveller with its vivid and picturesque scenes. Who does not remember the featherless divers who perform as a wonderful feat, and with the greatest gusto, the operation which was dreaded by ancient mariners as "keel-hauling"? Can the visitor forget the commercial gentlemen of acute instincts who sell the genuine articles— not those manufactured by the gross in Birmingham or Lisbon—but the real gold ring from Cape Coast Castle, on which the signs of the Zodiac, so well known to every traveller, are not struck by a vulgar modern die, but engraved by the neat-fingered black man of the Gold Coast? It is curious to see these charming evidences of the gentle art and scientific knowledge of the subtle savage.

Two facts about Madeira may be mentioned. These I learned from trustworthy sources. It appears that the chief industry, which of course is wine-making, is on the wane. Recently the vines had been attacked by phylloxera in an irresistible manner. The attacks seem to have begun in 1872, in which year over 10,000 pipes of wine were made. The produce of the year's vintage when I passed the place, in 1883, it was said on good authority would not exceed 1,000 pipes. The wine merchants, however, of the town have a very large—should I say inexhaustible?—stock of "Madeira" in their cellars, and by judicious "blending" or "mixing" (very mild terms!) there will be enough of the old-fashioned wine to supply the world even if the island vines did not produce a solitary grape. This result is one of the triumphs of the arts of advanced civilisation. What a blessing it is that we have so many ways and means of defeating the shortcomings of nature!

The bulk of the sugar crop is exported to Lisbon, where it finds a ready market free of duty.

The idea that Madeira possesses an admirable climate for affections of the chest has exploded since the experiment was made of sending out a number of patients in different stages of consumption from one of the London hospitals. The result proved that the advantages of the place were not equal to those of other health resorts nearer home, which were atmospherically much less humid, and consequently more conducive to the cure, or partial cure, of lung complaints.

We steamed away from Madeira, and shortly touched at St. Helena, which I would call the cabbage garden of the Atlantic, were it not almost profane to speak harshly of a spot which holds so prominent and hallowed a place in the world's eventful history. A detachment of the 58th Foot was quartered here at the time.

"How glad I am that this is the last day on board ship!" was my mental exclamation when we were thinning the end of our voyage.

Soon I found myself in Cape Town, walking under the shade of Table Mountain. What a satisfaction it was to think that at last I had actually arrived in Africa—the land of so many early visions of adventure! Yet there was little of the charm of romance in the proceedings, although a thousand thoughts ran through my mind relating to what I should do, and how I should do it.

What information could be gathered was a first consideration. Therefore I would telegraph to the farthest point reached by the sensitive wire, and draw interior news from the distant dwellers in the land of sparkling gems.

An answer came, flashed back over the dry karroo: "Hunters expected out shortly. Waggon and oxen reasonable." Again I tried, and from another source got the quick reply: "Hunters *not* expected out for some time." This was awkward. Another effort must be made, but this time I would be patient, for I would have to tap a more distant source.

Suddenly it occurred to me, "Where is Selous, the great hunter and traveller, whose admirable book 'A Hunter's Wanderings in Africa' had pleasantly wiled away my leisure hours when on the shores of the great Pacific near the Golden Gate? I must find him, for no better counsellor could guide early steps into this land of mystery. He alone, in the meantime, will be the object of my search." Another touch of the electric key, and a message was in the stage coach office at the Diamond Fields, with instructions that it should be forwarded to Klerksdorp, the principal trading and equipping station for traders north of the Vaal river. This was done, and I awaited results.

Going to the telegraph office I found the following message from Mr. James Leask, merchant at Klerksdorp, in the Transvaal Republic: "Drought raging in interior. Hunters cannot get out. Will be out on first rains."

An introductory letter to Colonel Montgomery, on the staff of General Sir Leicester Smyth, commanding the forces in South Africa, placed me in good hands. In a little time I found myself luxuriating in the groves and glades of lovely Wynberg, cheered by the most delightful society that one could possibly desire to meet. Pleasant recollections crowd thickly as I write, but they have an individual charm which cannot be transferred to the reader; although

I almost wish I could mention the names of those—and they were not a few—who showered so much kindness upon me.

Wynberg, with its picturesque surroundings of mountain, forest, and sea, is truly the garden of Cape Colony. But I must say farewell to the place, cherishing its ever happy memories of hospitable friends and their enchanting companionship, the kindly influence of which can never be forgotten.

I made inquiries at the most reliable quarters as to the probabilities of my success in accomplishing a journey alone overland to Central Africa. I did not get much encouragement. The arguments against the proposal were many.

"What will you do about the language?" said one.

"What will you do about the fever?" inquired another. "If it catches you when you are alone, it will soon stop the expedition."

"You can't pass the Diamond Fields," remarked a third, "for the small-pox is raging there."

And so the objections arose *ad libitum*. What was I to do? Stop in unapproachable Cape Town, and inhale the ungenerous winds of the south-eastern Atlantic? For the contrast, it must be remembered, between Cape Town and lovely Wynberg is remarkable. The mountain stands between them, and while the Cape Town side has a barren exposure to the merciless south-east "trades," which I had the misfortune to encounter once or twice during my stay, Wynberg's sequestered position is delightful in its shelter.

By the way, one man says, "Don't go to Port Elizabeth; it is by long odds the worst ash heap of the diamond cities of the south."

Was I blind to beauty, or indifferent to enchantment?

Was I in the oasis of Africa, or in its sterile Sahara? The words of men—Cape Town men—declared for the oasis, my experience for the Sahara.

I stand in the middle of Aderley Street, in front of the Standard Bank. The sand in circling storms wraps me in its gritty embrace. Where am I? In the Sahara, surely. And yet this cannot be, for through the blinding whirl I stretch forth my hand, and feel a rounded form of solid stone, fashioned unmistakably by the hand of man. What is it? Moving curiously forward towards the object, I find myself hugging a pillar, beside which I soon gain shelter from the searching sand, driven so mercilessly by the pitiless south-easter. After rubbing my eyes to clear them from the grit, I perceive that I am in the portico of the agency office for steamers. Happy thought! I will make inquiries about the departures for Port Elizabeth. I find that the earliest steamer will start in a day or two.

Most of the time was now occupied in studying maps. These I could see were far from being perfect. River courses especially were inaccurately defined; so, at least, I judged from their manifold variations. Few names marked the lands that lay to the far north-east between Matabeli-land and Lake Nyassa. It would be my aim to fill up, however slightly, some of these imperfections, and thus contribute something toward the geographical description of little known countries, should I be able to carry out the journey which I had purposed to do.

Hesitation soon vanished, and ultimately I determined to make the attempt to reach the lake regions of Central Africa overland by a northward course, and thence to proceed towards the Indian Ocean.

Dr. Holub, the eminent naturalist, was in Cape Town equipping an expedition which seemed to me, from the extraordinary array of paraphernalia, to be of gigantic importance. Dr. Holub strongly encouraged my plan.

As it was necessary to procure a few instruments I required, some days were occupied in going through the shops of the opticians; and although my expedition was to be carried out on the black-bag quantity, the articles of this description which I wanted were bound to be of the best quality and the highest accuracy. After searching the highways and byways of Cape Town, I succeeded in getting a good sextant and other instruments, and hastened to the Royal Observatory, where Dr. Gill and Mr. Findlay (of comet fame) gave me much information, so that ere many days had passed the first and most important part of the geographical and astronomical outfit was complete.

South-easters blew great guns; while dense, almost solid, clouds of sand swept over Cape Town on the day of departure. The place was at its worst. The "oldest inhabitant" had never seen the like before. Table Bay was seething with white caps. The steamer *Danube* lay in the harbour, ready for departure that afternoon, and in her I found my way to Port Elizabeth. The *Danube* had a notoriety for unsteady habits, and on this occasion her proclivities were painfully evident.

I gladly left the atmosphere of storm pans and spittoons and scrambled to the slippery pier at Port Elizabeth like a shipwrecked mariner. Landing at this modern haven during a south-easterly gale demands agility of no common order, although, of course, there is *every modern convenience for passengers!* The human cargo is handled as gently as is possible with the means at the disposal of the wharf masters. For the information of passengers disembarking at this port, I may say that by binding themselves with a pair of rug straps they will have a better chance of

LANDING IN A SOUTH-EASTER AT PORT ELIZABETH.

landing in safety than by trusting to the honesty of their tailors, or the firmness of their feet. If they depend too much upon these they will assuredly reach *terra firma* in the attitude of their ancestors in the four-footed life spoken of in science genealogy.

When I called at the telegraph office I found a message informing me that hunters were " arriving out." The first rains had fallen, and the time was propitious for making a start towards the interior. There would now be plenty of grass, as the lands had been freshened by the rains. Among the hunters I hoped Mr. Selous would be found.

Looking into a Port Elizabeth paper, I read of the tremendous explosion which had just taken place at the Diamond Fields. Its effect must have been prodigious, for no less than 33 tons of dynamite, 7 tons of loose powder, a quantity of paraffin, and 200,000 cartridges, were blown up.

From Major Deare, of the Colonial forces, I got every assistance, and, among other attentions, he kindly showed me the lions of the town. I cannot enter upon a regular guide-book description; but I may say that Port Elizabeth is an active and thriving town, showing a wonderful amount of life in the sixty-third year of its age—that was in 1883. The buildings are exceedingly handsome, and an especial feature is the new feather, ivory, and general produce market, which is a spacious as well as a fine building. The churches are elegantly built. There is a commodious and comfortable club; and, as a rule, the hotel accommodation and attention are unusually good. The place is healthy, but exposed to violent and piercing winds.

We must not, however, linger amid the scenes of civilization. We must be up and away to the north, the region to which the tremulous needle directs a course. Should the reader follow, we shall soon be roving free and unfettered over unbeaten tracks upon the virgin soil of rarely visited lands.

From the steamer we pass to the railway; from the railway to the post-cart; from the post-cart to the primitive ox-waggon. Then ho! for the north, on foot if need be, to the land of the honey bird, and the heart of the hunter's home! On to the Zambesi! We will wander through the umbrageous aisles of the primeval forest: we will roam over the vastness of the great plateau: we will saunter on the golden sands of Nyassa's lovely sea!

I had bidden a long adieu to the ocean and the trembling little *Danube* which had brought me from Cape Town. Soon, too, the railway had to be left behind, for it did not take long to reach the terminus at Colesberg.

When seated at the table of the Phœnix Hotel my *vis-à-vis* was a gentleman with spectacles, who was evidently very anxious, and, like some others, much worried by a feverish impatience to reach "the Fields." For we had just been too late. The post-cart had started shortly before.

"Bad luck to the man that dhrove it!" was the muttered remark of an irate Celt from Erin's isle, who had a very wide mouth and a low, receding brow.

It was soon evident that the city of Kopjies, or, properly speaking, Colesberg, was not a sufficiently attractive place for the spectacled gentleman. He was very energetic, and conspicuously a man of business. He swallowed his bumper of XXX, and then, correcting the dose with a cup of scalding coffee, adjusted his magnifiers and left the room, his purpose evidently being a search for a substitute coach. Hastily repairing to the Post-cart Office, he contracted for a Cape cart, something like a curricle with four horses. The driver had orders for relays of horses on the road.

Happy thought again! If I was lucky enough to be first I would doubtless be acceptable in sharing the journey and the expenses. No sooner thought than done; and on the next morning we were speeding rapidly on our way over the far stretching karroo.

I will at once pass over the 145 miles of country that lie between Colesberg and Kimberley at the Diamond Fields. We crossed the iron lattice bridge which spans the Orange River, and connects the state with the colony. Moving onward then through the Free State we passed the town of Fauresmith, and arrived at the Queen's Hotel, Kimberley, on the evening of the 11th of February, 1884, the journey from Colesberg having occupied two and a-half days.

The Diamond Fields are situated at an elevation of 4,050 feet above the sea. The surrounding country consists of undulating prairie land, covered with very short grass and sad-looking shrubs. Before the rains the country is about as bare as a well-worn macadamized road. At that time the rains had only fallen once in twelve months.

Excepting the diamond mines, the town is very uninteresting, although it has a club which is the best of its kind in South Africa. Only a few buildings are of brick or stone, the greater number being made of corrugated iron, one storey in height, so that when a full view of the town is obtained, it is apt to make one think of a resemblance to a lot of tin dog-kennels enlarged a few diameters.

Mining here, as is well known, dates from the first rush to the fields in 1870. Speculation of the wildest description was rife in the early days—almost as bad as it was in California in '74 and '75—but when I passed through the place the people were labouring under a depression as deep as their excitement had been high in more prosperous times.

Big companies had gone out of existence, and everybody spoke of hard times.

The principal diamond mines worked are the Kimberley, the De Beers, Du Toit's Pan, and Bultfontein.*

The Kimberley Mine is a huge quarry situate in the town. It is about 500 feet in depth, measured by plumb line to the centre. The mine was being worked by five different companies.

The mode of excavating was a simple system of quarrying and blasting, for which dynamite was used, the explosions taking place at mid-day and midnight respectively. The richness of the diamond treasure that has been taken from the crater is fabulous. Statistics say that from two to three millions of pounds sterling per annum have represented the aggregate value of the output of the mines.

Prospect channels and shafts seemed to be run, but to a very trifling extent. The excavations are sent up on steel wire rope "roads," the various companies having their respective hoisting works leading from the depths of the gradually lessening area of the basin. Two heavy wire ropes form the "roads." They run parallel, and are stretched tightly from the pit head through the air and down to an anchorage at the bottom of the mine. These ropes are the rails, so to speak, on which run the flanged wheels of the skip or cage. This system of hoisting is quite unique, and very effective for the class of work carried on at the diamond mines.

The soft blue rock in which the gems are found decom-

---

* A *Standard* (23rd April, 1886) correspondent, writing from Kimberley, gives the following statistics:—

Assessed Value of Mines.—Kimberley, £2,805,635 ; De Beers, £934,737 ; Du Toit's Pan, £1,283,591 ; Bultfontein, £682,266.

Value of Diamonds exported from Kimberley.—1883, £2,742,521 ; 1884, £2,807,288 ; 1885, £2,492,755.

poses under atmospheric and aqueous action. It is taken from the mine and spread over large spaces covering acres of land, where it is left exposed to the sun, while it is wetted at intervals by means of a hose, and broken by large hammers. This process of disintegration goes on for about two months, when the jewelled earth is taken to the mill.

An exceedingly simple and unscientific contrivance is this mill. The blue gravel first passes through a tapered cylindrical sieve, revolving in a horizontal position. It is thrown in at the small end of the sieve, and after its course along the inclined plane the refuse is thrown out at the other end. The stuff which falls through the meshes is conducted by a sluice into a sort of settler, consisting of a big tub about ten feet in diameter having a vertical central driving shaft, about which revolve four arms fitted with long teeth, which reach close to the bottom of the settler. This keeps the pulp constantly agitated, and, with the regular stream of water which is kept flowing, the waste and light sands are carried through an overflow on the inner edge of the settler. The refuse is akin to "tailings" in gold mining. Diamond tailings, I understand, are not worth much. The tailings flow directly into a small well, where a dredger, or bucket pump, lifts them to an elevation of about fifteen feet. From that elevation the trucks deposit them in all directions, so that they form a large sand bank.

The sands, or gravel rather, which are taken from the bottom of this tub or settler are passed over four wire screens of different-sized meshes, the last being very fine. All the gravel is then placed on iron-faced tables. By means of a kind of steel trowel it is sorted, and the diamonds picked out. The sand last screened, which is the very finest, is dried in the sun, and given to the Kaffirs to sort;

they being the best hands at picking out the smallest diamonds. These diamonds are sold to the licensed diamond buyers in the Kimberley market, and in this way the companies can immediately realise. It is said that there have been thirty or forty million pounds' worth of diamonds exported from the Cape during the last fourteen years.

The systems adopted in the working of these craters or gigantic deposits of blue gravel may have been very effective heretofore; but now the mines are attaining a depth that threatens to bring all such methods forcibly to an end; for the good reason that the shale which forms the surrounding walls of this basin is beginning to cave, and will naturally continue to do so until it finds its angle of repose, and of course it stands to reason that as they go deeper the area at the bottom will proportionately decrease, until it has run to nothing.

The hoisting engines in use were inadequate to cope with the vast volumes of floating reef gradually but surely coming down the deep abyss. Already there has been spent jointly by the companies £1,400,000 for the extraction of the falling reef. I am afraid that the day is not far distant when many a poor fellow will be prematurely buried under the inevitable fall of reef that must result from such an unavoidable mode of mining.

Naturally the question arises, What is to be done in order that the jewels may be got out remuneratively? There were many plans advanced for underground workings; but I did not find a single man there who understood underground work as it is carried on in gold and silver mines. In any case, the days of the present system are numbered. The people may go on until they are compelled to try another plan. Of course another system could only be practicable through the companies amalgamating, each mine being worked under undivided control. The scarcity of timber is a great drawback to underground working.

Various restrictions on diamond dealing exist. No one is allowed to buy a diamond without first obtaining a license, and only licensed dealers, or brokers, can sell them, although in spite of the vigilance of the detective department a great deal of illicit diamond buying is successfully carried on; hence the well-known symbols "I D B," which refers to the illegal trade. Men coming out of the mine have " changing houses," and they are searched before leaving work. The latter ordeal, I was told, was one of the grievances of the white people. They say it is degrading to a white man to be searched.

The Kaffirs are very good workers. I made a foreman " white " admit that they were far superior to the men of his own kind in every particular, and there was no trouble with them.

" But you must watch them," said he.

" Did you ever see any class of workers, either white or black, that did not require watching ? "

I think for the especial class of work the Kaffirs are very well adapted. I saw many pretty diamonds taken from the mine. One morning, soon after we had ascended in the cage, at De Beer's mine, a cave or slip occurred, burying three men.

An election excitement bustled the place during my stay. Kimberley returns three members to the parliament of the Cape. I spent the evening with a gentleman who was one of the successful candidates. His wife appeared to be much elated at her husband's success in being elevated to the position of a representative man.

One of the most amusing features of the election was the candidature of an unsuccessful champion of the " people's rights." His attempts to address the meetings were rudely stopped by showers of missiles as unsavoury as those which are even yet conspicuously familiar at similar scenes in the old country. Eight votes, in the long run, supported this candidate, who then abruptly left the town; so that the place that knew him, knew him no more.

Now we are to leave this feverish region, where the throb of labour and the nervous pulse of speculation are the signs of restless vitality: where the precious gems dazzle the eyes of those who in hot haste pursue the road to fortune; and where by day and night the heavy roar of blasting is heard rudely crashing above the hum of countless wheels. We are on to the home of the black man! There we will find charm in novelty, and in absolute freedom from the endless worship of the golden calf.

But first I must not forget that I am in search of Mr. Selous. Where is the hunter to be found? I must secure my place for the journey, and in the land of the Boers will soon discover what men and what news have come from the teeming hunting-grounds of the "Far Interior."

CHAPTER II.

THROUGH THE NEW PROTECTORATE.

Nearing a station—Klerksdorp—Unexpected meeting with Selous—His opinions of my project—The humours of Lo-bengula—The danger of shooting " sea-cow"—Hunters in trouble—Gold-seeking Americans—Equipping for the veldt—Kimberley again—" Cape Smoke"—Coach passengers—Starting for the veldt—Uncertainty of the future—Lichtenberg—Absence of hard cash—Odd trading—Jacobsdaal—Zeerust—Boer troubles—Small-pox and fumigation—A hasty departure—Linokana in Bechuana-land—Kaffir taxes—Linokana attacked by the Boers—Hermansberg Missionary Society—Moghose's station—Measures for the prevention of small-pox—Excessive power of a landdrost or chief magistrate—Religious zeal of the Boers—King Secheli—Dilapidated royalty—Hunting memories—" Camels, by Jove!"—Khama's Town—Shoshong or Bamangwato—Another "Lord of Boundless Dominions"—An awkward squad—Trade of Shoshong—Dread of Matabeli—Giraffe hunting—War preparations—Khama's wife—Little Kanyemba—A queer medicine chest—A worthless land—Irrigation impossible—The Shashi river—Matabeli-land.

VIGOROUS blasts from the small horn carried by the driver of the coach told that we were nearing a station. Our coach in every way resembled the typical yankee cee-spring stage of the west. As a matter of fact, it was an imported article of American manufacture. The station we arrived at was Klerksdorp, a small but comely town, the jolting journey to which had occupied two and a-half days and nights. The town, as I have remarked, is the principal trading station north of the Vaal.

Seeing in large letters the name of Leask, I thought that the owner must be the same who had telegraphed to me at Cape Town. Mr. Leask's stores formed the largest building in the place, and he is the biggest merchant in the Southern Transvaal.

A hospitable reception was given me here, and I soon discovered that Mr. Leask was a countryman of mine who had gone out early, and spent his younger days in elephant hunting in the interior. Our conversation naturally led to the question what brought me there with nothing but an insignificant handbag. This I explained in a few words. The journey I was about to take was a long one, and I hoped to augment my baggage to some extent. I had yet to fetch a few more things from Kimberley, which would be done as soon as I was able to get the information I wanted, and had made the necessary arrangements for progress. Now I was entirely away from railways and even post-carts.

I told Mr. Leask that I thought my scheme was, in theory, good; but first of all I desired to find a gentleman named Selous, whom I hoped to see among the hunters who would arrive out soon.

"My dear sir," was Mr. Leask's immediate reply, "Mr. Selous is in my house at this very moment. Look, there are his waggons! He arrived out last night with two waggon-loads of ivory, hides and horns, and a lot of other hunting trophies."

This was indeed fortunate! The path might become smoother.

When I told the great hunter and traveller of my project to reach the Zambesi by a north-easterly route, as yet unexplored, he courteously offered me all the information which his experience suggested—an invaluable advantage to me then. Mr. Selous also said that as soon as he could load up his waggons with the requisite articles for trade and exchange, he would again be *en route* for the hunting-grounds which lay two months' travel to the north.

We then and there arranged that I should take a cart and six oxen, if they could be got ready in time, and accompany him as far as Matabeli-land.

He thought that the chief opponent to my scheme of exploration towards the far north-east of Matabeli-land would be the powerful despot Lo-bengula, the defiant ruler of the country, whose name since my return to England has been more than once before the public in connection with the "deafening inanity" of South African politics. Lo-ben, as he is familiarly called, would be suspicious if he heard of a white man wishing to go through his country without asking permission to hunt for ivory or search for gold.

"Then," continued Mr. Selous, "there has been a good deal of trouble lately. The old man was in a very bad humour when I left. Some Hottentot hunters and one or two Boers had been shooting sea-cows (hippopotamus), which is contrary to the stipulation or agreement made by those who obtain permission to hunt. When the hunters came out to the king's kraal there was great excitement among the Matabeli people. Like the Zulus, they believe that the spirits of their ancestors dwell in the uncouth bodies of the amphibious hippo and crocodile.

"The result of the turmoil was that all the hunters were called to a great trial before the king, where they had to sit on the ground for whole days at a stretch while the case was being heard, their position being made more trying by the surroundings of a crowd of people who thirsted for their blood. This craving would have been satiated had it not been for the strong will of old Lo-ben. As it was the hunters were insulted, scoffed and jeered at.

"The verdict was that for each offence a heavy fine was demanded from every defaulter. Some of the hunters who had not even seen a sea-cow had to pay pretty heavily for the misbehaviour of their Hottentot subordinates; for in Matabeli-land the master must pay for the shortcomings and offences committed by his employés."

Some time previously a few Americans had asked permission to go through Lo-ben's country, saying that they did not wish to search for gold, which in truth was their object. Watched by some of the young warriors, they were caught *flagrante delicto* and brought back before the king, who summarily dispatched them out of his country to the south.

I found it was by no means easy rapidly to complete an equipment here. The time required for fitting out a waggon and oxen would be considerable, and delay might endanger the chance of reaching the Zambesi before the rains set in, that was to say about October. Here Mr. Selous assisted me greatly by offering a berth in his waggon.

By the return coach from Pretoria I was soon back at Kimberley to fetch the rifles and baggage. Here also, remembering the probability of geographical notes, I corrected the time by telegraph from the Observatory at Cape Town; Kimberley being the last point for telegraphic communication.

Again I was upon the old coach bound for Klerksdorp. Numbers of genial friends came to see me off. Once on the road the driver, who fancied himself considerably, started off in magnificent style, he being well primed with "Cape Smoke." Looking behind I could see in the dwindling distance the agent, who was shouting aloud and waving his arms in a most frantic fashion. We, or he, had evidently forgotten something. But the driver was deaf; and even to my attentive ears the shouts soon died away as we whirled swiftly over the swelling ground, the reports of our Jehu's whip ringing out like the sound of a live bunch of crackers.

Inside the coach a strong distillery-like odour pervaded the atmosphere, so that there seemed to be a danger that one might become tipsy without tasting. Of course we had with us the ubiquitous passenger who takes his seat with the self-satisfied assurance that he has paid his fare, and that he has rights which must in no case be interfered with, and therefore he resolutely smokes and drinks, while he fights for the coveted half-inch of room which the restlessness of his troublesome elbow incites him to dispute. How frequently do these eternal nuisances destroy the comfort of the sober passenger who has fewer wants, and who begins to think what an extraordinarily constituted beast man is, and how wonderfully well he is adapted to doing many things at a time!

On arriving at Klerksdorp a few days had to be occupied by loading the waggons with provisions and other necessities, such as cloth, beads, and so forth, for the purpose of exchange.

Then we were ready for the start. We had sixteen oxen yoked to each waggon, about fifty sheep, dogs, "salted" horses,* cows and calves. Our human supporters comprised a few black savages of different types. Among the others was a Mashona boy whom Selous had brought from his distant mountain home, and who was destined to take a prominent place in the course of my future travels. This boy, named Karemba, led the oxen of one of the waggons, he being adorned with a Boer hat and a coloured shirt, the only evidences of civilisation he could boast of, for poor

---

* "Salted" horses are those which have passed through the sickness which is so prevalent north of the Vaal river.

Karemba was accustomed to go naked. Mr. Selous and myself completed the typical South African Caravan.

What a fervour of fascination there was in the feeling that all before me was new! Where was the journey to end? That delightful uncertainty about filling the blank page of the future awakened in my mind a silent rapture that would be difficult to describe. Incident and adventure must of necessity arise: but here, at last, I was upon the threshold of the paradise of my boyhood's day-dreams: now I was to wander through the scenes of the mighty and mysterious continent!

It was on the morning of the 5th of March, 1884, that we bade adieu to that last outpost of civilisation—Klerksdorp—and bending towards to the north passed through the great waving grass plains of the Northern Transvaal, admiring as we went the lovely tints of their varying colours.

The town of Lichtenberg, at which we soon arrived, is situated at the summit of high rolling prairie country, which is so characteristic of all the southern and south-western portions of the Transvaal. Lichtenberg is indeed a dismal-looking place. Here and there a few houses are scattered as though they had been thrown from a pepper-box. Close to what is called—for what reason it is difficult to say—the Market Square, could be seen a square dog-kennel-looking building which proved to be the Dutch house of worship. Beyond that, a general merchandise store and a few tumble-down houses completed the township.

Grass grew high around the houses, and the market square is good grazing land. The roads, with the exception of the main highway, are almost hidden with grass.

The Government office is a little building about two feet

by eight. It looked like a sieve, and was a picture of dirt and disorder. The town has the same deserted and sorrowful aspect which may be observed in most of the small country towns of South Africa.

Money as a medium of exchange here is almost unknown, since prosperity departed with the English at the close of the war.

We visited Mr. Lane, a trader, who occupied one of the few remaining houses which had defied the elements, although as I wrote notes in my diary, a thin stream of water made its way through a weak spot in the bedroom ceiling. I began to think that the waggon was not at all a bad place for repose, as we could sleep on piles of blankets, and the tent cover was perfectly watertight.

Excessively wet weather delayed us for some days. The cattle, too, strayed into the field of a Boer to whom compensation had to be granted for damages. There was ample time, therefore, to talk over the situation on the frontier; of the freebooters; and the question of the trade route to the interior which was about to be raised between the British Government and the Boer Republic.*

Mr. Lane told us some interesting stories of his recent trading trip to Stella-land, and of the mob of freebooters, some of whom had been displaying their humour in the "noble art." He managed to do some trading, but the returns would not be very satisfactory to a Manchester merchant; for the transactions had produced a kind of currency that could not be readily carried in the pocket, consisting of a few cattle, and, for small change, two or three chairs with raw hide seats. Hard cash could not be seen.

* Since that time the British Government has thought fit to spend about a million sterling in this matter, a large portion of which has gone into the pockets of the Boers.

The waggons were sent on, and Selous and myself mounted our horses and soon left the desolate little town of Lichtenberg far behind, speeding on our way through the grassy prairie, past the little town of Jacobsdaal, with its small street lined with stores and the orthodox Boer church, until we entered the town of Zeerust, another trading centre within the Transvaal. Here we accepted the hospitalities of Mr. Greite.

We heard that great discontent was felt and manifested by the Boers with reference to the terms recently agreed upon by the Boer Convention in England, with regard to the question of the frontier line.

A number of Boers were met and some English traders. With one of the latter, Mr. Thomas, who had just returned from the interior, I passed a good deal of leisure time in the endeavour to overcome some initial instructions in the Matabeli tongue, which he very kindly agreed to teach me.

Mr. Selous had an awkward piece of intelligence one day. Small-pox had broken out in the town, and we would evidently have to undergo the disagreeable operation of being half-asphyxiated by the noxious fumes of sulphur, while we were shut up in a small room set apart for fumigation. Under these circumstances we lost no time in making a start.

Now we were nearing the borders of Bechuana-land, which lately has become the apple of discord among enthusiastic colonisers. Two days' journey brought us to the town of Linokana, the chief of which was Ikalafing, of the tribe of Bahurutsis. The town is divided into three parts. Each part has a petty chief. The population is about 3,000, and the language spoken is Sechuana, the same as is spoken by all Bechuana tribes.

Every Kaffir holding a hut pays ten shillings annually

to the Transvaal government. Just after the English war, in 1881, the Boers advanced upon Linokana with a force about 600 strong, and demanded 5,000 head of cattle—a robbery committed under the pretext that Ikalafing was building a wall round the town with a view to fortification. This wall, which was only partially built, was demolished by the Boers' command, who made the inhabitants build a monument with the *débris*, a structure which still stands, or did when I was there, to remind the black man that the white man's *might* is the devil's *right*.

A missionary station standing here, supported by the Hermansberg Missionary Society of Hanover, was superintended by Mr. Jansen, a Dane. That he had been industrious was clearly shown by the comfortable house he had built for himself. There it was, surrounded by magnificent specimens of the Eucalyptus, which he himself had planted eighteen years before. Gardens and corn-fields might also be seen. I heard little of spiritual rescues, but Mr. Jansen told me he had a good many followers.

Moghose's station, which we next arrived at, is thoroughly within Bechuana-land. The Transvaal was now left on the south. Chief Ramotsa rules Moghose's. He is the oldest chief among the Bechuana tribes (the name of his tribe is Maleti), and his station is larger than the others we have passed. It may be mentioned here that King Matebi used to rule all the Bechuana tribes, but now each tribe has its own chief.

At Moghose's we were joined by Mr. Argent Kirton, an interior trader, who intended to accompany us with his waggon to Bamangwato or Shoshong.

A man who had left Zeerust on the day after our hasty departure, told us that in the interval there had been seven fresh cases of small-pox. All the people, white and black, who left the town had to be fumigated. The few Kaffir houses in which the disease first appeared were burnt down, and fumigation was applied to all the Kaffirs in the town— a very trying ordeal, founded upon an exploded and ignorant idea. In the Transvaal, from what I have heard, the operation of fumigating is unusually severe through its being carelessly conducted; so badly, indeed, that there have been a number of cases of fainting, suffocation, and hemorrhage of the lungs induced by the aggravating and strong fumes of the sulphur. The person operated upon is kept in the room for thirty minutes. I have even heard of some cases of death resulting through weak-lunged persons being compelled to inhale the sulphureous gas.

In the Transvaal, the landdrost of a town, as chief magistrate, exercises absolute power. He can sentence any one, white or black, to be flogged, even without the preliminary of a trial, reminding one of Jedwood justice, "hang in haste and try at leisure," as Scott said.

I remember reading in an Orange Free State newspaper of an Englishman, fifty years of age, receiving fifty lashes for having given his drunken wife a kick, although not a mark could be found on the woman.

Religious zeal is extravagantly strong in the Boer Republic, and the outward ardour of the feeling has the happy effect of making travellers form golden opinions regarding the devout character of the people. One traveller, especially—and no mean literary authority—has evidently been strongly influenced by the pious atmosphere of a Boer's front room, which he breathed with refreshing delight, finding no doubt additional solace in draughts of Boer coffee. But the drop curtain was never raised to show life behind the scenes. And so the traveller when he is safe in his arm-chair, beside a blazing hearth in old England, draws

"OUTSPAN."

towards him his paper, pen and ink, to malign his white brother in South Africa, whom he stigmatises as being of evil repute and an oppressor of the holy Boer!

On the morning of the 21st of March we left Moghose's, travelling through a flat, bushy country, abounding with thorny acacias and very long grass. The sun was intensely hot, and its burning rays told heavily upon the struggling oxen.

When we arrived at Molepololi river—at King Sechele's—we at once visited the monarch, whom we found seated under the grateful shade of a large tree directly in front of his house. He was fanning off the flies with a giraffe's tail, and at his left side, leaning against the back of his chair, was his brass walking-stick or sceptre. On a log of wood before the king sat his interpreter, and towards the left, at a little distance, were a number of humble admirers, most of whom were very ancient-looking fellows.

The old king greeted us with much courtesy, and went so far as to show a little emotion when he saluted Kirton, which he did in a most civilised manner, by pressing the latter's hand and kissing him on the left cheek. Kirton was an old friend of the king's, having given him many presents, hence this outburst of natural affection.

Sechele seemed to be a man of at least sixty-five years of age, and was rather a fine-looking specimen. The hand of time, however, had not left him untouched. His hair was falling off, and his sight becoming impaired. Civilisation had exerted a sadly demoralising effect upon him, for he wore spectacles, and it even appeared that he had been using some hair-dye. Kirton had known him when his hair was grey; now it was of jet-like blackness.

Powder, caps, and whisky procured us the passport through his country. We visited his house, and spent some time talking to him, through the medium of the interpreter, a thick-lipped fellow, with an "all-over-the-place" sort of countenance, who sat on his haunches when speaking; his eyes being half closed, as though there was no slight mental strain in the effort of reproducing the speeches.

The king's house, inside, presented the appearance of a place that at one time, in long forgotten years, had been fairly furnished with all modern comforts, but now showed signs of desolation in its hopeless disorder, increased through want of glue and wall-paper.

The old man produced a number of rifles, which he seemed anxious to trade off for other commodities. A sideboard in the place wore a very dilapidated appearance, and was covered with a conglomeration of stuff that reminded one of the window of a three-balls' establishment. Most conspicuous of all were a brass basin and jug, in a condition that was calculated to give a supply of verdigris sufficient to poison the whole tribe. There were also a soda-water fountain out of gear, an ostrich feather or two stuck into a broken-down lamp, and a variety of other ill-assorted articles.

Leaving Sechele's, we trekked through the heavy beds of sand which are so marked a characteristic of northern Bechuana-land. Although game was far from being plentiful, we managed to keep the waggons supplied with meat.

This was a very happy part of the journey. From morning till night we were in the saddle hunting. The evenings were spent before blazing camp fires, whose light and warmth gave a glow to good fellowship, easing the run of pleasant converse, so as to soothe the sadness of lifeless solitude. Many a thrilling tale of adventure did Selous relate on these occasions, and many a funny joke and story from Kirton made our laughter ring high above the crackling of the blazing fire.

Water, which had been scarce, was plentifully found at Boatlanama in wells. Antelopes of several varieties abounded. It was here that I shot my first antelope—a fine impala (*Æpyceros Melampus*), with a good head.

The mode of hunting was quite new to me. It was full of excitement, and success was the reward only of the active and agile. The game is followed at full speed on horseback, and when the pursuer gets within seventy or eighty yards range—perhaps nearer—he dismounts, fires, and mounts again, reloading as he advances. The holes burrowed by the ground squirrels sometimes occasion heavy falls during the heat of the chase.

A number of Masarwa bushmen followed our waggons, waiting for odds and ends of meat. They are a very ugly type of mankind, and exceedingly short in stature, but they cannot be spoken of as being dwarfs. They proved to be extraordinary carriers; for although literally staggering under their loads of meat, they would walk for miles without a moment's rest. The hut the bushman lives in is hardly worthy of the name of hovel.

All of them carry small bows, and bark pouches with poisoned arrows, the points of which are of bone or iron. The poison is the milk of the herb *euphorbia arborescens*. Fire-making by rubbing together a couple of sticks—everybody has described the process—is general in this and other parts of this wonderful land.

One morning Selous, Kirton, and myself started off in search of blue wildebeeste (*Catoblepas Gorgon*). We rode for about an hour and saw nothing. Suddenly Selous shouted, " Camels, by Jove!"

This is the name they give to giraffes in South Africa.

They evidently saw us, but they did not start off until we were within about two hundred yards of them. Then off we dashed in pursuit, over the grassy veldt, and winding in and out among thorn bushes, holes, and heaps. The pace was marvellous. I soon felt that it would put my horse out, for he was not long in beginning to pump like a high-pressure engine. But I urged him on to the utmost of my power, and, dismounting, let fly both barrels of my 500 express without effect.

Selous and Kirton, who were on very fine horses, kept up the running; the former doing very good work with a small 450 Metford. Between them they soon brought down the two giraffes—two large bulls—the biggest measuring sixteen feet from the top of the skull to the soles of the fore-feet. They had run so far from the track of the waggon that we could not utilize the meat, although it would have been most acceptable, because we had a large number of hungry dogs. But we cut out the tongues, and also had one of the hearts, which are much esteemed.

While we were returning to the waggons we saw numbers of wildebeeste, but did not give chase, as the horses were tired. We found the waggons at a small vlei, called Selinia. During the night-time, lions prowled about the camp, and in the morning we saw the spoor. They had evidently been looking out for the oxen.

For some part of our journey we were now, through a scarcity of water, compelled to travel by night.

We arrived at Shoshong, Bamangwato, or Khama's Town, about mid-day on the third of April, and remained there for a few days, putting up at the house of Mr. James Dawson, one of the most generous-hearted of traders—a worthy Scot—who keeps open house for all passing travellers. By wandering about the place, I was enabled to learn a good deal about the customs and ways of the Bechuana people.

As some attention has of late been attracted to the place, in speaking of the new British colony of Bechuana-land, I will give a brief description of Shoshong. The town is not within the protectorate. It is situated on the northern side of a large open valley, close to the foothills of a black basaltic range of mountains, which, as you approach from the south, have a dark and dreary look.

Khama's Town is the name by which perhaps it is most familiar in England, through its having been adopted by "special commissioners" and newspapers. The name comes from Khama, the ruling chief, who is a son of Sekhome. Khama is a very good man, and singularly considerate to the whites. Such, in fact, has always been his character. He is supposed to be the king of the Bechuana people, and, like most of the black monarchs, he claims and boasts of a good deal more territory than he has any actual power over. Like Theebaw, Khama, in his mind's eye, is a "Lord of Boundless Dominions," but his modesty makes him speak of the Zambesi as his limit on the north-west!

The introduction of Christianity has caused a good deal of disturbance among the chiefs of Shoshong, giving rise to serious differences between fathers, sons, and brothers, and leading to separation, and even to fighting among those who had adopted the new faith and those who clung to the old order of things.

I met Khama several times. He appeared to be anxious to buy saddles and horses, doubtless for his cavalry regiment. Fifty years would be about his age, I should say; but he wears well, and in appearance and action is a gentleman. He dresses in European garb, as indeed do all the Kaffirs here when they can afford to do so. Those who cannot afford the whole costume of a fully-fledged European adopt as much as they can buy, no matter in what shape, so that a good many ludicrous figures may be seen on all hands.

The women wear numbers of bracelets of beads and brass wire; they have necklaces also of the same description, while massive anklets of blue beads sometimes extend to the calf of the leg. Usually they have a sort of cloak of skins, and round the waist, cloth and skins of all descriptions.

The old women are exceedingly hideous, and have no uniformity in dress. They seem to have the bulk of the hard work to do; such as carrying firewood, water, and the products of the field; in fact they are inferior pack animals.

No distinguishing form of head-dress is to be found among the people. Their hair is worn very short—perhaps as a sanitary measure, where combs and brushes are not toilet articles. Sometimes they have the head shaved, leaving a small patch of hair on the top, and this patch I have seen adorned with very small black and blue coloured beads.

There are about 3,000 people in the town. The huts are scattered over a large area along the foothills. I was told that in former days the town spread far out upon the plain, but through the restless dread of the warlike Matabeli of the north, the inhabitants have gradually huddled their huts closer together, with a view to gaining greater security against attack. There is a church in the place, capable of accommodating a small congregation.

The white man's occupation here is wholly connected with trading, of which the principal support is the traffic in skins and robes, or karosses made of skins sewn together with remarkable neatness. The people are very clever at their sewing, producing the finest work of the kind in South Africa. I was informed that the Makalaka, a number of whom live here, do all the gardening and blacksmithing work, and really are an industrious race, which cannot be said of the Bechuana people, who are thoroughly lazy.

Trade had been getting very dull for three or four years, and at the time of our visit was almost at a standstill.

The Matabeli, or more properly Amandebeli, under Lo-bengula, have long threatened to descend upon Khama, and for that reason the latter chief will not allow his people to go to the far-off hunting veldt, in proximity to the Kalahari desert, where ostriches still abound. The fear is that during the people's absence the invasion by the Matabeli might take place; so they stay at home, suffering from the hardness of their fate, while day by day and week by week they anticipate the long-threatened raid of their dangerous northern neighbours.

I am sure that, when it was over, such a war would be a boon to the white traders, for the continued dread in anticipation has paralysed every business enterprise.*

The slaughter of giraffes found in this country must have been very great. Within two years over a thousand hides of these beautiful creatures have been shipped to the colony, for the purpose of being made up into cattle whips for ox-driving. It was affirmed that at that time they had sufficient cattle whips to last for ten years to come.

An "old adjutant" would have been delighted to watch the manœuvres of the Shoshong infantry. I did not count their numbers, but it struck me that many were armed with

* Since then I have found reason to believe firmly that Lo-bengula's dreams of conquest relate to lands lying to the north of his territory. I think there should be no fear whatever of his attempting any extension towards the south. Some skirmishing, however, has taken place recently with Khama's forces.

old-fashioned rifles, which I felt certain in the majority of cases, judging from their general rusty appearance round the nipples, would not go off when required. Of course it must be remembered that their foes from the north were armed only with assegais.

Preparations for war were carried on vigorously. The infantry turned out every afternoon during our stay, but I should say that at no time was there a larger muster than 800 or 900, although I was told that Khama could raise 6,000 men. I do not think Khama could arm such a number. The cavalry, I was told, numbered 300, but only 150 had saddles. One morning, when I was taking my observations for longitude, I saw a number of them upon the plain in front of the town.

There was no uniform, either for cavalry or infantry. All put on what rags and old clothes of Europeans they could find. Under these circumstances it may be imagined that the back view of a company of foot was most ridiculous; some had shirts, while others were almost naked, but they all wore a cap of buckskin, black or white, the distinguishing mark of their companies.

Very peculiar was their mode of drill. A company would hustle together, and huddle up one to another, all marching with a sort of "mark time" motion, with very short paces. As they moved they sang in rather a quaint style, not altogether devoid of music. Suddenly two of the warriors started off ahead of the company at a rapid prancing gait and showing the bearing of defiance. After a few manœuvres of this nature the couple would return, and another file, from a different company, would sally bravely forth to go through similar movements.

How these warriors would bear themselves in front of a formidable Matabeli impi is too difficult a question for me to decide. But I have been told that they are frightful cowards. Here again, it may be the case that contact with civilisation has tended to make the people effeminate. Certainly it has not improved them in appearance.

Khama has but one wife, and she previously belonged to Lo-bengula, but had run away from him. I understand that when inquiries were made concerning her by her deserted

FREDERICK COURTENEY SELOUS.

spouse, Khama replied that she was "fat and had plenty to eat," fatness being the chief end of Kaffir ambition.

I cannot say that I regretted when the time came when we were to saddle up and take leave of Shoshong, or Bamangwato. Selous and myself, however, were sorry to part with Argent Kirton, who had proved such a merry companion. Now, however, he had to wend his way southwards.

The waggons had started ahead on the previous day, so we had a long ride before us. We were now about to enter the country termed by the Boers the "Thirst Land."

A short cut through the mountains immediately at the back of the town lessened our journey considerably. Tremendous conglomerations of rocks and boulders, of every description in size and shape, composed the rugged mountains on either side of our narrow track. These spoke of a mighty volcanic upheaval, and it would be difficult to imagine more imposing examples of some of Nature's old-world commotions.

We overtook the waggons on the north bank of the Mahalapse river. The heat was excessive, and the flies were out in myriads. At the waggons we found little Kanyemba, Selous' slave boy, whom he had got among the tribes near the Zambesi; a funny little fellow, the companion and feeder of the dogs and puppies. He was lying under a small blanket, trying to sleep under extraordinary disadvantages, seeing that the puppies were pulling and tugging at the covering, wondering, no doubt, why their playmate was so sulky, while the flies were swarming about his head, the pests being worse here than I had seen them in South Africa. The boy, it seems, had an attack of measles. So Selous produced his medicine chest, a veritable curiosity in its way. The extraordinary mixture of medicines contained in a very small cardboard box, formed a mystical arrangement which the owner alone could solve: there was no elaborate labelling of bottles and boxes which we have been taught to look for in every typical and well-regulated medicine chest. Notwithstanding this, the contents of Selous' "chest" were not less effectual, and in this case the results were all that could be desired. I must say that I had a great liking for this tiny black boy; he was so good-natured, and his happy little face always wore a winning smile, far from being unlovely, for he was by no means an example of the ugly type of the black race.

Inspanning immediately, we trekked through a country of very monotonous appearance, passing the Tchakani vlei, where Selous, in 1872, re-appeared after an absence of four days, during which he had been lost in the veldt, and had neither food nor drink. The small kopjie which stands beside the vlei was his beacon as he wandered about the trackless and sun-parched wilderness.

Black ants were swarming as we moved along, and a most offensive odour arose when they were crushed by the waggon's wheels. We hunted every day, but hardly any game could be seen.

Three or four hours at a time formed the spells of marching, and not a little progress was made during the night, in order to save the oxen, as the rivers all through this region are almost dry. Few of them have any running water, although about ten or twelve years ago they used to be well-flowing streams. Now, even after the rains, there is but little water.

What a strangely worthless land is this! Everyone who passes through the place must think so. There seemed to be few inducements to the investing of capital in any part of Bechuana-land through which I passed. This opinion encourages me to remark freely that some of the later travellers in these parts have been too cruel in picturing to intending colonists that health, wealth, happiness, liberty, equality, fraternity, peace, retrenchment, reform, and all the other visionary blessings which the modern social state hankers after, await them in this Edenless paradise. Why should the truth be hid under the tinselled veil of eloquence? Why should this region, above all others, be described as a land luxuriant in verdure, on whose vast tracts of fertile, well-watered soil the richest crops of golden fruit may rise, ripening under the genial influence of a cloudless sun?

Let the intending colonist go and look at the country, and he will find with a vengeance that he has

> "To force the churlish soil for scanty bread."

As a dupe of misrepresentation, he will search long for the wealth, agricultural and mineral, which is scattered through these regions of intense drought, and his capital will quickly disappear when he, perforce, begins to fertilize the land with his "lung-sick" cattle. When his money is expended, those who sent him out will be deaf to remonstrances, and the whole failure will be attributed to his lassitude and inability to grasp a golden opportunity.

Irrigation is the magic word shouted by every enthusiastic coloniser. Like the bottle of the charlatan, it means a cure for every evil. The actual significance of the word is ignored. The source of supply, of necessity the principal consideration in such a scheme, is never mentioned, not to speak of being indicated. The water is to be dammed, but there is no mention made of the class of dams, of their construction or their probable cost. Of course irrigation can be effected, but we must have rivers that will afford an abundant supply of water; then we must have suitable soil and contour, not too much rooting to be done, and a land adapted to ditching.

Now we find the nomadic tribes of Masarwa bushmen who rove in search of the solitary duiker, cooling their parched tongues by sucking through hollow reeds from the brooks beneath the sands. These inhabitants, as is well known, are stunted in growth, the dirt of years forms their covering, the bow and its bone-tipped arrow is their weapon, and wild grasses of the desert, thrown over bent boughs and saplings, shield them from the storm. Yet they are Nature's free men, for their land may be coveted, but it cannot be inhabited, by aliens. The rivers are sluggish, and are slowly but surely silting.

Remembering the long list of sicknesses to which domestic animals are liable, the vast tracts of unpeopled country, where the duiker and the steinbuck are the only species of game that can exist (their habit being to roam far from water), the scantiness of nutritious grasses, the boundless stretches of worthless bush and stunted forest, the long, winding belts of arid, yellow sand which mark the courses of once-flowing rivers—I say that, remembering all these features, there can be no doubt that they indelibly stamp the country as a great thirst land, a region lost to mankind.

Soon, however, we came to a fine hunting country, where giraffes abounded, also harte-beest (*Alcelaphus caama*) and zebras (Burchell), and where flocks of guinea-fowl and coveys of Namaqua partridges were seen.

Selous and myself bathed in the shallow pools of the river and in small vleis of the forest. The deeper pools were dangerous, on account of the crocodile.

The Shashi river was crossed on the 13th of April. It is said to be the dividing line between the countries of Lo-bengula and Khama, but I believe there is some ground north of the river which is claimed by both sides. Practically, however, it is ruled by Lo-bengula. We left the waggons here, and rode ahead. Now we were in Matabeli-land.

CHAPTER III.

IN LO-BENGULA'S COUNTRY.

The Tati Gold Fields—Dinner with the Jesuit fathers—A reckless traveller—The mines and their working—First appearance of Korana John—Game gradually disappearing—A disastrous flash of lightning —Among the Matabeli—Symptoms of horse-sickness—Lost in the veldt—A shot at a pauw—Unexpected aid—Return to the waggons— "Lo-ben is friendly"—An escort sent—Matabeli gardens—Scene at Magubuduani—Approaching Buluwayo—The "New Valhalla"—The country full of fever—An improvised hospital—Poor Whitaker!— The King in his kraal—Reception by Lo-ben—The Queens of the Matabeli—In the royal harem—Meeting a Yorkshireman—Interior of a queen's hut—Beef and beer with a vengeance!—"The King can do no wrong"—"Go well, Son of the Sea"—Poetical expressions of the Matabeli—Description of Buluwayo—Inxwāla, the great dance—Royal bloodshed—Matabeli morality—Selous attacked by fever—The Comte de Lapanose—Farewell to Selous—Lo-ben's origin—The King explains the country's customs—His final permission—Description of my party—A bad start—"Why, man, he's drunk!"—Breakdown of the cart—Start with waggon and oxen—John's penitence—Shiloh— Massacre of Captain Paterson's party—An apostle of work—Inyati mission station—Last outpost of the London Missionary Society— Kind friends—Farewell to the last white man.

As we approached the Tati Gold Fields we encountered a man who had long lived in Matabeli-land, but was compelled to leave owing to the frequent attacks of fever from which his family had suffered. He was a Boer and a polygamist. His two wives, his family, and his three waggons made a fairly representative Boer caravan. After partaking of a sumptuous lunch cooked by one of the fraus, we continued our journey until we arrived at a small mud-walled house, with a thatched roof, in the little village of Tati. It was Easter Sunday, and we were welcomed by the Jesuit fathers and brothers to a good dinner, the *menu* comprising stewed goat with sauce *à la Tati*, roast leg of mutton, French beans and potatoes, apple and black currant killboy tart, a finely-baked sponge cake that would rival one of Gunter's; also Cape sherry and *café au lait*.

The vegetables and water-melons were grown by the brothers in their garden, which was then in a flourishing condition after the refreshing rains. Father Prestage was the chief of the station, and he informed me that feasting was far from being a common occurrence, but it was natural on Easter Sunday.

A great deal of fever was here, especially down on the river's banks, Tati being situated on a gentle eminence rising, but at some distance, from the stream. The place was then very unhealthy.

On the following day we visited Mr. Sam Edwards, who had charge of the gold mines, a man well known and well liked by all the hunters and travellers who have passed here towards the interior. A young Canadian named Whitaker, he told us, had passed through on his way to the Victoria Falls of the Zambesi, with a donkey as his only companion: a very precarious way to travel, because the African fever attacks the strongest and reduces the most vigorous frame to helpless weakness by a sudden and resistless stroke. In the country which Whitaker was entering any traveller would be in dire difficulties, for should he have an attack and be far away from help it would be a marvel if he survived.

The New Zealand mine, a little to the east of the village, was the only mine in active operation. Working in the others had been temporarily abandoned. The outcrop of the veins on the surface here is exceedingly rare compared with other mining districts I have visited. It is therefore a very expensive country for prospecting. The auriferous quartz is of a rather low grade, and somewhat coloured with peroxide of iron. Slate generally composes the rock of the country. The gold is coated slightly with iron pyrites.

My opinion is that the process technically designated pan-amalgamation would be preferable to the method which the miners now follow, and would, besides, be the most profitable way of reducing these ores. So far prospecting has merely meant that the white man has followed the workings, or rather ground broken—it can only be spoken of as broken—by the Mashona and Makalaka, and long abandoned, the cruel hand of fate having driven these suffering races far to the north-east of Matabeli-land.

Doubtless the small holes which appear in these irregular fissure veins were made during the time when the Mashona and Makalaka were living peacefully in this country; that was before the days of the irresistible and indefatigable conqueror Umzilagazi, whose hordes became the land pirates of this section of the country, making their memories even in our day a trembling dread among all the tribes of the adjacent lands. There was ample cause for this dread, for captivity meant death, or worse than death, a cruel servitude for life in the bondage of the Great Black King.

Gold mining strangely infatuates those who know little or nothing of the ups and downs which men have experienced in life-long search for the precious metal; not only imperiling their possessions but actually their lives for the *ignis fatuus* of a rich lode. The chances are really a thousand to one against finding a really good one.

Here in Tati, however, we get an insight into misplaced

ambition, and a painful exemplification of absolute ignorance on the part of the principals. A gentleman whom I have mentioned before gets the credit of being the Quixotic adventurer who hazards his ducats, and who sent up the machinery for a small mill. We saw the parts of the steam-engine and the mortar-block lying promiscuously around the somewhat odd-looking waggons which had been sent out from England. The accumulation was the "headquarters" of the mining party, but not the faintest idea existed as to where the mine was to be found for which the mill would work.

At Tati we met a Korana elephant-hunter who had served his apprenticeship with Mr. Selous; the latter very kindly made all arrangements with the man to accompany me on my projected journey. The Korana went by the name of John Selous, which reminds me that among the Hottentots there is a singular liking for the name John. My new henchman presented all the peculiar characteristics of the Hottentot in his outward appearance.

We stayed only two days at Tati, being anxious to push on with all possible speed to Buluwayo, the chief town of Matabeli-land. The town was still ten days' travel to the north, and there I would have to make all arrangements about my future route. At Buluwayo I was to part from my good friend Selous.

Our track carried us through thick mopani bush and forest. Portions of the road had been badly cut up by recent rains, so that the waggon pitched and tossed like a ship in a short sea.

After a gradual ascent we reached a point 3,340 feet above the sea-level. Then we trekked downwards into the valley of the Inkwezi river, and crossing the waters camped on the other side.

While here I scoured the country for miles in search of game, but without any luck, although in bygone days there used to be abundance of sport found in these parts. That was before the war of extermination had been fairly started. Now, through the common property of gunpowder and the familiarity of arms to the natives, this region has been laid waste. You may travel not only for miles but for days in the veldt without seeing a living thing, save a few birds and, perhaps, a duiker. By no means a long time ago the shrill trumpeting of the elephant might be heard echoing among the kopjies which bank the river on the north; hundreds of giraffes browsed and found shelter in the luxuriant mopani forests; in short, almost every species of wild animal to be found in South Africa was common among the now silent groves which fringe the Inkwezi.

The native hunters, with their rude-looking arms, have been the exterminators. The finely-finished, specially-made rifles of the keen white sportsman have done little harm among the big game, compared to the havoc made by these imperfect-looking weapons, with their clumsy stocks covered with hide, and altogether resembling a gas-pipe with a frozen clod of earth at one end.

The utter want of animal life was inexpressibly sad. No one could help being impressed with the solemn loneliness of the surroundings on the banks of the Inkwezi, especially if they stood as I did at sunset and looked up at the reddish-coloured rocky prominences of the rude kopjies protruding boldly from their thorny bush coverings and flaunting the sunshine. Austere and immovable, they stood out stern in their original form, overlooking the vast, lone forests, soundless, without a murmur to break the stillness which reigned supreme through an empire of solitude and desolation.

At this place some years ago, when my friend had made camp, and was just inspanning for a start, a flash of lightning instantly killed fourteen oxen which were standing a short distance from his waggon under the shelter of a tree. He had been taking them down for a friend. The Kaffirs would not touch the beasts, as they thought the disaster was a special dispensation of some witch. Mr. Selous, however, cut the tongues out and took them with him as provisions. During the night, the dogs ate them all, and the superstitious Kaffirs doubtless thought the same witch had determined that no part of the cattle should become human food.

Early in the morning Selous left our camp on the Inkwezi river on horseback, bound for Buluwayo, the king's kraal, in order to tell Lo-ben of the arrival of his waggons, and also to state that he was bringing another white man.

This was a very interesting part of the journey. We were nearing the villages of the warlike Matabeli, and every day's progress became full of incident.

I have said that the recent rains had made the roads remarkably heavy, so that pulling the waggons was tremendously hard upon the oxen when crossing the Makhobe hills, where they sank almost to their bellies in the black and treacherous mud, the wheels being up to the naves. The old waggon groaned and creaked again grandly in the struggle, and at one time we nearly broke our dissel boom, which, for the benefit of the uninitiated, I may explain means the pole of the waggon.

Numbers of Matabeli warriors, with assegais and shields, passed us. They seemed to be a very good-natured lot of folk.

The country was of granitic formation, with white quartz cropping out here and there.

Passing on to the banks of the Mangue river we came to the house of a Boer—an old hunter who has permission from the king to live here. His wife was a victim to fever. I had sundry articles from my friend to deliver to him, and noticed with some interest the careful eye he kept upon the balance-scales as I weighed out his quantity of dried peaches* from America, and sugar—veritable luxuries in this country. The old Boer was a smart man of business in this particular. He told me that Lo-ben was in a bad humour, and had been blotting out a few lives lately.

Our animals all looked very well on the night of the 20th of April; but on the following day the yellow horse, as I termed him, fell very ill, and during the night died. He was a very good little beast, but had not had the sickness, in other words was not "salted."

I watched the symptoms carefully, but was at a loss to know what to do for him. This sickness seems to me to be a regular fever, with quick and violent pulsation. The nostrils are dilated, and there is evident pain in breathing. A copious discharge of a very yellow fluid comes from the nose, and, after death, a large amount of foam—likewise yellow—is blown from the nostrils and mouth.

By this time the weather had greatly changed. Usually I wore nothing but a shirt and light corduroy trousers, but now a coat and waistcoat were not out of place, and far from being too warm. We were getting high in elevation, the camp then being 3,850 feet above the sea.

A few mornings after this, according to my usual habit, I started out on horseback, leaving the waggons trekking in a north-easterly direction. My intention was to cross their spoor later in the day, as when I killed game I could

---

* The water in which the peaches are stewed is considered a valuable medicine in fever cases.

carry a portion of it on horseback to the camp. I had given chase to some antelope, but after going a long way I looked at my watch and found that I had been three hours in the chase.

Turning abruptly round, I made off in what I thought was the right direction to come up to the waggons. After galloping hard for some time I came to the conclusion, not having discovered the waggons' spoor, that I must have inadvertently crossed the track, so I started upon a new quest in a more southerly direction, keeping up a good pace, as I knew the waggons would now be far away ahead, and the boys would be out all over the country after me.

There was no doubt that I was properly lost. I would at once have to shoot something for that night's supper. Wandering for a time, I saw, about 200 yards off, a very large pauw, which is a big grey bird, larger than a good-sized turkey. I immediately jumped off my horse and tied him to a tree. There was a very bad place to cross before I could get to the bird, so I fired at 200 yards, and was fortunate in hitting it fairly on the breast. The bullet expanded, and glanced off instead of piercing: so much for the boasted hollow bullets; although it is right to say that mine were hollowed too much.

I started after the pauw at my top speed, for in spite of the shot, it was making good tracks, and I contemplated making my supper off him. As I advanced I was astounded to see suddenly a young Matabeli running alongside of me. It seemed as if he had sprung out of the grass. With his knobkerry he soon despatched the bird.

The young warrior's unexpected appearance was a surprise as pleasant as it was mysterious. I was delighted to see him. Now I would again find the spoor, and anticipations of a feast on raw fowl—I had no matches—were dispelled.

Knowing only a few words of Zulu, I used them to the best advantage, by trying to explain that I wished to find the waggons' spoor. I mounted my horse and followed the young warrior. He led me straight to his kraal, where I dismounted, and approached a group of old men sitting under the trees. They gazed at me with the utmost astonishment. After an interview during which I endeavoured to make myself understood by signs, words being exceedingly scarce, I offered my pocket-knife as an inducement to the head man to send one of his young men with me.

He agreed, and sent the young savage whom he seemed to own body and bones. The youth was remarkably cute, for after we had proceeded a little distance he feigned ignorance as to where I wished to go, and kept pointing to the long pauw feathers. I wanted to explain to him that he might have them all if he would only show the road, and at length I gave him them, much to his delight.

A very fine specimen of muscular humanity was this youth. In his right hand he carried a sort of battle-axe, and in his left hand some assegais and sticks.

At last we alighted upon the waggons' spoor. I then could see how far I had diverged from the right direction, for close to us was the large fig-tree under which we had camped on the previous night. The camp fires were still smouldering.

Of course I duly gave up the knife in payment for his services. I was glad enough to be once more upon the waggons' spoor, and after some hours' riding, late in the afternoon, I came up with them, just in time to prevent a general hunt being made for me. One boy had already started off in the search, but Jim, a Hottentot, saddled up, and went after him like the wind.

A messenger, sent by King Lo-bengula, now arrived from Selous. The object of his mission was to escort us past numerous Matabeli maize-fields and villages which now lay on our line of march to Buluwayo, the king's town.

The messenger handed me a letter from Selous, which was very welcome, because I was extremely anxious to hear something about the frame of mind of the monarch. Selous said, "Lo-ben is friendly, and prospect fair for your getting permission to go through his country."

Lo-ben's emissary was an immensely big fellow, and a good type of the young and stalwart Matabeli warrior, looking as though his life had been passed in a thriving land of plenty. His head-dress consisted of ostrich feathers cut short, and trimmed so as to form a large rosette, through which a long black feather was stuck. He carried a black ox-hide shield, interlaced with white thongs: he had three assegais and a knobkerry.

A Matabeli garden was close to us on the top of the hill; properly speaking, it was a patch of land under cultivation, for all the fields of corn in this country are, by the white man, called gardens. The garden, which was named "Mavuba," overlooked an immense valley, partly covered with trees, through which the road passed. I had a hurried meal, cooked by Sebina, the black girl, who had accompanied us all the way. Crowds of Matabeli people came to look at us, and some of them pounced with wonderful avidity at the remaining feathers of the pauw, which were long and pretty, being of a greyish colour, crossed here and there with white. They prize these feathers very highly as ornaments for their heads, and any one would admit that the decoration is remarkably becoming to the wild-looking, black sons of Nature.

Getting under weigh, and crossing the long valley, we soon ascended the southern slopes of the great granite mountains which form the division between the waters flowing to the Limpopo and Sabia rivers, and to the Zambesi. We came to a large kraal situated in the open, and having a background of jagged rocks. The place is called Magu-buduani. Here we stopped, and were soon surrounded by swarms of men, women and children, to whom our arrival was a cause of much curiosity.

Then began a bustling, chattering tumult. The flurried throng of men, women and children, forming an excited circle of naked humanity, pressed closely around us with their marketable produce, including Kaffir corn and meal, hemp, pumpkins, sweet reed, and so forth. For some small strips of cotton cloth—limbo it is called by the traders— we bought some potatoes and other articles. One cotton blanket was given for a goat, a transaction which occasioned a good deal of bargaining. The noise was tremendous; what with husbands and wives quarrelling about the amount of cloth they were to receive, girls chattering and holding out their hands for beads, and other uproar, it was impossible for any one to hear himself speak.

The whole scene was highly amusing. The fun of the fair was noisy, but nearly all the people seemed to be beaming with good-humour. All were well fed and happy. One woman was really pretty, with teeth as white as the proverbial pearl. She was full of sprightliness, and begged most persistently for white calico ("ilimbo elimhlopi") and beads. A small piece of white calico gave her lively satisfaction.

" I praise you " (Ngi ya bonga), she shouted, as she went on her way rejoicing.

Soon we left this lively fair. It was nearly dark, and

we camped in the forest beyond. We were now upon the great plateau of Matabeli-land.

During the next two days' journey we passed the villages of Inthlathlangela and Umganen—the latter a favourite village of the king—between which were interspersed rich fields of waving maize. This was a thickly-inhabited district, for we were now approaching Buluwayo, the town of the great black king, Lo-bengula, the most powerful monarch in South Africa.[*]

My curiosity was greatly excited as we neared the domicile of Lo-ben, who had so much power either to aid or thwart my effort. His subjects, masculine and feminine, of all ages and conditions, flocked around the waggon in scores, bringing tobacco and many other commodities likely to be wanted in exchange for the coveted cloth and beads.

They escorted us until we reached the "New Valhalla," the name humorously given to the house of Mr. George Fairbairn, a Scottish gentleman who trades in ivory, close to the king's kraal, on the southern banks of the Umkhosi river. A hearty welcome was given me here.

The country at the time was full of fever, and Fairbairn's house was temporarily an hospital. Several deaths had occurred in the immediate neighbourhood on the mission station, one who succumbed being Mr. Thomas, who was among the first of the white men who came to this country, and who had established a small mission station of his own, named Shiloh.

On my arrival I made inquiries concerning the progress of Whitaker, the young and adventurous Canadian, of

---

[*] Buluwayo means "the one that is slain." Gubuluwayo is sometimes used, the prefix Gu or Go, signifying *at, to,* or *from*. Bengula, the name of the king, means "defender," the prefix Lo signifying *the*.

whom we heard at the Tati gold fields as having been making his way towards the Zambesi.

"Ah!" said Fairbairn, "we buried poor Whitaker at Hope Fountain Mission Station a few days ago. He was very reluctant to take the medicines we offered him."

Fairbairn's abode was very full; but there seemed to be always room for one more. Of course in this country beds are unknown articles of furniture; cane mats being the familiar couches for the luxury of repose. Thanks, however, to the generous warmth of hospitality, we were soon comfortably housed, although I must admit that it was with regretful reluctance that I left the waggon, in which I had spent so many pleasant weeks, even for the better accommodation afforded by a house.

Fairbairn, Selous, and myself went up to see old King Lobengula. I was very eager to know in what sort of humour was the old gentleman. A missionary, Mr. S——, who had had a quarter of a century of Christian effort in Matabeliland, and was able to know the character of the people, had, when we met him in full retreat in Bechuanaland, given a dreadful account of the condition of affairs, saying that it was impossible to live in Matabeli-land since the difficulty about the hippo killing. The poor missionary's beard had been pulled, and he had to suffer other indignities which as an apostle of divinity he could not brook. But what special exemption could he expect? Many observers note that after five-and-twenty years of missionary labour there are no converts to the faith of our fathers. After so long a period of profitless contention with a people who are both deaf and blind to persuasion, it could hardly be expected that Mr. S—— would find more sympathetic treatment than other whites.

Fairbairn informed me that with the payment of all the

fines the troubles about the sea-cow row, to which I have referred, had vanished, and that now the old man was in a very good humour.

When we entered the king's kraal I could see him seated under his roof porch. A few of his people were around. All of us shook hands with him, and were received with more courtesy than might be expected from a savage king. We sat on the ground beside him, and his prettiest slave girls brought in beer. Kneeling before us they would drink first, and then hand the liquor to us.

Lo-ben seemed very friendly, and evidently had quite forgotten the troublesome episode of the shooting of the sea-cow. When Selous asked permission to enter the hunting veldt, the monarch granted his request with a smile, remarking, "Selous is a young lion."

Looking at me, he then asked what I was about to do. On being told that I was anxious to go through his country, and subsequently through unexplored Mashona-land, to the Zambesi, he simply remarked, "It is very far away."

A crowd of endunas began to assemble, and as it was clear that a "big talk" was about to ensue, we departed without making a further attempt to gain the desired permission. Walking to the back of the house we saw numbers of hive-shaped huts, the homes of the queens, the housing of the royal harem.

Here was a novel scene! Upon grass mats in front of the huts singly, or in bevies here and there, the queens of the Matabeli reclined gracefully and with careless ease, basking their rather *embonpoint*, but yet symmetrical frames like glossy seals lolling in the warmth of the sun. A strange but not unpleasant odour filled the air, for these queens are in the habit of scenting themselves with a perfume made from wild flowers and herbs rolled into balls about the size of small apples.

The picturesqueness of the figure-grouping, however, was somewhat marred by the occupation of some of the royal ladies, who were imbibing copious quantities of beer, and eating largely of meat. Yet they were a happy-looking company, beaming with good-nature, and all running to portliness, which evidently increased with years. We sat down and drank beer with some of them. They asked Fairbairn numerous questions about me, and with feminine curiosity seemed particularly anxious to know where my wives were, if I had any, and if so how many? One in a jesting humour called to some slave girls who passed, and turning to me said :

"Now choose a wife from among these; which shall it be?"

Fairbairn was well acquainted with all the queens. He seemed to have *entrée* into every part of the kraal. It is a very unusual privilege to be allowed to walk through the harem. Slaves of both sexes and of all ages and sizes were moving to and fro among the huts.

A new house was being erected for His Majesty, the material being bricks, and the builder an old British tar, a Yorkshireman named Johnny, who years before, while cruising on the east coast, had suddenly left his ship of his own accord, and found his way to the happier and freer atmosphere of the far interior. Johnny was a genial soul, and a very funny old boy. There he stood slinging mud like a Thames dredger, and yet in feeling as free and independent as an American senator. He has built the only houses that are worthy the name in Matabeli-land.

Many of the Matabeli queens were peeping in at the windows of the partially-finished house, and evidently made a good deal of fun of Johnny, who would turn round every now and then and give them the contents of his trowel.

I was astonished to see the interior of a queen's hut, which had a cleanly black polished floor, and everything arranged in the tidiest manner. Floors are composed of ant-heap, ox-blood, and cow-dung, which when set becomes very hard. The occupant of this hut showed me how the floor was polished, by means of a fine smooth, round pebble, which, held in both hands, was rubbed along the surface, the operator spitting every now and then to supply the necessary moisture. There was a rack on one side of the hut on which were placed numerous baskets and all sorts of little tricks, while against the walls, neatly folded up, were the cane mats on which the dwellers slept.

A queen's mark of distinction is unique. All of them shave their heads and wear at the top, and well at the back, a small inverted cup of about one and a-half inches in diameter made of red beads. Round their waists they wear kilts of black ox-hide, falling to the knees.

The kraal was full of slaves who had been caught during war, and brought to the king by his fighting men.

Some days elapsed before we again visited Lo-ben, so that we had ample time to think over the plans which might be successfully adopted in approaching him with my request. The most feasible seemed to be to present him with a very elaborate silver-mounted sword-knife, and a fine bull.

The day arrived when we should visit the king. We had heard that he was suffering from gout, doubtless through over-indulgence in native beer. He would soon leave for one of his other towns, so Fairbairn and myself again approached, and found him encircled by a multitude of endunas. Preferring to await a favourable opportunity for our request, we sat down beside the monarch. Patience, however, entailed great personal inconvenience. For four weary hours we sat drinking beer and trying to devour great chunks of beef handed to us upon the royal fork of His Majesty; who, while attending to the orations of his people, was busily engaged in gorging himself with a mass of meat which he held on a fork in his left hand, while with an enormous carving-knife he fanned off the swarming flies. Every now and then Fairbairn took a sly look at me to see what my powers of reception were in the beef-eating line.

Little slave boys, who had only recently been captured, and were nothing but skin and bone, crouched up beside us, and were glad to accept either morsels of beef or drops of beer that we did not want. Gladly enough would I have given them the whole lot; but I was well aware that the better I proved a capacity for eating and drinking, the more would savage appreciation smile upon me and favour my designs. The reader, therefore, may be assured that I tried to be sufficiently omnivorous.

Evidently a case of no slight importance was being heard by Lo-ben. All eyes were riveted upon him, and the facial expressions showed how eager every hearer was to catch even an echo of the weighty words which fell from the monarch's mouth. Occasionally, as he conversed with the assembled endunas, Lo-ben would utter some transcendent expression of infallible wisdom, which when given forth would get many responsive ejaculations of acquiescence and sympathy.

"Yebo, yebo, Kumalo!" cried the audience. "Ye, hay, hay!" *

---

* *Yebo* means yes. *Kumalo* is a courtesy title for the royal family. The other exclamations indicate approval.

THE ROYAL KRAAL OF LO BENGULA.

An oppressive subjection was evident among the crowd. They sat willing, should the potentate so ordain, and without a word of remonstrance, to see their own brothers die the death, for here could be found the most vivid illustration of the axiom, the "King can do no wrong." It was strangely noticeable that all who passed the circle of royalty had to cower to the earth, crouching as though they were about to collapse altogether.

Sunset was approaching, and as everyone, excepting those immediately connected with the royal household, were bound to be outside by that time, I was beginning to fear a further delay; but luckily the crowd dispersed, and as the king seemed to be in good-humour, Fairbairn deftly put to him the momentous question. A frank permission was the response; I was to be allowed to travel freely through the country. After this I presented Lo-ben the sword-knife, giving him at the same time the promise of a fine bull, for the purchase of which I had already negotiated.

"You may go through my country," he said, "but it is very far to the Zambesi."

I thanked him, and bade him good-bye.

"Go well, son of the sea," was his reply.

I thought this parting benediction of old Lo-ben was far from being devoid of poetry; but strangely enough I soon had other examples of the exaltation in this respect which assuredly characterises this remarkable people.

As I walked along with Fairbairn the far-off western sky blazed resplendently across the heavens its fiery farewell. The reflected glow of its light gave a crimson richness to the dome-topped huts of the royal kraal, and gleamed softly through the jagged spaces of the primitive citadel. The departing sun told that it was time for us to take our leave, and make our way to the outer side of the encircling fence before the "young men" would let the saplings fall so as to unite the two horns of the fortress, and make an endless line around the home of the monarch.

We had almost reached the wide portals of the enclosure, when suddenly stentorian shouts rent the air, making us pause in our progress. The shouts proceeded from a young warrior who stood in an attitude which reminded one of Ajax defying the lightning, looking a gladiatorial figure shining red in the evening light.

"Inkosa miama!" (black king) he exclaimed; and then continued to shout the following praises, which for convenience I will write in English, with the native equivalent.

"Calf of a black cow!" (*Inkoniama inkomo!*)

"Man-eater!" (*Ihlama doda!*)

"Lion!" (*Siluana!*)

"Thou art as great as the world!" (*Uena Ngaga gelizwe!*)

"Thou who appeared when people spoke confusedly!"* (*Uvela be vungasa!*)

"Star that shot through the firmament in the day of Zuangandaba!" (*Inkanyezi e ya tjega emini gwa Zuangandaba!* †)

"Thou art in the plains!" ‡ (*Uso bala!*)

"Black mystery!" (*Indaba emniama!*)

"Thou who pierceth the sky that is above!" (*Ihlabe Zulu elipezulu!*)

"Calf of the terrible!" (*Inkoniama gesilo!*)

"The Letter Destroyer!" (*Usa pula ngwalo!*)§

---

* In times of anarchy.

† Zuangandaba was the chief town of Lo-ben's enemies in the time of the civil war, and he conquered it.

‡ He did not hide.

§ The word *ngwalo* has reference to a correspondence of Lo-ben and his endunas with Sir T. Shepstone respecting Kuruman, the rightful heir.

"He crossed the great desert!" (*Wa dabula Ihalihali!*)
"The black duck of Umzilagazi!" (*Itata elimniama eliga Umzilagazi!*)
"The black calf of Buluwayo!" (*Itoli elimniama la gwa Buluwayo!*)

Such were the pæans sung lustily at the gate. Fairbairn and myself waited a little to listen; but getting tired of the endless shouts we pushed on homewards, the vehemence of the sound lessening and dying as we proceeded.

At the time, when I heard the interpretation of the sentences, I could not help thinking how barbarously delightful was the poetry of this warlike race! Their songs in laudation of their king were disinterested songs of praise. Perhaps a new Utopia was here, in which love was true and loyalty unselfish. I was particularly told that the people would come great distances to sing the praises of Lo-ben.

Was there any ulterior motive? The truly disinterested man cannot be found among us whites; was devotion so true an attribute of the blacks, and flattery at last sincere?

I asked Fairbairn about the matter.

"Oh," was his reply, "the old man gives them uxuala!"

Bah! that was it. The poetry was gone. Vulgar beer! Not a spark of the divinity of poetry! Henceforth I would not believe in exceptional blacks, but would regard them as ordinary mortals, as plain, practical men, with common cravings and with modes of gratifying them similar to those of the human family generally.

Returning to the "New Valhalla" we had a good supper on sheep's head and trotters, which I enjoyed all the more seeing that my mind was relieved from all doubts and fears regarding the obstructions which, with good reason, had been prophesied to occur here, but were dispelled through the courteous sanction and friendly demeanour of the much-dreaded Lo-bengula.

The kraal or town of Buluwayo is situated on the outer side of a great elliptic enclosure of about half a mile in length, which is entirely occupied by royalty, its adherents and belongings.

Once a year in this immense enclosure a great dance—Inxwala—takes place. It is a national event, and is considered the first and most martial sight in South Africa. The king stands in the centre of his 6,000 warriors, who are bedecked with ostrich-feather capes and otter-skin turbans, their arms being the assegai and the shield. Various warlike evolutions are gone through, such as darting their glistening weapons swift through the air, as all the warriors join, and together tap their shields with rhythmic beat, shouting and singing the while the song of the assegai and the praises of the great black king.

> "Come and see at Majobana's; come and see!
> Here is the display, display of the assegai!
> Come and see at Majobana's; come and see!"

Then stamping one foot, and pointing the assegai towards the heavens, they exclaim in chorus, "Sh—shu—shu," which literally means, "We stamp out—we will conquer!" This they never tire of repeating.

I was told that year after year the number of warriors at this dance is diminishing. Opposing factions have assumed or are assuming proportions which forebode a troublesome future in the reign of the present king.* The scions or

---

* Lately I have heard from Matabeli-land that much strife and bloodshed have occurred. In April 1885 the king sent an impi to Lake Ngami, in the west of his country, in reality for the purpose of acquiring a large stock of cattle, the lung-sickness of late years

connections of royalty are not permitted to have very large kraals. Their conduct is often a source of danger. Three months previously to our visit, Lo-ben put to death his uncle, Usikuana, and all his kraal, comprising about forty people, a doom which was brought on through the uncle exercising privileges which were only permitted in the royal circle to the king himself.

Another massacre, which was found to be in order, resulted in the merciless annihilation of a number of families. On the death of Umzilagazi, the father of Lo-ben, the body was buried with all the deceased's effects. His waggons and everything he had possessed were thrown into a cave called Ntumbani, which is the name for the grave of a king.* Near to this last resting-place of royalty a kraal was erected, and the inhabitants were told to watch the sepulchre that it might not be disturbed. But on burning the high grass to clear the ground for harvest, an evil wind arose, turning the relentless flames towards the grave of the old conqueror, until it was licked clean of everything,

---

having thinned the Matabeli herds. The army returned in August, but not triumphant. Many lives had been lost, but not a single head of cattle was brought to the expectant king, who was very angry, and accused the warriors of cowardice and also of robbing and burning a white man's house, a crime which was committed against his strict injunctions. This shows the justness of the dealings of Lo-ben in relation to the white man; for he decreed that for this particular breach of discipline the endunas should pay the full loss, in cattle. My informant also said that on the day previous to that on which he wrote, a fight had occurred between the Imbezu and the people of another town about the ownership of a boy. Before the combatants could be separated about twenty were killed and a lot wounded. "So," says the writer, "this shows you what a bloodthirsty lot we live among."

* The word Ntumbani literally means small mountain or hill. The people are so superstitious that they dare not speak of the death or grave of a departed potentate. Hence the indication of the sepulchre is included in the name Ntumbani.

the ironwork alone remaining to tell the tale of destruction. For such neglect there could be but one punishment. So at early dawn the executioners fell upon the unfortunate watchers, closing their earthly career, and sending their spirits to the crocodile and the hippo. Dogs and all were slain.

The morals of the Matabeli, from a British standpoint (which would take a Lord Chancellor to expound, and an archbishop, at least, to exemplify), are unquestionably in the lower scale. But in this respect they are far from being beneath other types of the African races. Polygamy is a recognised custom amongst them. Wives, in fact, mean wealth : their number is a sign of greatness in the husband. I would say that there is no immorality, for the knowledge of sensual vice has no dwelling in the really savage mind. His natural passions are not stimulated by subtle charms. He is not a *blasé* creature, but a simple son of nature, free and strong in the robustness of his manhood. There is no socialism, for various grades exist, as they do in other countries; but the king's license is regulated so that his subjects are not compelled to be vicious instead of natural.

Fever was very prevalent in the country. The missionaries were suffering greatly; and, much to my sorrow, my friend Selous was brought down by a very bad attack.

We heard repeatedly the dismal moans of the black people when in the early morning they bewailed for their dead friends as they went forth to bury them.

Selous' attacks were frequent, and very severe. It is wonderful with what rapidity a strong, tough man can be reduced to a state of childlike weakness. Pluck is most important in battling against this strange malady. Any one who has the slightest fear is almost sure to succumb. But my friend was not troubled with the latter feeling, for while exploring in remote regions, where neither medicine nor even the common necessaries of life could be obtained, he had pulled through a succession of fevers which would have killed the strongest of men.

During our stay here we sometimes rode to the mission stations, and to some of the principal kraals. While on one of these excursions we encountered a French gentleman living in a small shanty, with a few Kaffir huts near his door, at which he sat in his shirt-sleeves, for he had evidently been preparing his dinner. He appeared to be perfectly happy, although his mode of life was indeed a great change from the brilliant gaieties of Paris. I discovered him to be M. Comte de Lapanose.

Time was passing, I thought somewhat unprofitably. It was with the greatest difficulty that I procured a cart of very small dimensions. Keeping in view the fact that I inevitably would have to abandon this mode of conveying my stores, I did not wish to have the encumbrance of a waggon. The cart looked quite unsuitable for a journey such as I was about to attempt. But making up my mind that we would get through somehow, I fitted it up as well as I could with some kind of makeshift gun-racks and other conveniences.

The load consisted of blue and white calico, and beads of different colours (these commodities being the necessary articles of exchange), some coffee, tea, and sugar (a very limited supply), rifles, and ammunition. Some idea of the slenderness of the store of trading goods and provisions may be arrived at when I say that the total weight of everything on board was 450 lbs. The cause of this was that the conveyance would certainly have to be abandoned, and carriers become a *dernier ressort*.

It was now about the middle of May. Selous having quite recovered from his serious attack of fever, started on a hunting trip towards the Mababe and the Chobe rivers, which lay about two months' travel to the far west. I was very sorry to say "good-bye," for we had "hit it off" together most pleasantly. We had many exciting hunts, and those weeks I spent in his waggon I shall never forget. Neither shall I forget the help he afforded me in overcoming many vicissitudes which necessarily confront one who begins a journey of this description. "Your principal difficulty," he said at parting, "will be in getting carriers. Remember you don't take any Matabeli men, as in that case you will be sure to have trouble with the Mashona tribes."

Next day, in company with Fairbairn, I rode over to Umganen, whence the king had gone to recover from his fit of gout. A trader, Stewart by name, whom we met there, was thoroughly versed in the Matabeli tongue, so I seized the opportunity of getting him to interpret a few questions which I wished to ask the king, seeing that I had already imposed on Mr. Fairbairn's good-nature to a very great extent in interpreting for me at all my previous interviews.

This seems to be a fitting place to say something of Lo-bengula. He is the son and successor of the great and warlike Umzilagazi, the redoubtable conqueror of the country, and the founder of this nation. His wife—Lo-ben's mother—was a Swazi Zulu.

Lo-ben is about eight-and-forty years of age. When a boy he herded bucks in the Transvaal, at the time his father was achieving conquests in the north. Kuruman, another son, and the rightful heir, when quite young had been secreted in some spot far from the country, a common custom with savage heirs-apparent, to avoid the probability of their being assassinated, or some other evil befalling them. When Umzilagazi died, Kuruman could not be found, and it was supposed by many that he was dead. Lo-bengula, as the second son, was then made king, the report going forth that Kuruman had died in the Transvaal during the previous year. But on more than one occasion I have heard that there are still those who cling to the idea that Kuruman yet lives, although he has never dared to come forward to claim his rights as king.

If he still lives, his caution or cowardice may be due to a vow which was made by all the natives at the coronation of Lo-ben—a vow which announced that the name of Kuruman should die, that all who spoke of him should also perish, for now Lo-bengula was king of the Matabeli for ever.

I met a man who had been sent to fetch from the east coast the salt water used as an ingredient in majesty-making medicine. I tried to get some information out of him regarding the east coast lands, but although he was of a very communicative disposition, he evidently thought my questions irrelevant; so he amused us by relating tales of hunting the lion and other beasts, in which pursuits he had evidently distinguished himself with the assegai. It is a favourite sport with these people to attack the lion with spears. All over his body this man was a mass of scars, but they had not injured him much. According to my custom, I strung him up on the ivory scales, and found that he turned 200 lbs. He had not, I should say, an ounce of superfluous flesh.

In conversation with the king, through Mr. Stewart, I asked him:

"What is the law of Hlonipa?"

"My mothers-in-law," responded the king, "cannot look upon my face; they must cover their faces when they pass me; they cannot use any word resembling my father

Umzilagazi's name. For instance, for the word *amanzi* (water) they would substitute the word *miaha*, for *angazi* (I do not know) they would say *angani*."*

"What is the law with reference to twins," I inquired. "Do not the Bechuana and Basuto kill them?"

"Yes," was the reply, "the Bechuana do, but we let them live; it makes no difference with us. With the Bechuana, when the lower teeth of any child appear first it is all right —a good sign; but when the upper front teeth appear first it is bad, and they kill them."†

"What do you think becomes of you after you die?" was my next question.

"The Zulus believe," replied the king, "that they turn into some wild animal."

From the way he spoke, I could infer that Lo-ben did not himself believe this; at any rate, it did not seem to trouble his mind.

"What do you think of the missionaries and their belief?" I asked.

"I suppose it is right," said Lo-ben, "because they say so; but then they are paid for saying so."

At this juncture a man came in, and bending before the king reported that sixty more cattle had died of lung sickness, a plague that is very prevalent throughout South Africa. I heard that over fifteen hundred head of cattle were reported dead to the king in one week. The man's announcement had the effect of checking our conversation. I imagined, however that Lo-ben had little sympathy with missionary efforts. One of the missionaries had told him of

---

* This, however, I found to be an ordinary rule in savage etiquette—a rule, *but not a law*.

† The reason of this is, that they think if the child grows up, bad luck and calamity will attend the kraal; all will lose their lives, the man alone surviving.

a heaven abounding with milk and honey. This was a mistake. Such an ideal is hardly compatible with the blood-thirsty appetite of this tribe of warriors, who are not allowed to touch milk after coming to man's estate.*

On resuming our conversation, I asked the king what the war-cry was. He was, perhaps naturally, reluctant to state that of his particular tribe, but told me that every tribe had a cry peculiar to itself. Mr. Stewart then asked him about the name "Amandabeli."

"Amandabeli," said Lo-bengula, "is an Abusuto word, the proper name for my people is Zulu."

This ended our interview with the king. I bade him good-bye, and he said: "When you come back to my country I will send boys to meet you." We parted as the best of friends, his farewell words being:

"Go pleasantly, and come back quickly, son of the sea!"

On our return, Fairbairn, Stewart, old Johnny and myself had a parting dinner together at the "New Valhalla."

The king, generally speaking, had a very fair notion of Britons, distinguishing them readily from the Boers, whom he invariably holds in great contempt. One day Fairbairn had puzzled Lo-ben very greatly by predicting an eclipse of the sun. He took care to be with the king when the phenomena occurred, which was witnessed with unbounded astonishment, the monarch having scorned to entertain the idea that a prophecy of this description could be realised, except as a purely accidental verification of the word of the white witch.

Often, however, he would say, "You white men are very artful, but you cannot cure the fever."

---

* It is stated that the Matabeli warriors are fed on raw meat, but this is inaccurate. There is a certain ceremony gone through at the great dance at which they cut pieces of raw flesh from the living ox.

Upon the following day I was to begin my travels alone.

Morning brought a good deal of busy, bustling work. It took some time to pack the cart and to fix the rifles firmly in the racks in case of breakage should an upset occur, which was more than likely, as the vehicle to my eyes looked very rotten; indeed, from the first, I did not like the appearance of the thing.

Sagwam.   Karemba.   Korana John.   Taroman.   Windvogel.
THE "FAITHFULS."

Now to describe my party—all told. Korana John was to be driver, interpreter and companion, for he could speak broken English; then there was a Makololo, called Taroman, whom I styled the india-rubber man; a Makalaka, named Sagwam; a Mashona, named Karemba, of whom I have spoken before; and a Bushman, the higher ape, as I dubbed him, a creature of disputed origin, and a very extraordinary mortal, whose fancies in dress lay entirely in the line of head ornament, for he bedecked his marvellously-formed cranium with all sorts of articles, chiefly feathers. This character had many names, among others Windvogel.*

The party was small, but I had learned that to take a following of Matabeli people would be fatal to progress, besides being dangerous, as they were constantly at war with their neighbours.

Preparations being over, and everything complete and ready for the start, I despatched the little caravan, and after a lapse of a few hours Fairbairn and myself started after it on horseback. When we were within half a mile of the Umkhosi river I was astounded to see John coming along towards us looking as though he had been grossly insulted.

"Great thunder! what is the matter? Something broken on that old rickety cart, I'll be bound!"

I noticed that John's face had lost a shaving of its outer covering, and from his general limp appearance I concluded that he had been wrestling with the cart, and decidedly had come off second best, hence his extreme indignation. Much to my disgust and astonishment Fairbairn quietly said:

"Why, man, he's drunk!"

Just at that moment a little Matabeli boy came running up, and said that he had found my driver, interpreter and companion having a serious fight with a thorn bush. By this time he was making such a row that there could not

---

* I think it necessary to give these particulars regarding the party, so that the reader may become familiar with their names, as they each have an incidental individuality during the journey onwards. Besides this, they were now my only companions.

be the slightest doubt that the cursed black snake had found its way to my party in some surreptitious fashion.

The misgiving that first flashed through my mind was a fear lest my chronometer and rifles had been broken. While shaking his head in a most dismal manner, John kept on reiterating the doleful tidings that the cart was in the river, the news being varied by strong declarations that he was not drunk!

Arriving at the river we found that our conveyance had become a total wreck. The dissel boom had broken off short. Fortunately the cart was not actually in the water, but it stood just tipped on the brink of the high bank. With the tools I had I at once went to work to repair the dissel boom. John sat amidst a group of admiring blacks who had followed in the wake of the cart, and who seemed beside themselves with delight at the entertaining scene. His ailment had reached the whimpering stage, and he tried to show his penitence by intermittent fits of weeping and swearing, while ever and anon he would send forth a spasmodic and violent shriek.

The heat was extreme, but I worked as hard as I could, and in due time finished the repairs. Happily, nothing important had been broken or lost; the rifle-racks had proved an immense success. Now, however, I made up my mind that a decrepit cart of this description was wholly unfitted for the journey upon which I was only now at the threshold. A waggon must be had, but where?

Inspanning the oxen we crossed the river, and after making camp and giving John instructions to await for my return, I rode back to my friend Fairbairn's house. Ever ready to assist, he at once came to the rescue, offering me his light waggon. Mr. Stewart, whose waggons were close beside Mr. Fairbairn's house, kindly lent me his oxen, so that before night I was in a position to despatch the waggon to the place where John was camped. Afterwards we spent the evening in talking over the country, its people, their habits and customs. I was up betimes: the sun had not yet risen, and the leaden mists of dawn were hanging over the cosy little domicile of the New Valhalla when I bade a last farewell to the place and to my friend Fairbairn, under whose hospitable roof I had spent so many pleasant days, and whose friendly aid had helped me onward.

Mounting a very good little horse, I galloped off towards the Umkhosi river, and reached the waggon-camp just as the sun peeped up in the eastern horizon.

John had his head tied up in a red pocket-handkerchief. He was a picture of woe, and no doubt felt very "coppery." His forehead was all torn through his plungings in the thorn-bush. I could not help thinking, when I looked at him, of a wooden god, with the paint badly rubbed off, which I had seen in a Chinese joss-house. But I asked no questions, neither did I condole with him on his pitiful appearance, busying myself with the transference of all the goods from the cart to the waggon, the former being returned with Mr. Stewart's oxen to Mr. Fairbairn.

Once we were off I felt relief, even happiness. The feeling of rolling along over four firm wheels was infinitely better than sitting haphazard on the front of a small, over-loaded cart, giving frequent chances of coming abruptly to grief by being precipitated between the hind legs of an irascible ox.

A difficulty which I had hardly foreseen soon became apparent. The six very small oxen which had barely been able to draw the cart, were, of course, far from being equal to the work of dragging a waggon through the heavy river-beds that lay ahead of us. My only chance of procuring trained oxen was at Shiloh, twenty-two miles distant, so we pushed on with all haste, and that evening we arrived at the house of Mr. Thomas, the gentleman to whom I referred as having just died of fever when we were at Buluwayo, and the father of the young man who was killed with Captain Paterson's party. Mr. David Thomas, the deceased's eldest son, gave us a hearty welcome. He was a brother of the young trader whom I had met at Zeerust, in the Northern Transvaal.

In 1878, Sir Theophilus Shepstone, administrator of the Transvaal territory, wrote to King Lo-Bengula, complaining of some assumed grievances of the traders. The delivery of the letter was entrusted to Captain Paterson, who was accompanied by Mr. Sergeant. The contents of the missive, as well as the conversation with Lo-ben, were somewhat injudicious, judging from the written copy of the transactions which is in my possession. They could not fail to arouse the suspicions of the endunas, as well as the doubts of the king. The "big talk" ended in nothing but bad feeling.

Captain Paterson, Mr. Sergeant, and party, resolved to make a journey to the Victoria Falls of the Zambesi, if permission could be obtained, and with this object they asked the assistance of Mr. Morgan Thomas, who was acquainted with the native tongue. Lo-ben's reply to the request for permission to go through the country was to the effect that Captain Paterson should first return with the message to the great Queen, after which he might return and make a journey to the Falls. Invariably friendly to the white man, Lo-ben doubtless gave this advice knowing the hostile attitude of his endunas, whose wildest suspicions were aroused by the extraordinary mission from the British.

Influence, however, at length seemed to prevail with the king, and Captain Paterson, Mr. Sergeant, and Mr. Morgan Thomas left on a journey towards the Falls, Lo-ben protesting to Morgan's father against his allowing his son to accompany the party.

A month after the party had left, Usinduana, a Matabeli, returned, giving news that on the eighteenth day of their journey they had suffered greatly from thirst, and having entered the country of Zanki, called Ubenanzwa, of the tribe of Amaholi, one of whom they encountered, they, against the man's will, compelled him to show them where water was to be found. Thereupon he led them to a pool in the mountains, and all being parched, they drank immoderately. Very shortly every member of the party fell sick, the result being the death of Captain Paterson, Mr. Sergeant, Mr. Morgan Thomas, and seven coloured colonial servants.

My informant respecting this occurrence was the brother of Morgan Thomas, who was one of the victims. The messenger who brought the news also reported the death of five of the Matabeli escort. White traders and others in southern Matabeli-land asked permission to go and bury the dead, but Lo-ben would not grant the request.

Evidence respecting the matter was very conflicting, and young Mr. David Thomas has spared no pains in trying to unravel the mystery. To divulge a secret of the king's meant immediate death, but a man—the brother of a rain doctor—privately said to Mr. David that when Umlugulu, the headman of the town of Oyengweni, arrived with his party at the king's kraal, they were despatched by Lo-ben to overtake Captain Paterson's party and destroy them. Usibigo, the man who explained this, said that Captain Paterson's mission was distasteful to Lo-ben and his endunas. This story was corroborated by Umhelo, who belonged to the town of Buluwayo, and was of the king's regiment—Amahlogohlogo.

The voluminous evidence which Mr. Thomas's journal contains, and also the word of men living in Matabeli-land, and who belonged to the party, distinctly proves that the people were not poisoned, but assegaied by order of the king, who was compelled to act in accordance with the wishes of his endunas. Bearing in mind his fair dealings with the white man, however, it may be assumed that the order was involuntary on his part.

I must say that this was the only place in Matabeli-land where I observed signs of any real industry. The endeavour to make a home and improve was very apparent. Young Mr. Thomas worked hard, and had a large tract under cultivation, with plenty of fruit-trees—banana, orange and lemon —all bearing well. He also irrigated on a small scale.

Such a man may well be emulated by the black people who live around his home; but industrial emulation is not one of the predominant traits of their character, which looks up to excellence in the art of war as the only goal of life's purpose. I must be excused for thinking that a man who shows the fruits of his labour in a form so substantial and comprehensible, should in time be able to exercise a very powerful influence over the warlike aborigine. He manifests in a tangible way that there is something real in the white man's ascendancy, showing that it is not a mere matter of story, but a fruitful experience, carrying with it the blessings of prosperity, and indicating that there is something true in the labours of that best pioneer of civilisation and progress—the practical teacher of the gospel of Work.

Mr. Thomas kindly said that he would assist me in any way he could. The oxen, however, that he was good enough to offer as a loan were at the mission station, Umhlangene or Inyati, twenty-five miles to the north-east. So saddling up the horses, and sending the waggon on with the same oxen, we started.

The weather had looked very threatening; heavy black clouds went scudding across the sky, and just as we arrived at Mr. Elliot's house (the mission station) they suddenly burst, and down poured the rain in torrents. When the waggon arrived, the boys all looked miserable enough. This station is the last outpost of the London Missionary Society. The mission has been in Matabeli-land for about a quarter of a century.

Mr. Elliot, a most estimable gentleman who is now alone at this station, will make a good impression upon the natives, for he is an excellent doctor, and willing to dispense all kinds of medicine if the people will only accept it.

We were most fortunate in collecting twelve good oxen, the property of Mr. Thomas, to whom I was and am indebted for this as well as many other favours. Had he not come to my aid at that time, I do not know what could have been done, trained oxen being very scarce.

As I now had little or no hope of seeing a white face for a very long time, or of being able to procure any of the articles necessary for exploration work, I busied myself for the next two days in preparing sketch maps, drawing-pad, and so forth, and also made some observations of the sun to find the variation of the compass, and test that all the instruments were in working order. Mrs. Elliot kindly made me many nice things for the road, and on the evening of the 27th of May all was in readiness for a start.

The kindness shown to me by all was remarkable. When I took leave of Inyati, and was saying good-bye to the mission, Mr. Elliot said, as he handed me a letter :

"Should you reach the Lakes in safety, please deliver this letter to the missionaries there. You will be the first to convey words of greeting from us here to those in the Lake regions, who are working in the same good cause."

In the morning the weather had cleared; for the last time I bade adieu to my white friends. With unearthly shouts and yells from Korana John (who had quite recovered his senses, and was using his great cattle-whip with startling effect), and the oxen straining in the yokes, we headed to the north-east, and were soon hidden in the dense gloom of the forest. The sun was sinking as we camped in a small tree-environed plain, where we could hear the welcome music of a small rill of crystal water.

CHAPTER IV.

THE "BIG GAME" COUNTRY.

Stocking the larder—My "C. L. K." rifle—A zebra hunt—"Gijima, gijima!"—Hollow bullets—An unpleasant ducking—The mountains between the Zambesi, Sabia and Limpopo—Difficulty in lion hunting—Humours of ox-driving—The Sepaque river—Out of the track—Clearing under difficulties—Elephant spoor—Fruitless pursuit—Umvuli river—A catalogue of miseries—Story of Windvogel's victim—John and the wolf—Lion incidents—A dangerous ford—An elephant hunt—The honey-bird's note of warning—Thrilling moments—A good day's work—Kaffir gluttony—Game and honey—Selous' deserted camp of 1883—Taroman missing.

OUR party was now so small that every man had his special work "cut out:" the occupation of hunter devolving upon myself. The reader may be assured that every effort was made to keep the larder well stocked. As yet the majority of African mammalia had not appeared in my records of the chase, so that everything had the subtle charm of novelty; and we were now in a great game country. Anything between a duiker, with its tiny feet and diminutive horns, and the gigantic African elephant, with its world-coveted tusks and formidable ears, which could be likened to the wings of a gigantic eagle, might become the object of the chase. It is not, however, a part of the purpose of the present work, to deal largely with descriptions of hunting adventures. Already much has been written, and well written, in various works devoted entirely to the subject of the wild and exciting sports of Africa. Now and then, however, I must refer briefly to a few of the principal trophies in sport which fell to my rifle.

The weather was lovely, the thermometer registering on an average 50° at sunrise, and in day-time from 75° to 85° in the shade.

We held an average course N.E., passing numerous rivulets which give their waters to the rivers flowing northwards to the Zambesi.. Forests of *machabele*, the food of which the elephant is so fond, *mopani* and other strange varieties of trees were passed in our route.

As a rule, I left the waggon in the morning, Karemba being my only companion: our arms consisting of a shotgun and 500 Henry express rifle, the latter being ycleped C. L. K., the initials of my father. The weapon was a present from him when I left home. A most valuable article it proved—certainly the most valuable in my whole outfit; becoming the life of the expedition, through being the means of supplying to the party the necessaries of existence, all through the long journey until I reached the sea.

Late one afternoon, when the sun was fast nearing the tops of the tall forest trees, we came upon a large herd of zebra (Burchell zebra). The herd was quite 150 yards off, and had evidently been frightened, for they were going at a good pace. The chance for stalking therefore was gone; but I fired at the leader, and having aimed carefully at the shoulder, was astounded to find that the shot had not the slightest result. I at once made up my mind that I had missed him; but Karemba kept saying, "gijima, gijima," which meant run, run, and although thinking the pursuit a forlorn hope, I started off at my best speed through the tall rank grass, which in some places was higher than my head. After a run of nearly half a mile I began to feel utterly "winded." But Karemba pointed to a small clump of trees, and there, sure enough, stood the zebra. I gave him another shot, and away he went again, spinning along another 500 yards, during which other three shots were sent after him. I then began to think that my long-tried powers of endurance would soon come to an end, but to my surprise and satisfaction the zebra fell; Karemba then making quick work in despatching life with an assegai. Afterwards I discovered that nothing gave greater satisfaction to Karemba than the act of extinguishing life.

Examining the fallen zebra, I found that the first and second shots had both hit the shoulder. The bullets, however, being hollow, had been flattened to the thinness of a sixpence. This, and many other experiences, proved that such bullets were nearly, if not quite, useless for game possessing the extraordinary vitality which distinguishes the zebra and the antelope of Africa. In this matter I remembered some words of Selous, who remarked that the bullets were hollowed too deep, and that the lead at the apex was insufficient.

Darkness was falling when Karemba and myself left the scene of our adventure. We hurried off in the hope of being able to find the waggon on the south bank of the Goque river. But on arriving at the drift, on the south bank, where the hunters' waggons always cross, Karemba said that the waggon must have gone on to the north side. There was a good deal of water in the river, and as Karemba was almost nude I got upon his back and guided him forward. He stopped at the brink like a donkey at a fence. Without comprehending what he said I urged him on, and very soon down we went into a deep pool. I fell off my carrier's back, and just at the same moment the fact struck me that, of course, all these silent river pools were infested by the slimy and loathsome crocodile. At once it flashed across my mind that this was the cause of Karemba's unwillingness to cross, although the poor fellow had spoken in words which I could not understand.

It was very dark, and the sensation of immersion was anything but pleasant. Scrambling out, we soon came up to the waggon, where we found John seated beside an immense fire, comfortably, and in dignified leisure enjoying his evening smoke. John informed me that it was not safe to wade in these rivers. He was under the impression that I was ahead, otherwise he would have waited on the southern side.

Much to the delight of the boys (male servants, no matter what may be their age, are always "boys"), the next day was spent in cutting up meat and drying it in the sun.

We were now passing through a forest country, with granite kopjies here and there breaking through the alluvial land. Towards the south-east we beheld the rugged chain of the granite mountains, which form a conspicuous and clear dividing line between the waters of the Zambesi and the waters of the Sabia and Limpopo rivers. Away to the north-west, about a day's march, was the tsetse-fly country, which abounds in big game of every description.

We soon lost the spoor of the hunters' waggons which had gone in towards the Hanyane river a year ago, and which Selous had told me to follow; for by that means I would be enabled to reach the borders of Mashona-land in the shortest possible time.

A little to the north of the Gwailo river we stuck fast in a small swamp. Oxen are often of a very stubborn disposition, which some of ours on this occasion showed to perfection; but I could plainly see that the poor beasts had a rough time before them during the next month, for the rivers which we had already crossed had tested their strength with painful pitilessness.

Various ramblings in search of game showed the spoor of lions and leopards, also their lairs. Lions I think must have been plentiful; but it was almost impossible to get at them without dogs, as the grass was then so high that there was some difficulty in distinguishing even the largest antelopes. On one occasion, however, while on the way back to the waggon, I came across a troupe of harte-beest, and bowled one over as it ran past. Following in hot haste, I saw, with no slight surprise, that I had a companion in the chase, in the shape of a yellow dog, which seemed to enter with great gusto into the spirit of the sport. The half-starved angular figure of the tyke was not unfamiliar to me, as many a time had he spoilt my opportunities for a shot. So as he bounded through the grass I took a snap shot at him, with the intention of giving him a good scare; but much to my amazement the shot took effect, killing him in an instant. I was really very sorry for this mishap; especially as the Kaffir boy to whom the dog belonged looked so dreadfully unhappy when he heard of the demise of his hot-bottle, the favourite being one of a group which huddled together at night in order to sustain their warmth. However some cloth, a few beads, and a large chunk of meat soon dispelled the sorrow and lightened the heart of the mourner.

John having informed me that he was ill, I now for the first time in my life assumed the responsibilities of an ox driver. Many and many a time had I used the short-handled cattle whip employed in herding on the western prairies of America, but I had never used the gigantic and indispensable whip common to all South African caravans. In becoming initiated into the mysteries of its use, I left numerous marks upon my face and neck, and was more than once nearly strangled. While vigorously pressing on the leading oxen I would fall heels over head into some deep hole. Sometimes the oxen would wheel quickly round, rushing through the forest and breaking the young trees, while the old waggon rolled along like the grounding of a wrecked balloon. When evening came after such experiences I felt as though I had been mobbed and hustled at an election.

At the crossing of any of the large river-beds, however, John's aid was indispensable. He could crack the whip and make a report like an Armstrong six-pounder; while his shouts and fiendish yells resounded wildly through kopjies in such a manner that even the hoarse roar of a foghorn, or the shrill shriek of a steam-whistle would have had no chance against him.

By this time we had an enormous supply of the zebra and harte-beest meat stowed in the back of the waggon, in uncomfortable proximity to the place where I slept. The odour reminded me, in an uncertain sort of way, either of Wombwell's Menagerie, No. 1, or of Smithfield Market; perhaps neither one or of the other, distinctly, but a little of both. The boys and the dogs had plenty to eat, so there was a chance of their getting fat and hiding their stark staring ribs which stuck out so prominently when we left Inyati.

As we trekked further towards the north the nights became much colder. After fording the Sepaque river, and passing the heavy pool through the Umnyati, two of our oxen became footsore, so that the strength of the span was now reduced to ten.

The caravan, otherwise, was becoming somewhat demoralised. We had now completely lost the tracks of the hunters' waggons. Having gone too far to the north, we were compelled for days to cut our way through the forest, and this heavy work had to be carried out with a single small hand hatchet, as our equipment for foot travelling was as light as I possibly could have it, and was totally wanting in heavy axes or other implements suitable for clearing. This work was very wearisome, although, fortunately, the trees were of slight dimensions. As we neared the Umzwezwe, some of the country through which we passed was exceedingly rocky. Numerous kopjies, like piles of broken stone, edged the river on its southern bank.

The lessening rays of the setting sun were kissing the tops of the mopanis when we descended towards the river. Far in the eastern sky the moon was rising, and the view from the spot where I stood in the centre of the water was beautifully striking. Lower and lower the sun sank in the horizon, casting, mirror-like, over the sky its ever varying hues of lovely colours. On each side of the position rose precipitous banks, while luxuriant foliage hung gracefully over the silent pools of the stream, which in other places dashed in crystal clearness and in merry mood through the countless boulders and jagged rocks which formed the ford over and through which we had to pass. A picture so lovely, glowing beneath the glories of so beautiful an evening sun, I have rarely seen.

On the succeeding day we came across the spoor of what was evidently a large troupe of elephants. Trees were uprooted, and their branches broken, while great boulders were unearthed. Some of the broken trees, must have been snapped by the united strength of two or three of the animals. John and myself went on the spoor from morning till night, but returned to camp with nothing except ravenous appetites. The weather was cold, so that unless we found the spoor very early in the morning, the chances were against our finding the elephants—I believe they will travel great distances in cold weather, without the mid-day halt which they invariably make during the days of heat.

Several hunting excursions of this nature were taken. On returning from one of them, an incident occurred which may deserve notice. John, unconsciously of course, walked straight up to a wolf which lay asleep amid the long grass. The appearance of the recumbent animal, which seemed rather reluctant to move, took John thoroughly by surprise; so much so, indeed, that he stood stock still, and uttered some screams so thrillingly horrible that by imitating them the divine Sara herself might have given to her audiences a new and telling experience of terror. Running up, for the shrill notes of the man's awful voice had struck the chords of my inmost feelings, I saw the wolf —a large one—bounding through the grass. I took a flying shot, but only grazed the brute. He gave a growl, and with another bound disappeared amid the sea of impenetrable vegetation.

"My gaut, master," said John; "I tink it was lion!" The waggon was camped under some large trees, upon a favourite spot for hunters, who usually left their impedimenta there, before going down into what is called the "Fly Country" (referring to the tsetse fly) to look for big game.

At this spot, too, was the grave, covered with wild creepers, of one who had died by the capricious hand of Windvogel, the bushman, or the higher ape, as he has been called. Here Windvogel was initiated into the mysteries of shooting; his first experience resulting in the fall of a playmate, whom he shot stone dead in an instant. The event occurred only a few years previously, and even now the reckless assassin looked like a boy; but on my saying so to John he answered :

"Master, he is an olt man, and a very bad leetle man."

The course of the crime was as follows: Arming himself with a regular Baron Munchausen blunderbuss, which belonged to the father of the poor boy he killed, he started for the hunting country which was not more than one hundred yards from where the waggons of his party stood. He soon "cut the spoor" of his playmates, and, knowing well his game, gave them warning that he was about to fire. The others, being unarmed, found they were handicapped, and bolted. Unfortunately the "higher ape's" first shot was a bull's-eye, and ended the life of a poor playmate. Perhaps he felt towards his young Korana comrade as the Boers felt towards his forefathers, when, but a few short years before, they would go out in search of bushmen, and considered them "fair game."

This adventure led to the bushman's being "christened" in a somewhat rough and ready manner. Tied to a waggon wheel, in the cruel fashion practised by the Boers, when their jaundiced humours are more than usually acute, he was christened Windvogel; the recollection of the christening being impressed upon the subject by the stinging lash of the shambock, a name given to a rhinoceros-hide whip. This ceremony reminds one of the manner in which gamekeepers "christen" a dog. When this story was laid before the king, he ruled, as was the custom of the land, that the father of the slain boy could either kill his slayer or keep him as a slave. It was in this way that Windvogel fell into John's hands, whose slave he now was.

But to resume the personal narrative. Three days more (June 12) brought us to the Umvuli river. Our catalogue of miseries was pretty full. John was sick; two oxen were footsore; Karemba had been kicked by one of the oxen, which he had been endeavouring to throw in order to examine its feet; Windvogel, the "higher ape," had dysentery, and lay on his face writhing and groaning with pain, by all odds the most dismal and dejected looking creature I ever set eyes on; Sagwam had the sulks; and Taroman, the india-rubber man, had so over-eaten himself, that he gave up looking after the sheep and cattle, and overcome like a cobra, with an overcharged stomach, had lain down to sleep and so lost the live-stock.

The old drift through the river, where the hunters' waggons used to cross, had been scoured out; leaving a deep hole on the south side, while in the centre of the water was a high mound of soft sand, making the place quite impassable. The banks, too, were very steep.

Under these peculiarly adverse circumstances a short halt had to be made. But as it was still early in the day we made the best use of our time, by cutting branches, and by preparing a ford to take the waggon over.

John and myself returned from our work on the river, and were not a little surprised that no sign of life could be seen near the waggon. It was nearly dusk, and as neither boys nor oxen appeared, John and I started in different directions to scour the country for the absentees.

This neighbourhood abounds with lions, and consequently my anxious mind pictured horrible visions of the cattle becoming a prey to the king of beasts. Only the previous year, Selous, while hunting here, had stopped on the north bank, his cattle being tied in the customary fashion, with large fires encircling the camp, while the boys were seated in a group close to the animals. In a little time a lion came up close in front of the party, having passed the fires with the utmost indifference. A moment later the lion seized upon one of the fattest of the oxen, and brought it to the ground; but the contents of a double-barrelled shot-gun discharged at close quarters immediately checked his meal and his earthly career at the same time. When a lion is thoroughly hungry there is no limit to its audacity and daring. I know of an occasion about the same place, of a lion having attacked a man, in the night time, while he was seated before a blazing fire.

After an anxious walk of about two miles, I shouted, and much to my astonishment, an answer came from Taroman, whom I found under a tree where he had evidently been taking a nap. The sheep were beside him, and in his hand he held an enormous chunk of zebra. The time was now approaching when Taroman wholly lost the use of his eyes, which were of no service in the slightest shade of darkness. On such occasions he even could not find his way, and this I discovered to be true beyond doubt.

From Taroman's attitude at that time it was evident that he expected to be thrashed; but as I do not believe in whipping or kicking as a means to any satisfactory end, I merely asked him about the cattle. In reply he made signs of a very vague character, and I hurried back to the camp taking the sheep along with me, not, however, without frightening Taroman by telling him to go and search for them, knowing as well as he did it was Lion Veldt. When I returned to camp I sent a boy to fetch the old humbug home. I was aggravated at the time, for the loss of the cattle would have been irretrievable. We were twelve days' good travel from Inyati, and still very far distant from the borders of Mashona-land. John by this time had found all but two of our oxen.

It was a cold and stormy night. The wind blew with terrific force, threatening to unroof the waggon, and leave only the pitiless canopy of heaven as a substitute. The wolves howled on every side, one approaching very near the waggon, although I could not get a shot at him, as he was wholly obscured by the shade of the trees.

The missing cattle having been luckily found, we, on the following day, about noon, made a forward move towards the ford which had been prepared. Starting down the steep bank the oxen plunged into the water.

The ford was chiefly composed of small branches, among which the legs of the animals sunk very deeply. At one time both of the hind oxen fell, and looked as though they would inevitably be crushed by the waggon, the fore wheels of which were just on the brink of the river, giving the whole affair the appearance of standing on end.

Awful thoughts weighed heavily upon my mind, regarding the probability of a total wreck of the waggon in the middle of the river. All hands had to be piped to keep the cattle in a straight course. No one could help feeling for the poor beasts as they strained their strength and contorted their struggling bodies; sometimes splashing in the pools, but often sinking up to their bellies in the soft and shifting sand. We had, however, to get out of the river, no matter in what fashion.

While ascending the north bank, for there was no track except that which we had scraped out with sharpened sticks, the oxen in spite of the efforts of Karemba and myself, who were pulling the leading yoke, suddenly swerved to the right, breaking through the thorn bushes on the steep bank, and amidst the thicket we were sent sprawling and scrambling, to be cut and torn by the sharp and prickly thorns.

At length, after very hard work, and a great many demoniacal 'shouts and yells, with the old waggon cracking

ACROSS THE UMVULI.

and creaking, and the oxen grunting and groaning all the time—the yoke stays threatened to choke them—we with one grand final effort reached the top of the bank.

After a brief period of rest, we were again on the forward move; and that evening I breathed more freely, as I sat before the blazing camp fire, and pondered over what had passed.

One morning happy thoughts dawned upon my mind when John said he could see elephants in the distance. At the time we were trekking through an immense sea of yellow grass, fanned by a gentle breeze into waving billows, through which the party, as it passed, left a wake behind, like that of an ocean steamer tossing the glassy sea into a turbulent foam. At intervals the grass was dotted by thorny acacias and small clumps of trees.

Sure enough, as John had foreseen, we shortly came upon the fresh spoor of what seemed a large troupe of elephants. Anxious as I was to press on, this was too great a temptation to be resisted. Outspanning the oxen, I set out with my Reilly, double eight-bore,* while John accompanied me with his waterpipe, as I termed it, much to his disgust, although the description was tolerably true, as the weapon had a suspicious resemblance to a branch service-pipe, and he invariably sluiced it out with water after the day's work. Karemba and Sagwam were gun-carriers.

We were soon tracking up, and every sign tended to show that the pursuit would not be a long one. From the zig-zag appearance of the spoor, we judged that the elephants were feeding.

To a hunter imbued with the spirit of the chase, there is something intensely exhilarating in the feelings which are

* Eight drachms Curtis & Harvey's best, and 3-oz. conical bullet.

aroused as he nears these monarchs of the forest, who roam free through the wilderness of nature, without a considerable rival save man. The inexpressible glow of excitement is perhaps a selfish feeling; but it thrills through every fibre of your system as you approach nearer and nearer to the object whose life it is your ambition to take. Does not this, almost with vividness show, that the instincts of the lower forms of animal life, from which it is said that all mankind have sprung, bud out through the higher intellect, even in all its severely cultivated forms?

There was a lull in the wind, which is an indispensable agent to a successful stalk, and close to the left I soon observed a moving object. The dull leaden colour of the elephant serves admirably as a protection from the searching glance of his pursuer, and in this he resembles most of the wild animals, whose colour is akin to that of the vegetation in which they live. There was soon revealed to our view a large elephant cow; and I had just brought my rifle to the shoulder, when John pulled my sleeve and told me not to shoot, because it was a "kooes-cop," *i.e.* an elephant without tusks.

Whether she had scented us, or had been startled by the honey birds,* which continued to chirp and lead us all the way I know not, but suddenly, with gigantic strides and curling her trunk close up under the mouth, she made off towards her companions, who were standing huddled together under some large gonté trees, fanning themselves with their huge ears.

There was no time to lose. Happily the fugitive did not trumpet, so that we were able to get within fairly good range before she raised the alarm. I fired at the nearest

---

* These little birds are very troublesome during a stalk, for if the game hear them they recognise the cry as a note of caution.

elephant, and the shot threw him into a state of the wildest excitement, shown by successive shrill trumpetings. Wheeling round and round he came heavily to the ground; while away went the panic-striken herd, sounding aloud their far-reaching bugle-call of retreat, and clearing all before them. I never saw a quicker piece of roadmaking. They literally crashed and ploughed their way through the young forest, piling up, on each side of their track, mopani-trees, stacks of rank grass, and great heaps of scrub bush.

Thinking, and as it proved rightly, that I had mortally wounded the first elephant, I ran after the herd as fast as I could, and coming within pretty close range fired, but this time made a bad shot, hitting a young bull too far back, after aiming at the shoulder.

John was now close to me in hot pursuit of a cow, which he had hit several times. She had fallen behind the rest of the herd, and just at this moment had almost stopped. Turning towards us, John shouted:

"Look out, master, look out!"

At this evidently critical moment I was endeavouring with all the energy at my disposal to reload my rifle; but, as on many other occasions, of which one or two might have cost me my life, the empty cases had stuck, and do what I might, I could not extract them for some time.

Meanwhile I heard other two shots, and when I last saw John he was flying like the wind through the bush, while his gun-carrier fled in another direction, shouting like a demon. Karemba had left me, and rightly too, for he was unarmed, and the noise made by the elephants sounded as though they were actually upon us. Behind, and uttering sharp screams, was the first elephant I had shot, while that which John had wounded was in front, dashing wildly about, and trumpeting with her angriest power, as she revengefully searched for her pursuers.

I had not had such a time of excitement for many years. I pulled and tugged at the cartridges, but for a time all such efforts were of no avail. Amidst the confusion, I heard John roaring as though he were being torn limb from limb. I had by this time succeeded in reloading, and, of course, made off at my highest speed, for I really thought that John was caught. On getting up I found that the cow had charged him, and, John having run out of bullets, had been obliged to take to his heels, in order to escape from the infuriated monster.

A lively time had evidently been passed, for both John and Sagwam looked dreadfully exhausted; the former, too, was quite crestfallen, because he had lost his elephant.

I had but one rifle with me, and a wounded elephant still close by, but I pushed the weapon into John's hands, and away he went, at once, on the blood spoor. Hurrying back to the camp, I snatched up C. L. K., and returned to the wounded elephant, which I found standing under the shade of a large tree.

Just as I came within range, however, I heard the sharp report of the eight-bore, and, before my eyes down went the elephant with a heavy thud. As the animal was not dead, I quickly ran up and gave the *coup de grâce* to end the poor brute's sufferings.

The elephant wounded by John had been soon overtaken by that worthy when he got my rifle in his hands; and after despatching it, he had gone towards that wounded by me, firing the shot I had heard just as I arrived from the camp with C. L. K. After cutting out the hearts, we returned to the camp, situated two miles north of the Simbo river, and there in dreams I, over and over again, went

through the eventful and exciting scenes of the day's hunt, chasing in nocturnal fancies the phantom forms of multitudes of the forest's denizens.

Very early in the morning we were again upon the scene of yesterday's exploits, and all hands went to work cutting up elephant flesh, and chopping out the tusks. The Kaffirs, according to their custom, had a fire lit; and during their intervals of rest they warmed (it could not be called cooking) what they considered dainty morsels from the inside, which they would devour much in the same condition as they found them; for cleansing, or any other culinary preparation, was unknown. As feeders, the Kaffirs are the foulest people imaginable; it is not saying too much to affirm that they will eat nearly anything, and pretty nearly in any condition. After they had devoured their *bonne bouche*, they would disappear once more inside the carcase, in order to cut out the fat, which is much valued as a curative salve for rheumatism and other ailments. Special morsels which they came across were taken out by alternate members of the party, in order to be warmed at the fire and demolished. Inside the carcase the happy rascals would wallow in blood, bathing and rubbing themselves all over with it, which seems to be a custom among the people. The blood is left on, until it naturally wears off.

After we cut out the first pair of tusks, we inspanned the oxen and departed; telling Karemba and Sagwam to proceed to the carcase of the other elephant, and cut out the ivory. On their return to camp, they reported that on their arrival at the elephant, they found two large leopards, "impisi," feeding upon its flesh. I felt sorry I had not accompanied the boys.

Now we were in a land of plenty. Game was abundant, and honey seemed to be inexhaustible. Whenever the boys had an opportunity, they would disappear, so that they might watch their little winged friends, the white-backed honey guides (*Indicator major*), the unfailing pilots to Nature's sweetest stores. The honey was remarkably good, with a strong flavour of wild flowers.

From the Umvuli river we had been followed by lions. They could be heard at night, but did not come close to the waggon.

We were now within two days' journey of Selous' farthest hunting camp to the north-east. Crossing two small rivers, the Sarue and Karemwe, we took a course more to the north, cutting our way through low, light forests, until we emerged into a beautiful open, park-like country. The variegated colouring on the trees, that hemmed us in on every side, was very striking.

Away in the far distance we could faintly see the smoky, yellow haze of the prairie grass fires, lit by the Mashona people. Towards the north-east could be seen the distant leaden outline of the Umvukwe mountains, towering high above the level of the plateau. Of these mountains we were destined to know much in the future.

A long and very fatiguing trek, tiresome alike for men and oxen, brought us to a suitable spot where we pitched camp, just as the light of parting day was throwing its darkening shadows from the great forest trees, which surrounded the position.

Another step of the journey was accomplished. We were now upon my friend Selous' deserted hunting camp of 1883, situated at an elevation of 4050 feet above the sea, and on the southern bank of the Hanyane river; the banks of which were clothed with high forest, shutting out our view to the north. Taroman, with the sheep, and two foot-sore oxen were missing.

Our present position was very far in the interior, so far indeed that henceforth the journey would be a course of exploration.

What a sombre and dreary scene surrounded us, with its quietness undisturbed, even by the slightest tremor in the voiceless air! I sat on the front box of the waggon, waiting to make an observation for latitude. Looking at the flickering flames of fires, around which the boys lay fast asleep, I could see that the little hunting camp had become grass-grown, with wild hemp intermingled, while a rich garden of pumpkins studded the ground, and creepers innumerable, and of every description, hung gracefully from the boughs, kissing the tops of the grass sugar-loaf huts, which rose slightly above the netted vegetation.

I succeeded in getting two successful observations for latitude, and the following day was devoted to fixing the longitude, finding the variation of the compass, and arranging other smaller matters with reference to survey work; for onwards, from this point, it was my intention to map the country as accurately as I could.

CHAPTER V.

INTO MASHONA-LAND.

Food supplies—John's concertina—Stirring dreams—Protection at night—John has an eye to the future—We leave Taroman behind—His revenge—The prairie on fire—A close escape—Matabeli raids—Sudden appearance of Mashona hunters—Chibero's—Description of a Mashona stronghold—Matabeli war tactics—Desolating results—Advantages of silence—Chibero is stubborn—The carrier difficulty—Stupid advice—Little Unyamwenda—One of Nature's dungeons—Native trading—Recruiting volunteers—"Villum" or Chirumutu—Writing unknown—Harassing bargains—"I melt de fat of de olifant, Master"—That exasperating fellow Taroman—Harte-beest hunting—Mashona mode of hunting—Netting game—General appearance of the Mashona—Mashona girls—Weapons—The assegai—A persecuted race—Diet—Cattle—A dilatory start—The waggon abandoned—"Tussa, tussa!"—Baggage for the journey—The body-guard—Taroman incensed—Helplessness of the whites among the blacks—The company start on foot for the north.

EARLY in the morning I sent John in search of Taroman, whom I had not seen during all the previous day, when I had been hunting. It was not long before John returned with the wanderer, and also with the missing oxen.

"Master," said John, "dat olt man go back to de olt bones of de olifant what we keel!"

Taroman's general appearance might have led any one to believe that he had spent the night in a dust-bin, for he was coated with an ashen hue, while his face showed unmistakable signs that the honey-birds had piloted his steps to sweet stores of plenty. He looked on this occasion as he always looked after a return from absence without leave;

that is to say, with a guilty expression suggestive of the dog which has been hunting on its own account in your favourite pheasantry. Sometimes he looked as if he had lost something and was anxious for an immediate search.

"Umtagate!" (which means anything but a gentleman) was the subdued chorus which rose from the group of fire-squatters on such reappearances.

Enquiry got no response from this unrivalled torment, who generally excused himself by saying he had heard lions. Perhaps his sight had left him unusually early in the afternoon, and he had sought refuge in a high tree, where he had spent the night. On my suggesting that he had better go and feed, the stolidity of his face thawed; it broke up, grew wider than it had before been long, through the lively emotions of anticipated bliss.

We had a very busy day. To our stock of provisions was now added a number of pumpkins, forming a very welcome accession, as the supply of vegetables was remarkably poor. Of meat we had a superabundance; the waggon was filled with it, in almost every variety, piled up in absolute confusion, so that everything appeared to be upside down. Close beside my head, where I rested, was an immense piece of an elephant's trunk. The sight of it was becoming tiresome, but in spite of the most strenuous efforts of the boys they could not "wear it out."

The wind rose towards evening, and brought on a thick mist. I was thoroughly fatigued, for I had again been hunting, and, notwithstanding the confusion around me, was glad to lay down on my somewhat limited bed, where I was lulled to sleep by the wildly erratic tones of Korana John's concertina, sounding as though it was screeching in defiance of the impediment of a chronic asthma.

All the surrounding conditions, and in fact even the

atmosphere, reminded me that we were in a game country. The thought conduced to create thrilling dreams of sport, especially after a supper of elephant's trunk, when the digestive organs would be sadly impaired, and would send tumultuous throbs to the brain, awakening the most awful visions of imagination. At one time I would be breathlessly creeping up, like a snake, to some fearful monster, and just as I came close to him my gun would not come to the shoulder. In a second he would be upon me, but I was off, whirling through space, as though I were shot from a Krupp; jumping, in one bound, rivers which had taken hours to cross: and at length dashing meteor-like through the ethereal sky, only to see my dreaded enemy, in the shape of a larger world, directly before me, and coming nearer and nearer with a velocity equal to my own. Of course just as we were about to collide, with terrific force, I awoke.

I then found that the drawing board which I was accustomed to place at my head, to protect me from the wind, as it blew through the waggon as if through a funnel, had fallen upon my cranium, bringing down at the same time the lantern, while the sail flap at the end of the conveyance was lashing and cracking about my ears, being agitated by the heavy gale.

What a gipsy life this was! But it was pleasant withal, almost captivating, one might say, for hitherto no real or serious obstacle had come in the way.

When morning broke the mist lifted, and the grey of the dawn proved the harbinger of another lovely day for our journey. Breakfast, before starting, consisted of tea, and about six inches of elephant's trunk, which I worked on strenuously with my teeth for a quarter of an hour; but making no impression upon the stuff, and noticing the "higher ape" watching for an opportunity to try his powers, I flung the bit to him, and saw it go down his throat like a worm into a young sparrow, for by this time he had quite recovered.

John had succeeded in making a small tent-cover for my bed, using for the purpose some cotton drill (trading stuff that I carried). The cover was necessary, because the dews were now very heavy at night, and we would soon have to abandon the waggon. This was the only way to avoid having constantly, or rather as long as the climate would allow me, to sleep in wet blankets. Damp means fever.

I was not sorry when the time came to leave the camp, as my Kaffirs would soon become useless through their excessive feasting. They had been eating at every spare moment, and the fire had always a pot full of pumpkin, while long pieces of meat were being roasted. The "higher ape" at this time was a fearful looking picture, his outline resembling that of a drowned man. Poor Taroman had assumed the aspect of a well-developed pumpkin, and was forced to find that there was a limit to the elasticity of the walls even of *his* wonderful paunch, which he continued to rub with earnest fervour, groaning all the time, as he declared that he had a pain in his head! Like other people in all parts of the world, it is noticeable that as the Kaffir grows fat he becomes lazy.

Karemba was now in his own country, although his home was a great distance towards the south-east.

At 6 o'clock in the morning the thermometer registered 40°, the dew laying heavy on the grass. Before noon we made a start, although it certainly was rather difficult, for one of John's harassing peculiarities was his at all times far-calculating disposition; his keen eye to future business being always wide awake, as he thought of the happy day when he would return to Buluwayo with a waggon-load of interior produce. This idiosyncrasy was at times very funny. He would often say, "Master, I want harte-beest skins," but this morning he had been gathering together the pumpkins, and just as we were about to start he said, "Master, I have a beeg load on; pumpkins I am going to take back when I go home. The waggon will stick this day." Home, it should be observed, was John's brightest star of hope.

It was now my intention to travel on the southern side of the Hanyane river towards the south-east, until I reached some of the Mashona kraals.

Striking through an open, undulating country, characterised by a succession of low, wave-like hills, and showing avenues of stunted forest growth fringing the edges of its innumerable narrow watercourses, we shortly made a halt beneath the shelter of a small clump of trees. The sun was excessively hot. We were surrounded by plains covered with long rank grass, portions of which had been burnt by the Mashona people.

After a short rest we shouted for Taroman, and cracked the cattle whip, which is a custom in South Africa in letting the herdsmen know that it is time to bring the cattle to inspan, for the report of the whip can be heard at a great distance. Taroman, however, was nowhere to be seen, although we succeeded in finding the cattle after a long search in the high grass.

So we were forced to start without our herdsman, abandoning him to whatever fate might be in store for him. After a little time I gave a last look behind, thinking I might perchance see the notorious absentee.

Instead of that I was startled to find that the whole

prairie was on fire. It was evident that old Taroman had awoke from his lazy sleep, and, whether through spite at being left behind, or for some other reason unknown to me, he must have taken a wand from the camp fire and ignited the long grass, which burnt with great rapidity, the conflagration being borne swiftly towards us by a brisk wind, which fanned the furious flames and drove them impetuously onward.

We at once saw that we were chased by a dangerous and relentless enemy, and a very annoying time we had during the pursuit. John's really vigorous endeavours to urge the oxen forward seemed to be inadequate, for the fire kept steadily gaining upon us. What I was afraid of was the waggon and all the valuables for trading. Previously we had always taken precautions against such emergencies, but only at night. Usually the grass was fired surrounding our camp, so as to prevent a surprise. Where the grass is low and thin, the fire can be fought pretty successfully with branches of shrubs; but with long grass in flames, furiously swept forward by a mighty wind, it is obviously impossible to stand near it. Now and then, when ploughing through streaks of wet, black, loamy soil (where, by the way, we saw the spoor of black rhinoceros), the waggon stuck fast. At such times my anxiety was intensified to a troublesome degree. To be overtaken meant immediate ruin.

I was seriously thinking of pitching all John's pumpkins overboard, when we fortunately pulled out, and striking a very dry belt, put the oxen at a run, and presently, crossing a small rivulet, found ourselves in a position of safety, where we could bid defiance to the devouring rage of the pursuing fire.

Two days' travel brought us to the outlying kraals of the Mashona tribe.

During this journey we passed over numerous deserted Mashona fields, which had evidently been devastated during the frequent raids of the Matabeli impi (army or warriors). The savage invaders had driven the more industrious Mashona away to the eastward, killing all who came within reach. Thus the once well-tilled fields were left to assume again the unprofitable wildness of their primitive condition; the furrows and ridges of the formerly cultivated land alone remaining to tell the sorrowful tale of conquest and desolation.

While hunting for rhinoceros one morning I came upon some antelopes, one of which I wounded. In the course of the swift pursuit which followed, I was thoroughly startled by the sudden appearance in the chase of two men, who turned out to be Mashona hunters. Both were armed with flint-lock muskets. Their persons were adorned with bracelets of buffalo hide, and necklaces of bone and claws, also pieces of the hoof of the small gazelle. Round their loins they wore sporans of leather, interwoven with beads of iron and brass. They carried their powder in horns.

As I could not speak the language, I signed to them to come to the waggon, which we could see indistinctly, almost buried in the long grass. On coming up to the caravan they asked for caps, and in reply we told them that we were going to the Zambesi, and if they would accompany us we would give them caps there. But they shook their heads, saying that it was very far, offering, however, to go on a hunting trip to get meat.

I was quite glad to see a strange face, for since leaving the mission station at Umhlangene, nearly a month before, we had not met a single soul. The hunters informed us that there was a Mashona kraal close by, and hinted that perhaps the chief, whose name was Chibero, would give us help.

After about three hours' trek we came upon numerous

little patches of cultivated ground. A stream of human beings kept pouring towards us, gradually swelling to a large crowd, until at length, with the babble of innumerable voices, varied by the strange notes of Mashona musical instruments, which some of our happy escort carried with them, we entered a lovely green valley where a few cattle could be seen grazing. The valley was walled in by low mountain ridges, and overlooked by the rocky fastnesses of the Mashona chief. We camped about 500 yards from where the town stood.

Taroman, the "thorn" of our party, had not appeared since the prairie fire. The sheep, of which there were only three left, and one goat, were such pets that they followed close under the waggon without herding.

The people were all very friendly, and eager to get some of the white man's treasures. They are a very different type to the bloodthirsty warriors whose country we had just left, and of whom they live in constant terror. Judging from first appearances, I could perceive that the physique of the Mashona was very inferior to that of the Matabeli. Their skin is darker too, and altogether they have a greater resemblance to the genuine negro. I sent word to the chief that I would visit him in the morning, and was not sorry when morning came, for the night was very stormy, and the waggon had its head to the wind, which passed through with great power, so that I might say that my lullaby was the loud voice of a hurricane.

Karemba and myself started across the plain, and walked into the fastnesses of a rugged mountain, composed of immense boulders, over and around which wound a tortuous path running right and left, up and down, and screwing in all directions, so as to avoid the rocks that jutted out over this wonderfully intricate track of the mountaineers.

Situated on the highest point of the mountain was the citadel. The spaces between the massive rocks which formed an impregnable barrier around the town, and whose sides were so smooth that even a cat could not scale them, were filled with stout posts interlaced with thorny bushes. It appeared to me that it would be impossible to effect an entrance without the aid of someone inside. All this powerful fortifying is carried out in order to secure their lives against the murderous attacks of their dreaded foes. Undisputed by the owners and tillers of the soil, all property in the form of corn and cattle must be abandoned to the caprice of the conquering Matabeli.

Attack is entirely a matter of cunning and stalking. A Matabeli impi (army) will approach as stealthily, and as invisibly as snakes, crawling as closely upon the ground, and concealed by the undergrowth, they watch the movements of their intended victims, the timid Mashona. Then, when a favourable opportunity occurs, up they rise like a wild black cloud of destruction. Hissing and shrieking their fiercest battle cry, they bound and leap like the "klipspringer," * from rock to rock, dealing with fearful precision the death-giving blow of the assegai; and ever and anon shouting with thrilling ecstasy, their terrific cry of triumph, as they tear out the yet beating hearts of their victims.

After a pursuit of the flying and panic-striken horde, the ravagers herd in the straying cattle, and then the devastating cloud moves away, gathering, in its circuitous route, other nebulæ in the shape of slave girls and boys, as well as the cattle from perhaps hundreds of hitherto quiet and smiling valleys. They return to their king with news of victory; dancing as they sing the story of their soul-stirring and daring deeds, while in feasting they drink the beer made by

* A small but extremely agile antelope living in the rocky kopjies.

the hands of the girls whose parents' lives and property were the fruits of the chase, their bones lying bleaching in the sun amid the weather-worn rocks of the deserted highland home.

On such occasions the king rewards his generals much in the same way as is done by the English. He gives them the currency of the country (cattle), although perhaps blood does not call for so high a premium in a savage country as it does in our own land.

The gateway of the barrier seemed to be the only access to the town. It was composed of trunks of trees laid in a horizontal position, one above the other, and the whole "shored up" from the back by strong poles.

Karemba soon succeeded in persuading the inhabitants that we were on a friendly mission, and had come to consult the "old man." Satisfied with this assurance, they, after a good deal of work, pulled away a sufficient number of the logs to leave a small opening, through which we crawled with a little difficulty.

Our appearance caused not a little curiosity among the crowd of Mashona, great and small, who witnessed our entrance. Immediately on our left, and half hidden under the shadow of a huge rock—against which were laid whole stacks of assegais, battle axes, and clubs—sat the chief Chibero. His position was close to a large fire, where a number of his vassals, exceedingly wretched, half-fed looking creatures, also crowded in their efforts to absorb in their miserable bodies some share of the scanty heat, for the morning air was bitterly cold.

I felt, and I am sure I looked, like a mummy. We seated ourselves, with awful solemnity, upon the ground, looking and acting all the while as though our mission was of a most funereal character. It should be remembered that

in the company of the savage the longer you remain
mute, the greater weight will be carried by your words,
whenever you deem it fitting to divulge the ruminations
of your mind. Does not this bear in some degree upon
certain features or frailties in civilised life? Many a
man, but few women (for obvious reasons), have high
reputations for wit as well as wisdom built upon the
negative but commanding virtue of silence. The virtue
seems to be exceptionally useful—golden not silvern—in
the world of business. In my position at that time
any appearance of anxious solicitation would have been
disastrous; just as it invariably is, in dealings with our
white brothers, who are ever ready to take advantage of
human weaknesses.

At length, with all the decorum due to so important an
assemblage, for to me the occasion and its results were of
the greatest moment, Karemba inquired if the chief could
give the white man boys to go to Kunyungwi, that being
the name given by these people to Tette, the Portuguese
settlement, or rather outpost, on the Zambesi, which in
the meantime was my intended destination.

Chibero, however, declared that he could give no boys,
while all those who were beside the fire laughed with disdainful heedlessness. The Mashona have not the slightest
idea of the lapse of time, their days being passed with purposeless indifference, and even with less exertion than is
shown by the degenerate Mexicans.

It soon became evident that nothing could be done with
Chibero and his "boys," so we left the stubborn chief, and
retraced our steps through the intricacies of the path
towards the waggon.

I had failed to satisfy my wishes; but I had learned a
useful lesson. In future I would not say, "I wish the boys

to go with me to Kunyungwi." As I judged from the surprised faces of the natives, the distance to them was too great. Then and there I determined to find out through the medium of Karemba the name of the next chief, whose country lay towards the north-east, and thus, from one chief to another, gradually work my way through to the Zambesi. The little failure about getting boys, reminded me of the warning words uttered by Selous, who said, " Your great difficulty will be to get carriers: they do not like to go far from home."

This assertion greatly differed from the statement contained in a letter I received while yet in the vicinity of the Diamond Fields. The letter was from a friend, who informed me that he had just met a gentleman who had arrived from the Victoria Falls of the Zambesi. On that account this gentleman considered himself an infallible authority on African travel, and said that he thought there would be no trouble whatever in getting boys. Here it is advisable to remind the reader that there is a traders' waggon route—as wide as the very broad road that is so familiar in pulpit oratory—reaching to within a couple of days' journey from the Victoria Falls, which are situated on the great southern bend of the river, about 360 miles (as the crow flies) N.N.W. of Shoshong. My present position was about 450 miles (as the crow flies) N.E. of Shoshong, so that I was yet 220 miles, in a direct route, from Tette on the Zambesi, which was the ultimate point of this section of my journey. The actual distance, however, which I traversed even here was more than doubled through the intricate wanderings and reverses experienced during my progress through an unknown country.

These facts are mentioned only for the purpose of showing how readily some African travellers, who are but freshmen on the field, will venture opinions upon modes of travelling in regions of which they have no experience, and unsupported even by the dictates of common sense.

On reaching the waggon we soon spanned in the oxen, and a short trek brought us to the town of Little Unyamwenda, which was under the rule of a headman, or enduna, of the chief Unyamwenda, whose town is further on, being situated close to the southern bank of the Hanyane river.

I had already made up my mind that on no account would I risk taking the waggon across the Hanyane river, as all our future movements where enveloped in obscurity. No one could say how our journey was to proceed. Therefore I concluded to make this town the final halting place for the waggon and the animals; for it was well to anticipate the difficulties which lay before us to the northward; among other obstacles being the dreaded tsetse fly, which would certainly kill our oxen.

We pulled the waggon as near as we possibly could to the apparently inaccessible town, the track being of a most uncomfortable description, full of sharp corners which we had to round with the greatest care in order to avoid collisions with rocks, while in some instances we slid over slippery boulders whose treacherous sides provoked many a mishap. At length we reached a secure spot, and it was indeed a miracle that the waggon had not been upset or smashed. Taking everything into consideration, I was very well satisfied when we came to an anchor.

It would have puzzled anyone who was not thoroughly familiar with the peculiarities of these rugged mountains to tell how we had ever managed to gain our present position. We stood in the centre of a small basin, enclosed by immense boulders whose massive summits, bold and grey, frowned upon us on every side. In colour they admirably matched the dull leaden hue of the atmosphere, impregnated with smoke from the forest fires. The smoke seemed to be prevented from rising by the heavy clouds which hung overhead, making one think of the state of affairs which, with the pith of proverbial slang, is called a "blue look out."

We seemed to have wound our way into one of Nature's dungeons, and the resemblance was the more striking owing to the changing weather having brought a spell of cold, with occasional drifts of searching misty rains.

The waggon was here to be abandoned, and I could not help looking upon it with all the affection usually given to an old but comfortable arm-chair, on which every grease spot, and every charred hole, showing where the mild regalia had fallen during drowsy moments, bring to one's recollection the memory of special stories, which in their turn revive other associations, all tending to cheer the weary mind, and make us forget for the time the presence of dreary surroundings.

There the old waggon stood, reminding me strongly of a worn and torn craft which had braved the buffeting billows during a long and tempestuous voyage. The sail which formed the cover now hung in shreds, torn by the angry thorns of the dense forests through which we had ploughed our way. The top was covered with the skins of wild animals. The dissel boom, or pole, was a rough unhewn tree, and the wheels were thickly caked with black sun-hardened clay.

The whole turn-out looked shabby and dilapidated, but I watched with a happy heart the poor foot-sore oxen (whose bones were now forming sharp angles and threatening to break through their hides) as they wended their way down the narrow, rocky trail to the fresh green valley beneath, where I knew that for months they would be released from work.

Animation was soon given to the scene by the arrival of the Mashona people, who began to crowd around; the young men all being eager and anxious to know what the white man was going to do. "Was he going to hunt for meat?" "Did he wish to trade?" and so forth, were the class of questions asked.

Gradually the crowd of visitors began to swell to considerable dimensions, and we had quite a lively market scene, which brought with it a shower of light to our gloomy spirits, enlivened by the turmoil of countless voices. Produce of all descriptions common to the country was brought forward. We had rice, corn, meal, sweet potatoes, ivory, ostrich feathers, and assegais. On every rock the native merchants and their friends were perched like living statues, watching our movements and commenting upon us all the while. Abundance of light and shade could be seen in the style of conversation and in the mode of trading. Indeed their ever-changing countenances formed a special study. A great deal of acuteness was shown in trading transactions. They wrangled boisterously even about the value of a small wooden saucer filled with meal, or about the quantity of beads they had received in exchange for any special article which they sold.

Indignant at times, they would stare wildly at their associates, looking as though they meant to break for ever the link of friendship. In hot dispute their tones would show the highest excitement, succeeded by the lowering frowns of sulkiness, and anon by wild bursts of uproarious laughter; all showing that the barometer of their temper was of a thoroughly mercurial character, subject to rises and falls of no ordinary abruptness and extent.

As I at all times kept in mind the fact that a day would inevitably arrive when serious obstacles must cross my path, I was anxious to make the most of the time at my disposal; for I knew that the prospects of long marches in the high, wet grass of the Zambesi valley would certainly be realised should the rains overtake us.

Remembering this I at once commenced to engage volunteers who showed any real willingness to proceed. While they seemed to be in a favourable mood, the sooner I could catch them the better; at least so I thought.

One of the first to come forward was a very strongly built and extremely fat man, extraordinarily so for a Mashona. John said he knew him as one who had often gone with hunters to the fly country. The man had been nicknamed "Villum," but his real name was Chirimutu.

Five others quickly followed the example of our first recruit, all saying that they would go with me to Kunyungwi. These I found were Chibero men, who had followed us from the town at which we last stopped. In this way I continued to enlist the boys, as long as the novelty of the occasion captivated and enchanted their childish minds.

My *modus operandi* was as follows: Taking out a sample cotton blanket and two varieties of beads (small red beads with white eyes seemed to be the favourites), I tried to come to terms with each individual; and in an effort to instil some degree of method and discipline into the wild and babbling crowd, I wrote each man's name in my note book. All this time, however, I was pestered by annoying interruptions of a most extraordinary character. The man who had just been at my shoulder, anxious to know what he was to receive, after giving me his name, and seeing it written down—an operation which afforded him pantomimic delight —would wander away as though nothing had taken place;

in all likelihood thinking that when I was writing his name I was merely consulting my spirit as to the advisability of accepting his services.* Before he had gone fifty yards, the whole transaction was obliterated from his erratic mind.

He would wander off and meet a friend who, after a snuff, would inquire if he had seen the white man. On receiving an emphatic reply *in the negative*, they would return to me in company; the man I had just arranged with coming up unabashed as a distinctly new man; and, looking as though he had never seen me before in his lifetime, he would ask for quite a different and a fresh lot of things, thus upsetting all the former agreement which I had written against his name, for I was especially careful not to give anything away until all was in readiness for an immediate start. It seems to be indispensable that the natives should get presents. In fact they must get them, or they will do nothing; and even afterwards they must have promises of other donations to follow.

Sometimes it would seem quite hopeless to try and do anything with such volatile and insensate beings. Any number of them were ready to go on a hunt for meat; but the fact of being required as carriers seemed to be utterly beyond their comprehension. Sadly perplexed by such troubles, I turned round to look for John, especially as I was coming to terms with an unusually tractable black. Where was he? Certainly nowhere within the range of vision; but, after looking about for some time, I found him behind a rock, in company with the higher ape and Sagwam, melting down elephant's fat, and at the same

---

* The natives have not the slightest idea of the meaning of writing. So far as I can make out, they fancy that the white man discovers everything in his papers, and these he finds "ready made."

time busily chewing the gristly bits, that would not liquefy into a money-getting commodity.

"What are you doing, John?"

"I melt de fat of de olifant, master, to take back when I go home. Dar is man in Natal, dat give me one pound for de small cup full."

Hurriedly taking the melter away from his absorbing occupation, I ran back with him to the place where stood the hesitating recruit, who had just been on the eve of accepting the bounty. He was gone!

Where was Karemba? There he was dancing with a group of brother Mashona, who keep time as he deftly touches the iron keys of the native piano; for Karemba was budding out, and here he unexpectedly turned up as a musician of note among his own feather.

Amidst all this confusion and distraction, the reader may imagine how difficult a matter it was to keep the temper within the bounds of reason. And yet, just as I was struggling against the formidable flood of annoyances, another provocation to wrath made its appearance in the person of the long lost and incorrigible old scoundrel Taroman, whom we had not seen since he had sent the prairie fire careering after us to accomplish our destruction. In my present state of worrying excitement I could have annihilated the fellow; and yet there he stood, grinning from ear to ear, and calmly saying that he would " like a blanket!"

Words cannot express the wildness of my feelings at this particular moment. Without egotism I can repeat the oft spoken simile that compared to my outward resignation Job's patience was not a circumstance. The patriarch would have gone "bald crazy" had he been similarly situated. More than once I felt inclined to retire and have a solemnly independent dance, by myself, during which I would endeavour to remember some lines of Dante's "Inferno," while I hummed the strains of Beethoven's "Funeral March."

Having heard that meat was an indispensable article as an incentive before starting on a journey, I lost no time in going forth in search of it. Taking C. L. K., and followed by a number of Mashona who carried their bows and arrows and spears, off we went, crossing the small range of mountains which lay to the north of the town, and then descending to a large plain, which was completely black through all the high grass having been burnt. Only antheaps, like huge molehills, could be seen to vary the dead flatness of the blackened surface.

My garments here were the cause of some consideration. I had donned a new pair of corduroy "unmentionables," a flannel shirt, and a cartridge belt, which, with a Boer hat, completed my costume. I fancied myself "quite too much" like a clothes pole in front of a Hebrew store in Oxford Street, altogether too clean for hunting, as I stood like a white pillar upon the jet-like blackness of the ground. This chalkiness, however, was soon ebonised by rolling my body freely in the charred straw. After this charcoal shampoo I felt more like my work, and noticed that the Mashona highly appreciated the little stroke of hunter's policy; doubtless thinking that the white man was getting a good "ready" on, like the cock which stamps and jumps about before he is pitted.

During this operation the keen-eyed mountaineers had espied a herd of tsessebe antelope (*Alcelaphus lunatus*) at about 600 yards' distance. Stalking on these flats is very nice work. We make use of the ant-heaps, and crawl alligator-like along the ground. I dropped two fine bulls, but the second was lost after having chased him until my store of wind had completely run out, and I had taken an involuntary plunge into a small black bog, that threw up coarse-high reeds upon which I was nearly impaled. Smeared with green slime and black mud I emerged from this pitfall, using language which I am certain could hardly be characterised as that of meek affliction.

On my way back I found the Mashona in great glee carrying off the meat. I was not sorry when the sun had set. The day's work had been hard and trying, but at the same time when I closed my eyes I had the satisfaction of thinking that what I had done would facilitate our departure, which I sincerely hoped would be managed on the succeeding afternoon.

The Mashona mode of hunting is principally by netting the game. This they do at night by staking out long lines of nets, towards which they drive the game so as to become entangled in the snare, and render the capture an easy task. The Mashona say that the nets are sufficiently strong to stop an eland, the heaviest antelope in Africa. The rhinoceros and elephant, however, make playful havoc with the obstruction. The nets are very neatly made from the bark of the machabele-tree, extensively used by these people for many purposes, which I will endeavour to explain in succeeding pages of the present book.

The Mashona is careless of his person generally, with the exception of his head, covered with curly and crisp hair, which he loves to adorn in a manner that shows no inconsiderable degree of skill and even taste. Artistic arrangement is rarely absent, and the observer is forced to acknowledge their power in the department of hair-dressing. The women are the adorners and barbers. With a pointed piece of bone they divide the hair into a great variety of fantastic shapes. Sometimes the partings are made from back to front, showing cockscomb-like ridges which form a most becoming head-dress. Another fashion is the separation of the hair into circular tufts. Pulling it out to the full length they bind it round with the fine mimosa bark, so that it stretches outwards from the head, leaving a tuft of curly hair at the end of the newly-formed stalk. A very liberal supply of the fat of some wild animal, or perhaps of the oil of the ground-nut, is then employed to anoint the head-gear, showing the finishing touch of the master coiffeur's hand, the appearance of the whole adornment being shiny and fleecy, and resembling in a peculiar manner a luxuriant bunch of wild blackberries.

The women shave their heads, while the young girls have a fashion of stringing beads in their hair, and by the increased bulk cause their tops to look like the hooded bantam, especially as they shave all round the sides and back, leaving nothing but this odd-looking mop-like tuft.

Many of the youthful Mashona charmers, while very young, have lithe and graceful figures, although their features are far from lovely.

So far as I could see and learn, the morals of the people were much superior to the morals of the Matabeli, of whom I have already spoken in that connection.

It was interesting to notice the tribal or distinctive mark of the Mashona, which was shown by the practice of filing out spaces between the two upper front teeth, the aperture having the shape of the letter V inverted.

Their weapons are the bow and arrow, the axe and the assegai. Of the latter every man carries two or three of various sizes, but all, as a rule, much larger than those used by the Zulus; they are also much broader in the blade. The butt end of the assegai is shod with a piece of pointed iron, which is utilized for all manner of purposes, such as making holes in which to place the stakes of their game-nets, and other kindred uses common in the fields. It is rather a clumsy weapon, very different from the assegais of warlike tribes, in which the shafts are as light and as springy as whip handles, while only the spear-head end is used, the head being fitted into the shaft and bound neatly but firmly with pieces of raw hide, which is allowed to dry, so that by the shrinking process the binding holds with a vice-like firmness. The weapon I describe is a weapon solely intended for bloodshed, either that of animals or of men.

A persecuted and a hunted race are the poor Mashona. Dwelling in the mountain fastnesses, where their towns are hidden in most inaccessible spots amidst the great igneous belts which form such a prominent characteristic of the landscape, their huts are exceedingly primitive in construction, thatched with wild coarse grass, and usually perched upon the summit of isolated rocks. The only means of communication are, in some cases, a rough notched pole, which they can pull quickly up in the event of attack so as to make their retreat secure, or through innumerable intricate windings among their almost impenetrable rocky environment.

Many a time, as I dodged through the wild, goblin-like caverns of the place, did I think how thoroughly harassing, if not demoralising, it would be for an aggressive army to fight its way through the maze. Single rank would be the only formation that could advance, and men looking for their next uncertain foothold would be sure to be annihilated either from above, or from the innumerable black devils' gates which abound on every side, and in which the Mashona crouch during the attacks of the foe. In spite of all these natural advantages for defence, the Matabeli always seem to be able to out-general the unfortunate inhabitants.

Almost every nook and cavern of these well-nigh inaccessible mountain fastnesses contains a village or town of this hunted people, who never build their kraals on the flats or in the valleys. Here we see the struggle for existence admirably portrayed—not the individual struggling for life, but also the tribe, which is likewise a unit among African races. History repeats itself, and even the savage community must have its birth, infancy, maturity, decline and death. Mashona unity is broken; they have no longer such power of organisation as their neighbours, the Matabeli. They live in detached tribes, each one being a little kingdom in itself, and only looking towards its own existence. It seems as though the ambition for supremacy amongst them has faded from their minds, and that their only prayer is now for a quiet life. For them all glory has fled.

The diet of the Mashona consists generally of maize, meal and nuts (*Arachis*). They are particularly fond of the latter. A special partiality is also extended to meat of every description, which they cook in the crudest manner. They are not at all particular as to the time when it was killed, provided it has not wholly assumed another form of animal life.

Their cattle are very diminutive, but peculiarly hardy. Some have even been trained and used by hunters in their waggon work, and have been found to be very tough creatures, not so liable to get footsore as larger cattle, such as the Boer trek oxen. Towards nightfall the timid people herd their cattle and goats into the town, the nimble-footed beasts scrambling up the narrow rocky paths with the utmost ease and confidence. Before the sun has set the gateway is barricaded with immense trunks of trees.

Respecting these people, the impression left upon my mind is that they are a declining race, exemplifying strongly the Darwinian doctrine of the survival of the fittest. The stronger blood of the tribes of Zulu origin they cannot resist; consequently their adversaries have been encroaching upon their lands and liberties for many, many years, and in all probability will continue their depredations unchecked until the memory of the oppressed Mashona is but a thing of the traditional past.

Another day dawned, and the morning light shone brightly upon fresh scenes. Great numbers of people came to visit us, bringing ivory, skins of baboons, and all kinds of earthenware pots, also long sacks made of bark, woven in the most ingenious and neat-fingered fashion, and quite watertight. I bought some of the sacks in which to carry cartridges, so that the powder would not be damaged by wet.

I am sure that it would be very tiresome for my reader were I to attempt to describe the scene of confusion, disorder, and utterly hopeless abandonment of discipline which lay before us, showing the perplexing impossibility of doing anything. The babel even stopped the chance of hearing one's own voice.

"Oh dear, oh dear, oh damn! There is the sun again moving slowly down the clear western sky, carrying with it every prospect of a start for to-day! But I must positively get off to-morrow." And with the latter consoling thought lingering in my anxious mind I sank, but only for a few hours, into the peace of a refreshing oblivion.

Daybreak saw us again at work, packing into small bundles all the actual necessities for our journey. Many things had to be left behind in a padlocked box in the waggon. They consisted of ivory, feathers, hides, and a number of trading articles, some of which I was very reluctant to leave, but did so because I felt that the lighter the equipment the quicker would be the progress. A kraal, too, had to be made, into which the cattle could be brought every night for shelter.

Amidst all the skurry and turmoil of departure, it was painfully evident that the natives thought such a moment an especially favourable one for begging "presents." Oh, how the eternal repetition of that word "tussa" (present) rang like a chronic singing in my afflicted ears! You may talk of the "backsheesh" of the Arabs if you like, but I will back the duskier denizens of southern Africa for genuine all-round begging against the world. Their greed is insatiable, for the more you try to gratify their desires the more they are encouraged to demand.

On the eve of our departure, Chibero, the chief, turned up from the other town. As he sat down on a rock a ring was immediately formed around him, and every one of the company clapped their hands, such being the Mashona mode of saluting a visitor.

At length everything seemed to be ready for the start, except, of course, the indispensable Mashona escort. My baggage, I am afraid, would have made but a poor show beside the enormous stores carried by some expeditions to the interior of the dark continent; and, far away from even the slightest evidence of civilisation, there was, as a matter of course, no chance of replenishing should the supplies be exhausted. Provisions taken with us from this point consisted of some meal and rice, a small packet of tea, about thirty pounds of sugar, three pounds of coffee, three tins of salmon, one box of sardines, three small tins of condensed milk, two bottles of "three-star" brandy, two boxes of Huntley and Palmer's biscuits, two pounds of sago, five packets of maizena, and two bottles of lime juice. In case the system might be overtaxed by such luxuries, relief was to be found in the following medicines: One bottle Eno, one small bottle of spirits of ammonia, two ounces quinine, one ounce podophylin (the most effectively industrious searching medicine in the whole pharmacopœia, and principally used to dose those who were shamming, and who after one trial rarely called a second time at my drug store), one small bottle of chlorodyne, and two bottles of castor oil. The ammunition comprised two hundred and fifty rounds of elephant-gun cartridges, five hundred rounds of C. L. K. brass shells, ten pounds lead, reloading apparatus, and a few boxes of Curtis & Harvey's best powder.

The articles for trade included cotton blankets, white calico, blue calico, fancy handkerchiefs, four varieties of beads, a few yards of very pretty cloth kept for extraordinary occasions, as a gift perhaps to a cantankerous chief or a youthful princess. I also had some books—a small edition of Shakespeare, a Nautical Almanac, logarithmic tables, and Proctor's Star Atlas. The remainder of the effects were made up by instruments for observation, etc.

The total weight of the baggage was about four hundred and fifty pounds, which gave to the twenty-five men about eighteen pounds each as their share of the burden, and even at that many of them grumbled. What a contrast to the Zanzibar porters, who lift and carry for immense distances fifty pounds weight—aye, even more—without a murmur!

The body-guard consisted of the Royal Household of blacks, headed by John, who was followed by a young Mashona, also carrying a weapon. Sagwam bore upon his unwilling shoulder the "80-ton gun," which he hated with all the intensity of a lazy man's dislike to burthens. Karemba, with C. L. K. and fifty rounds of cartridges, was my immediate attendant. The higher ape, whose duties were now to be those of a cook and royal dishwasher, had a load that could not be considered trifling, especially as he carried on his head so many ornaments in the shape of a large and wonderfully worked hat, adorned with long feathers, his lower parts being enveloped in a shirt which I had given him, and which reached nearly to his heels. Besides this natural burden, he carried my shot gun, upon which were hanging a small kettle, two tin plates, two axle grease pots (now used for cooking in place of a cast-iron pot), a small gridiron (a Buluwayo production, suspiciously like an old preventer of rubbish in the mouth of a drain), and two tin bowls for tea, for ours was a teetotal caravan. John informed me that this itinerant kitchen had a love affair on, so that we should have to keep an eye upon him in case he should elope.

Personally I carried a compass, watch, and telescope, the latter having an unusual and melancholy interest through its being the last to signal the fading lights of the unfortunate *Captain* before she went down in the Bay of Biscay.

I also carried a small Matabeli stabbing assegai, which Karemba, with throbs of sanguinary delight, invariably used in giving the *coup de grâce* to expiring game.

I now paid Taroman, giving him a cotton blanket, and telling him that if the cattle were all right on my return, I would give him another, also plenty of beads. The old man was highly incensed. Working up his passion, he fumed and stormed, showing more energy for the time than could be noted in the aggregate of his exertions since I had enlisted his services.

What ridiculous capers he cut! With exclamations of utter disgust he was constantly turning away as though he intended to leave us to the tender mercies of an inexorable fate. Then he would return, primed and ready with a new and a more powerful charge of withering words, which he poured forth with astonishing volubility.

Although the attack slightly disturbed my arrangements, my equanimity was not upset. I was resigned, and bowed even to the aggravating circumstances, having long before become aware that I was utterly unable to frame a sentence which could in the slightest degree do justice to the occasion. Even in an inflamed vocabulary there was nothing sufficiently sulphurous.

Like a gipsy pedlar I kept on, undoing bundles perhaps to show a piece of cloth or a blanket to a man who said he would like to see what he was to get at the next town, not to speak of what he received before he started.

Amidst these scenes of bargaining John's temper and countenance had undergone many changes. In the heat of his rage he would call every one thieves. His face would change from a livid genuine yellow Hottentot rage to a stolid and sickly imperturbability which told of the sheer abandonment of despair. It was painfully evident that the comforts of philosophy had not touched the mind of poor John. When most was expected from him he would sit down as indifferent to all his surroundings as a monkey with the colic.

Oh, how often I wished that the man could understand me, when after one of his outbursts I would look at him in despair, and say, "What is the use of your trying to worry at the words, when you know that I have tried it and ignominiously failed?"

How helpless are the whites among the blacks when the latter are in their own lands! At such times we must pocket indignation, and thoroughly temper impatience, only dreaming of the blissful time when we shall be released from the bitter thraldom of dependence, and once again find ourselves free to give effect and direction to our wills among reasonable beings.

At length after much wrangling, and after paying each of the carriers a fathom of cotton calico, without which not one of them would have moved a single forward step, the caravan started for the north. As I anticipated desertion, we had thirty-three "regulars," and a multitudinous rabble of nude creatures of all sorts and sizes who followed in our wake.

Karemba and myself remained behind until all had left. I then gave two fathoms of fine striped cloth, which might almost be called beautiful, to the head man of the town of Little Unyamwenda, telling him to see that the cattle were coralled every night, and the waggon carefully guarded after our departure. Under its shelter I left numbers of things to be delivered to Fairbairn at Buluwayo, whenever John should make the homeward trip.

As for myself, I had made up my mind never to return to the waggon. Henceforth our journey through this wild land was to be performed on foot. Nature alone would decide the places for our rest. Although I had not literally "burnt my boats," I had done so in mental determination. Come weal, come woe, the object of my journey would not be abandoned!

CHAPTER VI.

MASHONA-LAND.

A funny ceremony—Working on superstition—Hypocritical Taroman—An immense prairie fire—Meditations on the journey—Cold dews—The slumbering camp—Unyamwenda, the chief—A tough-skinned fellow—Desertions—Bundles of wisdom—Old Sebaii appears—The charred plain—The Zururu river—John's success in hunting—Gorging the crowd—Furious quarrels over meat—The best way to manage natives—Sterile rocks of Mashona-land—Making a skerm—Mashona music—Karemba's repute as a performer—Native dancing—Pleasure in primitive life—"Ah, master, I never see people like here!"—Craving for limbo and beads—The Umvukwe and Rusaka mountains—Etsatse river—A troublesome goat—Curious hut—Prospecting for gold—Mashona ablutions—Honest natives—Unexpected appearance of Mehesa, the Vulcan of Mashona-land—Pursued by grass fires—Blacksmithing in the wildernesses—A primitive forge—Ironstone of the country—Troubles in camp—A night scene—Clannishness—Threat to kill Sagwam—Quarrels in camp—A doubtful expedition.

Much as I was impressed with the natural honesty of these simple aborigines, I still thought it unadvisable to neglect precautions for securing the safety of property. To effect this, a somewhat curious and highly amusing ceremony had to be performed.

Before we set out, the wily Karemba suggested that I should stand in front of the waggon, and merely show the people my watch. The sight, he said, of such an extraordinary fetish would make them afraid to steal during our absence. To put into effect this shrewd notion of Karemba's was the work of a minute. Standing in front of the waggon, I assumed a portentous demeanour of a most Satanic description, looking all the time devilishly upon the upturned face of the watch. I then walked slowly and solemnly round the waggon, describing a fair circle, from which I mysteriously waved the crowd away, tacitly intimating that within the charmed radius mortal man dare not come. I then stood still, and again gazing at the watch declared in fearful tones that whoever stole during my absence would be known and overtaken by a dreadful vengeance. It was amusing to observe the terror and awe depicted upon the faces of the astonished crowd.

We were hardly half a mile on our way when Karemba gave out the interesting news that we had forgotten the sheep and the goat. No time was to be lost, so back we went at "the double." Again the endless question turned up, "Where, in the devil's name, was Taroman?" Only after a long search did we discover the scoundrel talking to some Mashona women.

He said he had lost one of the sheep, so that now we had only two left, besides the poor goat, which was just like a dog in its tameness.

Had the old humbug lost all the sheep I could have understood the calamity, but to lose one, when the little beasts were always inseparable, was beyond the limits of comprehension. I could not help thinking that Taroman, with his rascal instincts, had one of the animals slyly hidden for future "lifting."

"Ah!" said the hypocritical delinquent, "I shall never see master again."

"And lucky for me, too!" I thought; for I would certainly become prematurely aged if he remained long in my train.

We soon overtook the party, which by this time had reached the southern bank of the Hanyane river. The waterway at this point was about sixty yards wide and averaging three feet deep. We crossed to the northern bank, and much to my delight I found that the majority of the camp-followers—altogether a troublesome incubus—had remained on the other side of the river, being averse to the wetting.

Crossing the Umtenge river, a small affluent of the Hanyane, meandering through a country splendidly adapted

MODE OF CROSSING RIVERS.

for farming, and overgrown by coarse, yellow-tinged grass closely resembling fields of ripened wheat, the party suddenly came to a dead stop, the chorus being that they would camp and sleep on this favoured spot. As a matter of course, John lay down, and said that he was sick, very sick indeed! But I was both anxious as well as determined to proceed, and would allow no loitering or malingering at this point. A vigorous protest was necessary; so I at once declared an intention to reach the town of the chief Unyamwenda that very night.

Just as the day was over we camped, and could look back upon the great granite crags and rugged mountain sides up which we had clambered, and which were now glowing with the streaming light of a magnificent evening sun. The first day's march was over, and, so far, had brought nothing but fresh troubles to my mind.

After a very light repast in the shape of supper, I left the camp's oddly uninviting scene, with its rabble of vociferous natives, and climbed high among the gigantic rocks, until I reached the topmost point of one of the many huge granite eminences which were so prominent in the surrounding scene. While there I looked about, and suddenly saw before me one of the grandest sights I ever witnessed.

It was an immense prairie fire. Far away, stretching for many miles, nothing could be seen but a vast chain of lurid fire, showing a wild appearance, as though the whole country was enveloped by its devouring flames. It was indeed a sight of awful grandeur. The long and fierce red line advanced like the phalanx of a great living and destructive army. The conflagration seethed and hissed horribly as it was swept onwards by the impelling force of a hurricane, while tortuous tongues of fire leaped upwards in flashing redness to pierce the dense black clouds of darkening smoke which rolled in volumes over the scene and intensified the blackness of the night. Burnt stalks fell like black snow-flakes on every hand.

Quite alone, without a fear of mortal disturbance, I crept into a small crevice in the rocks, and there, sheltered from the elements of mischief, I sat and viewed with charmed eyes the fiery panorama which lay outstretched before me, over growing wider and wilder as it coursed along. In this position, wild as the wind whistled, angrily as it howled, and fierce as was the scene, I felt a pleasing sense, even of repose, far different from the agitation produced by the noisy babble I had left in camp.

Naturally I meditated much upon my project. Reflecting upon what had occurred during the day, I thought that, although we were but a short stage on our journey, I could already detect among my party signs which were decidedly antagonistic to the plan of reaching the Zambesi by the intended route. The position was odd. I had no companion, no one even upon whom I could unhesitatingly rely. I was a helpless wanderer, directed by the mysterious hand of Fate.

Why had I not gone to Mababe to hunt with Selous, at once the best of companions and friends? Aye, why?

An answer might be found in the fact that I still had an almost absorbing interest uppermost in my mind, namely, to study the life-surroundings, and satisfy myself as to the character, of the black man in his aboriginal home. I also wished to gain as much knowledge as I could regarding the *real* value of the Dark Continent to the countries of Christendom.

To stop now was utterly out of the question. I had started, and was determined to get through without turning my back upon the far extending prospect of the new but wild regions. Adventure at all times has its charms.

Thoughts such as these flashed rapidly through my uneasy mind, until, overcome both bodily and mentally, by the fatigues of the day, I dropped off into a sound sleep. Not until the early hours of the morning did I awake with a start, to find myself still in the crevice of the rocks.

The mountain was enveloped in smoke and mist, and I

soon became painfully conscious that my body was saturated with an ice-cold dew. In the highlands of the Mashona country these dews are very heavy at this time of the year (June), while the morning air is sharp and biting.

Giving myself a good shaking, just to see that I was all there, because I had little actual feeling left, I returned hurriedly to the camp, where no sound broke the silence of the night except a general round of snoring, rising with drone-like monotony from the somnolent company, distributed upon every available space around fires now reduced to a few smouldering embers. Rolled in blankets, I soon was as unconscious as the rest of the slumberers.

Unyamwenda, the old chief, visited us in the morning. Seating himself upon a boulder, he said he wished to speak with the white man.

I approached with John and Karemba, who acted as interpreters.

The dusky old gentleman had paid no attention to the niceties of the toilet. Mark Twain has said somewhere that the "women of the Sandwich Islands wear a long, loose, coarse garment; the men don't," and certainly little description is required for the costume of Unyamwenda, whose figure the Lord Chamberlain would, without a second thought, have banished even from the modern British stage, and that is saying a good deal. The said apparel consisted of a small skin carried over the shoulders, while a sporran of the same material completed the simple garb.

His Highness was exceedingly dirty, and might be considered a thoroughly good specimen of smoke-dried, well-cured humanity. With a back resembling a side of corned beef, his skin was literally baked, this being attributable to a custom of the people, who sleep with their bodies exposed to the heat of immense fires, which often entirely destroy the epidermis, giving a fearful disfigurement to the poor souls.

As Unyamwenda sat silently looking at me for some time, I judged from his indulging in extraordinary facial contortions that he was suffering from surprise and injured dignity; perhaps being impressed by the notion that the white man had treated him with too much levity, for I had not even sent him a present in advance of my arrival.

Thinking that I would anticipate his reproaches I presented him with a fathom of striped calico of a very dazzling pattern, also two empty cartridge-cases. The latter are used as snuff-boxes by these people, and are worn hanging pendant-like from necklaces.

He then looked round at the other pieces of partially-cooked humanity who were grouped as his escort, and who all this time were exercising to an awful extent their frightful chattering faculties.

The gift appeared to unhinge his mental equilibrium; but he soon recovered the balance, and, not because he wanted anything more, but simply from the evidently hereditary conception of the race that the chief end of man is to beg, he asked for another snuff-box, a very moderate demand, which was at once acceded to.

"Have you a waggon?" was the next question.

"Yes," I replied.

"Then why did you not bring it here?" asked the chief.

"Because you have not made a road for a waggon; so I had to come on foot."

Unyamwenda rose on hearing this reply. He scratched his stomach for a little time, then shook himself, and drawing his shaggy leathern cloak about his shoulders, he disappeared, without uttering a word, towards the inner recesses of his rocky den.

For hours I now tried to effect a forward movement; but, as I had ominously anticipated, the "roll-call" showed an extraordinary reduction in the strength of the party. I had to lose no time in making overtures, as winning as possible, to the expectant crowd of Mashona, who stood eyeing, with the hankering stare of avarice, the white calico which lay at my side.

Elbowing their way through the encircling crowd came some old grey-haired men, who by their interminable loquacity seriously delayed our arrangements. These old bundles of wisdom were unconscionably tiresome; they would sit and talk by the hour, and, assuming the appearance of transcendant sagacity, would contradict everything that was said by others, a weakness of vanity that is by no means confined to the untutored savages of remote regions.

I managed, however, to single out one whose word appeared to have most weight with the boys, and giving him a present of some white calico, I soon had the satisfaction of finding him a staunch advocate of my cause.

The old fellow looked as though he could number a hundred years of life. From constant roasting at the blazing fires, of which I have just spoken, his hide had taken the appearance of gold-beater's skin, stretched upon layers of rich leather, and looking as though it could stand, without a flinch or a quiver, the application of a fiery poker, or the touch of a flaming torch.

After a tremendous amount of talk, we managed to find recruits to fill the deserted ranks; but it required not a little energy and tact before a start could be effected.

The old man never left us for a moment. Karemba said that he was wishing us a good journey, and telling the boys that they must go well and come back well with the white man. If talking could have done anything towards the realisation of our object, we would have gone on like an express train.

This reference to talking reminds me of a singularly solemn and rather small-looking man named Sebaii, who joined us here, and offered his services as a guide. He had a very remarkable gift of speech, and said he was a son of a chief called Macheangombe, whose town was not very far distant.

He had heard of me and had come, of course in a disinterested way, to see if he could be of any service. Sebaii knew the Zambesi well; he knew all the mountains; he knew all the rivers; in short, he was a walking *vade mecum*, a doubly-concentrated itinerant encyclopædia of African knowledge. As he was engaged to direct our way, his load was to be as light as his responsibilities were heavy. Therefore, excepting his own meat, his pillow, and assegais, he carried only our canteen, which consisted of two bottles of brandy.

Parenthetically it should be observed that all the Mashona people carry a small carved wooden pillow, measuring about nine inches in height, and perhaps about three inches wide, the article being intended, not only to keep the head from the earth, but also to prevent so dire a disaster as the disarrangement of their wonderfully artistic head-gear.

From our rock-bound camp at Unyamwenda we descended to the great plain which lay towards the north-east. On the level everything smelt of fire. The whole atmosphere was obscured by thick clouds of ashes, rising from the burnt grass, which were wafted hither and thither over the parched and blackened plain. As I peered through this heavy smoke-like mist, I felt an unusual depression of spirits; indeed, little else could be expected in such a scene.

Sometimes the immense waste seemed to have the appearance of an Indian shawl of gigantic dimensions; the yellowish brown grass encircling the blackened spots, and thus forming a curiously eccentric pattern, varied by the fickle freaks of the wind, or abruptly decked out by the moist places in the verdure.

We now steered about N.N.E. in direction (magnetic).

Intending to spur on stragglers, I was purposely in rear of the party. The first waverer I came across was a man who had become tired of carrying a load of cartridges, and had quietly laid them down. I met him on his way back. He said the load was very heavy. Consigning him with weighty words to a snowless region, I got his abandoned burden placed upon one of the spare men, whose actions, when he raised the bundle, occasioned grave thoughts that he, too, would cave in and follow his brother homewards. It was not so this time, however, and we forthwith proceeded to drive on the remainder of the party.

We had marched only about three hours when we came to a small rivulet called the Zururu. The afternoon was now well advanced, and I could see from the demeanour of the Mashona that they had not yet comprehended the fact that we were actually *en route* for the north, intending to push on in right good earnest.

I consulted with John as to what was to be done. The result was that John went off, taking C. L. K., in search of game. It was necessary that I should stay in camp.

"Good luck, John," I called out; "for Heaven's sake get meat, even if you shoot away the whole belt of cartridges! We must keep up our names as hunters, or these people won't follow us."

I then pitched the small tent which I formerly described, stowing inside most of the things I wished to keep dry.

Big fires, the great essentiality in Mashona comfort, were built by the boys, and soon after dusk John returned. He had killed one eland (*Oreas canna*) bull and two cows. John, as he often proved, was a splendid hunter, and in the present instance I warmly congratulated him upon his success.

No sooner did the Mashona hear of the meat than they were off in numbers, nearly all carrying firebrands, bent upon gorging themselves all night, and bringing what was left to the camp in the morning.

A silvery sunrise, which brightened the vast plains, found the camp in an active bustle. Of course, as usual, I was anxious to be off, but I had to curb impatience until the necessary distributions of meat had been carried out.

When it was all brought in, Karemba began to give it out in portions to all those who said they would go further; but of course there was no knowing how far any of the carriers would go. After they had been served, the followers from the town were let loose into the wild-looking shambles, and then the meat seemed to fly in all directions. Squabbling and wrangling over what were considered dainty bits, they reminded me of a herd of wild dogs, especially when now and then one of the number would wriggle out of the crowd and rush with his portion to some secluded spot.

As I had taken the precaution to keep a lot of meat in reserve, I was ready, should it be necessary, to give some to those unfortunates who, spiritless or feeble, would come out of the scramble without a bite, for a few of the more energetic had made a "corner" in the meat market, and seemed to have established a monopoly.

At length there was only one "bone of contention," and that happened to be a leg, at which two men hauled and jerked with might and main, making a single "tug of war" of the affair, which was watched with much interest, until the stronger man of the two walked triumphantly off with the gory trophy.

The defeated one immediately began to shout most lustily, and being joined by three or four others, there was soon noise enough for any indignation meeting, even at home. Thinking the meat was all gone, the fellows seemed beside themselves with rage. The scene baffles description. The men seemed to be talking against time; they threw their arms wildly about, and positively foamed at the mouth.

Excepting on one occasion, I had never seen a human being foam at the mouth, and the man I had seen had been drinking. But these combatants had nothing to imbibe except pure water, so that their symptoms of rage could well be considered as a prodigious, even a masterly, effort.

On inquiry, I learned that all this maddening row resulted from the circumstance of each being allowed to help himself. The men who were left out were headmen of Unyamwenda, who had expected me to give them the meat to take back to the chief. They said we had been killing game in their country, and had not given any to the chief, to whom the whole country belonged. Hiding, therefore, had proved auspicious. The store in reserve settled the whole difficulty.

With the same noise, turmoil, and trouble we again managed to get off. This time, however, I felt that all those who were with me were for the day my men. The hungry rabble had returned meat-laden to the town, carrying with them food for the families of those who were accompanying us.

Some readers may think that I always seemed to be in a great hurry to push on; but, under the circumstances, activity in that respect was absolutely necessary. I had a very long journey to do, and very little to do it on.

I have already described some peculiarities of the Mashona, and may now add that they will carry only very light loads, and require more to eat than any people I ever saw. They must have meal, and when they get plenty of meal, which is rather heavy and has to be carried, they must have meat, and this you must kill every day, for they will only carry very small pieces when they are with you. As a matter of course, the more men, the more provisions. A corresponding weight has to be provided for, and, besides, there is a limit to carrying capacity in connection with the very bulky and heavy medium of exchange, such as cotton goods, porcelain, beads, &c.

On every possible occasion the natives will ask for cloth, and they are not such fools as not to see keenly how thoroughly you are in their hands, if not at their mercy. True to the instincts of human frailty, they in many ways take advantage of their position, so that, in my place, patience, perseverance, and never-ceasing energy were the all-important qualities which might help to carry me through. With all such primitive-mannered races there is nothing so influential as a perfect self-control in temper.

Another momentous fact had also to be borne in mind. If my small stock of goods became exhausted before I reached the Zambesi, I should be in a mightily awkward predicament. The people there do "nothing for nothing." Remuneration is not called "pay"—it is "present;" but these "presents" mount up to an indefinite extent, assuming at last the proportions of unlimited loot.

The country through which we were passing at this time resembled a tract of Scottish moorland from which the heather had been burnt. The wind was high, and ashen-hued clouds were scudding over the desolate-looking plains. All the country had a bare, flat-like appearance, almost destitute of vegetation, while the ground was covered with small stones, brightened here and there by patches of short coarse grass.

Away to the eastward lay expanded a very sterile country, of extreme flatness, until the horizon was broken by a chain of craggy mountains—stark upheavals of spire-like rocks, whose wild recesses concealed Neanda, a large Mashona town, of which Setouro was the chief, and he was said to be friendly towards the Unyamwenda people. As I have previously remarked, these heights of rock are peculiar to the country; they often tower hundreds of feet above the land level, and almost invariably guide the traveller to the sequestered towns of the oppressed Mashona.

Though not very late in the day, the boys were making constant halts which boded that a camp would soon have to be formed; and as I always preferred to anticipate the wishes, and not allow them to "run" me altogether, which in reality they were doing, I announced that we would make a camp close to the nearest water.

We soon arrived at the sloping banks of a small swiftly running river, called the Gwiwi, which flows towards the Hanyane.

Wading through the water, we had to force our way through tall reeds which grew as thickly as grass. We passed through a small black swamp, and, reaching the other side, climbed the slopes, from which we could see a small kopjie surrounded by young forest trees.

For a camp the place had quite an inviting appearance, and consequently a halt was made.

As all the Mashona carry a small axe (the blade of which, at the cutting edge, is not more than two inches in width), they soon succeeded in clearing a comfortable spot; forming indeed a capital enclosure (skerm) of young trees, and branches which wound in and out; the whole being a circular fence about six feet in height, having a small opening as a sort of gateway, which at night was closed up with scrub.

Although the night was dark, its gloom seemed to have but little effect upon the spirits of the company, which were very much improved since the word-storm of the morning.

Immense fires were soon alight, with forked sticks on either side, and another stretching across. Upon the latter were hung long strips of eland meat, so that the little camp was a great kitchen, redolent with the odour of savoury roast, but never too strong, because there was no trouble about ventilation so long as the mighty star-lit sky was our only roof.

The scene was novel in every way. Indeed it was noticeable that, although I had now been camping for months, newness in surroundings and experience was continually present. Such changes might almost be called kaleidoscopic in their variety. At present I was wandering with a following of Mashona whose every act was new to me, and supplied many oddities to arouse all sorts of quaint reflections.

John and the worthy trio were the only companions whose character and peculiarities I knew well.

Animation of a very lively description brightened the camp as soon as the first repast was finished; and it must be noted, that with the Mashona, dinner is not over until everything in the shape of raw material is demolished, or the gormandising powers of the carnivorous horde have been defeated by repletion. A rebellion of nature alone can curb the appetite of the insatiable cormorants.

Another indispensable part of the peculiar enjoyment of

the Mashona is their music. They never forget their
pianos. Karemba, as I have said before, was quite an
eminent musician, and every day his reputation as a performer was becoming greater and greater. He was invariably
the first to touch the keys, and to pipe the wild opening
notes of their weird-toned song, which began with a high
long-drawn sound, and then suddenly dropped an octave,
to mount again shrilly on high as the most coveted notes of
a Mario.

All the time he was singing he danced vigorously, now
facing to the right, then to the left, and throwing out his
feet sideways just as a fat brood hen does when she is
making a nice big basin nest in your favourite border.
Sometimes, as if mysteriously moved by a sudden impulse,
he would bound rapidly forward, holding out one leg in
front while jumping with the other. On the elevated limb
he continued to gaze intently, as though it were something
particularly new, and of marvellous beauty. He would
circle about two or three times, and getting thoroughly
warmed to his work, as well as strongly excited, he would
stoop forward looking earnestly upon the ground, and then,
quickly throwing his body back, he would gaze into the
starry sky.

With leaps and bounds he described a small circle,
around which by this time all the company had gathered
closely, and in sympathetic admiration enjoying the performance, clapping their hands and singing, while each
one who entered the circle vied with his predecessor in
endeavouring to reach the highest perfection of emotional
dancing.

The "higher ape," not to be outstripped by Karemba
(who was in himself a veritable show), jumped into the ring
trying to look dreadfully fierce. He span round like a top,

first from the left to the right and then *vice versâ*, until, giddy and exhausted, with great beads of perspiration rolling down his body, he fell out of the ring to make room for another aspirant to the honours of the native ballet. During the course of the dance the " higher ape " enlivened his efforts by hideous imitations of all sorts of wild animals.

Entertainments such as these may be spoken of as being the drama of the people. Through them our little camp was cheered by the mirth of its wild inmates, who alternately slept and awoke, ate, sung, and danced throughout the livelong night.

Possibly it may seem strange to those for whom "roughing it" and wandering have no charms, when I affirm that the memory of a night of this description is ever cherished in my breast, and a mental revival of the scene always arouses feelings of grateful pleasure. Oh, how thoroughly have I enjoyed those hours of relaxation in camp after a long and tedious day! Perhaps it may have been a day rendered miserable by indescribable difficulties and troubles, which as a rule I do not care to dwell upon in thought, they being past and buried.

It is only natural to have a feeling of happiness when one finds himself unfettered and free among a primitive race in a primitive country, where all the evidences of the human kind speak of the natural (that is the wild) state of man. To me there always has been, and I suppose ever will be, a pronounced fascination in the circumstances of a genuine wild life. My readers must not misapprehend my meaning. I do not mean " roughing it " on a bottle of soda water and a ship's biscuit in a frail skiff on the upper waters of the Thames; but away in the core of some marvellous region whose land has rarely been trodden by the feet of civilised man and whose story is unrevealed. Each day in such a country brings a new intercourse with unspoiled Nature, new adventures, and new knowledge, all giving ample and important subjects for steady reflection in times present and times to come. In the condition of life which men call civilisation it is indispensable that the mind should be regularly occupied. That strangely inexplicable soul-yearning which is inherent in every man's nature should never cease to urge us on to the accomplishment of the purposes of life, and to the acquisition of a knowledge of its circumstances.

In this way, as years roll by, one's little pile of knowledge will be ever increasing. We may not aspire to reach the higher rungs of the shining and slippery ladder of fame, but our accumulation of knowledge will be sure to comfort us at some depressed period of our lives: it may also perch us a step or two upwards with a secure footing. "The mind of man in a long life will become a magazine of wisdom or folly, and will consequently discharge itself in something impertinent or improving."

But what am I thinking about! By this time the sun is high over the little kopjie at the back of the camp and we must be off. John sits motionless beside the fire.

"What's the matter now, John?"

"Ah, master, I never see people like here! They want to take all de tings. My Gaut! my Gaut! Limbo and beads, limbo and beads, limbo and beads, everee day all de same! What shall us do?"

I will not weary my readers with details as to how we settled such difficulties. The story would be far too long. Amidst all our annoyances even the administrative power of a Napoleon would have been frustrated. I began to think what such a man would have done under the circumstances; but soon came to the conclusion that he would never have placed himself in such a weak position, so again I turned round to face the facts, the too palpable too hard facts.

The sun near meridian, and not a soul moving! On every hand I have to accede to loud and incessant craving, so that limbo (calico) and red white-eyed beads are distributed all round.

Some Mashona who had been driven from their homes during the latest raid of the Matabeli came to see us. They said that there were some ostriches on the plain beyond, and they brought numbers of the prettily-striped skins of the little ground squirrels. Much as I would have liked to have bagged some ostriches I could not suffer the delay, so after the usual pangs had harassed my temper in the endeavour to effect a move, we were again tramping northwards over the bare earth, which was parched and smooth through the grass being burnt.

We held on the same course during the following days. The nights were spent in uproar caused by the singing, dancing, and wild gorging with meat which I have previously described. These evening entertainments became so familiar, that they hardly disturbed me, and I think I could now sleep serenely amidst any surroundings, even amidst the fervour of an "Irish night" in Parliament. That is to say if I was not troubled in mind.

At that time there was enough to trouble the mind. The Unyamwenda men were an ever increasing source of anxiety and bother. They were then trying all they could to frighten the six Chibero men, who, up to the present, had done tolerably well, but were now becoming nearly as bad as the others.

The course carried us through vast undulating plains, broken by bald hills, and very sparsely dotted with solitary-looking, scraggy upland trees. Numerous rivulets were crossed, such as the Akanizita, Watadzi, Inyaoko, and the Mswatadze. The shimmering and murmuring waters of these tiny streams run a winding course, north, south, and west, until they fall into the Umquadzi which conveys all the water of this great valley into the Hanyane. The immense dome-shaped mountains, conspicuous on account of their naked summits, belonging to the prominent Umvukwe range, suddenly spring into view on our left. These rough eminences form the western barrier of the Umquadzi valley. Our line of march was on the elevated but flat-looking eastern side which sloped gently towards the river.

Game, such as eland, bastard hartebeest, roan antelope, and so forth, was very plentiful, but the herds could not be spoken of as being large. Hartebeest were seen in the largest numbers. Birds of any description were very scarce. In the forest belts small baboons were numerous.

We passed another town, lorded in this case by a chief named Mchesa, the Vulcan of Mashona-land. His town was another example of the vast monumental looking groups of granite blocks, tossed and tilted in every direction, with deep rents yawning in their polished adamantine sides.

After Mchesa's town was passed, the country became more broken. On either side, suddenly, the view opened out larger, for we were now on the great watershed between the Umquadzi valley in the west, and the rugged country which extended far to the east, and abounded with rough and barren-looking heights, showing no resemblance to the massive solid-like slabs of rock which composed the hills we had recently passed; they could only be compared to gigantic piles of shapeless broken stones.

These ridges are known as the Rusaka mountains. They skirt the Grumapudzi, which winds its way through the foothills, and flows in a north-easterly direction to discharge into the Amazoe, a tributary of the Zambesi.

Many a good hunt was missed in this part of our journey, simply because I had to be constantly on the alert among the party, knowing that the less time they had for trifling talk the better were the chances of making them work and push on. At one time a Koodoo cow, which John shot, did a little in the way of keeping them at rest; but on reaching the Etsatse river the Unyamwenda men declared they were tired, and that they wished some days of rest.

Well did I know what that meant! The cormorants were calculating upon having an out and out game of plunder.

With the greatest difficulty I had been able to induce them to pass Mchesa's town. Now, however, I silently acquiesced to their demands for a halt, although I was at all times extremely loth to do so. The fact was I felt rather tired, not on account of the marching but through the constantly recurring difficulties, which ever and anon threatened to become insurmountable obstacles.

To relieve the tedium and anxiety of a halt, I went out in search of game, a usual resource in such circumstances. Luck in this case was obstinate. I had two good stalks, but missed; evidently I could not see straight, although on the way home I shot two reed bucks (*Cervicapra arundinacea*).

Remembering that ere long we should reach the tsetse-fly country, we now killed the two remaining sheep, sparing the goat which by this time had taken up Taroman's place as a nuisance, although the four-footed beast was preferable on account of its livelier nature. We had plenty of provisions for the next day, and I made up my mind never to kill the goat, which was as tame as a dog, choosing to let him run his chance of becoming a victim to the deadly flies, and then give him a decent funeral.

The night was dark and very dreary. The dismal air deadened the spirits of the whole party. Even the sprightly levity of the Mashona seemed to be buried. Up the valley the wind blew "great guns," bringing with it a penetrating, wetting mist. Wrapped in our blankets, John and myself crouched close to the hissing, badly burning fire.

Melancholy experiences once more made John think of his home and his "leetle wife" far away in the Tati gold-fields. Lugubrious meditations respecting the girl he left behind him were evidently surging through his depressed brain when he would give vent to an expression of this kind:

"Oh! my master, I go well all de years; but dis year I go varee bad. When de master goes to hunt, de people wants to fight wid me all de time."

Knowing that sleep would be the most beneficial thing under such gloomy circumstances, I crawled into the diminutive tent which Karemba had almost filled with sacks of meal and other stores that had to be kept dry. At my head was the chronometer; on one side were the rifles, gun, and cartridges; on the other the provisions, the latter being packed so closely that very little room was left for the old goat, who had pretty much of his own way in the tent, seeing that I was always happier when he remained inside, for the simple reason that when he was outside he invariably chewed the cords, so as to demolish the humble erection, an effort which was more than once crowned with complete success.

On this especial night, some time after I had got soundly off to sleep, I was startled by a sharp blow on my back, which was quickly followed by the collapse of the whole tent. This was not my first experience of similar catastrophes, but my restive lodger had never before treated me quite so ungraciously. Annoyed by being cramped to an unusual extent, the old goat must have moved up towards my head in order to get more room, and meeting with disappointment he was consequently in proper form to fight for his rights; so he banged away in a most unceremonious manner, I all the time making wild clutches in the darkness, expecting to seize a horn or a leg. But no: my irate companion was struggling to get out of the canvas, and as I was bent upon the same object we had a regular rough and tumble set-to. The old goat managed to make things pretty uncomfortable for the remainder of the busy night.

Before noon next day a good deal more game had been shot, and numbers of people, from a town hidden in the recesses of the contiguous hills, came up to us, bringing with them a most varied store of commodities for sale, or rather in exchange for meat. Like a couple of butchers, John and myself stood over the heaps of game, carving and cutting off the pieces, for which we got in exchange sweet potatoes (very good when roasted), and other provisions for the party.

Not a few of our visitors, too, brought with them gold dust, stuffed in large quills stopped at the end with small pieces of bark. Of this gold dust, and of the gold-yielding region generally, it is my intention to speak more fully further on. For the gold dust I gave cloth in exchange; but, commercially speaking, I found that I had invariably made bad bargains, the people placing an extraordinary value upon the stuff, as they made signs that they had worked very hard to procure it. For two fathoms of white calico I bought a very fine assegai, of the kind used in elephant hunting.

An afternoon was spent in prospecting, my object being to see whether I could find quartz reefs in the immediate vicinity. With this purpose in view I roved observantly through the rocky hills—they could not be called mountains—which lay a little to the west of our camp, taking the aneroid with me.

I found that the divide between the Umquadzi valley and the Etsatse (where we now were encamped) was 4450 feet above the sea. Although I did not succeed in reaching the Umquadzi river, I inferred from natural evidences that it should have a large volume of water. The area drained by the river is of great extent.

A curious hut was seen during the course of this wandering. It was built of green branches closely matted together, and running up to a point. The structure was not unlike a North American Indian's hut, although it had no aperture for the escape of smoke, nor was there a visible means of getting in or out. We shouted here for some time before we received any response. Finally the timid inmates became convinced that we were friendly, and assured of this made a small hole by pulling aside some of the interlaced branches.

I crept through the opening, and found myself in what seemed to be the near atmosphere of a strong kitchen fire. Breathing or seeing was impossible, owing to the intensity of the smoke, which of course had no outlet with the exception of the crevices between the leaves and branches of the walls, which formed the remarkable fortification.

Inside the Mashona were all cowering over the fire. A few small boys and dogs, busily knawing bones, completed the select and very high-smelling circle. The men were smoking wild hemp.

The boys who had been hunting with me also had to

enter. I suppose it is Mashona etiquette that no stranger should remain out of doors. A Kaffir hut seems to be another of those extraordinary places which always has room for one more: a tram-car, for example, in which an emergency is seldom known when one extra passenger cannot be squeezed in. The only difference I could see was that the unenlightened black quietly allowed his neighbour to be accommodated without looking at him as though he was a dangerous intruder, perhaps an escaped, deeply-dyed defaulter. In those wilds, happily, there are no austere-looking dames whose withering looks are calculated to make a hardened heart quiver through conscious depravity when the possessor takes his rightful seat in a railway carriage, an omnibus, or a theatre.

The company and the quarters were not in this instance sufficiently attractive to enthral me for more than a few moments, so we were soon on the move. After a tramp of over ten miles we once more found ourselves in camp. I had not found metalliferous rock of any description; the gold-bearing veins are evidently on the Amazoe river, which lay to the east.

The scene in camp contrasted strongly with that of the previous night. A babble of numerous voices broke the stillness of the night air; the stars shone out brightly; and the gleam of the wood fires was reflected in the ruddy glare of hundreds of glittering spears.

A whole community seemed to have sprung up during my absence. There must have been at least a hundred and fifty strangers from the Grumapudzi river. All had flocked to see the white man. Each carried three assegais, and every one sat round the fire eating and chattering vigorously.

John said that during my absence he had bought some

gold for me with cloth. Meat we exchanged only for meal or other provisions.

Something of more importance, however, was his telling that he had overheard what the two leaders (Shedabarume and Saiika) of the Unyamwenda had been saying. From their remarks he did not think that they would go any farther without a further supply of cloth. At that rate, I thought, I should soon be bankrupt.

Amidst all the inconvenience I managed to get an observation of a star, and so fixed the latitude. Using the top of the sextant-box as a table, and kneeling—for the shelter was only three feet high—I plotted my route on the rough chart, which I kept filling up as I proceeded, giving for each day the distance accomplished. One fact made me feel very uneasy. The position showed that we were holding too much to the north; and although I had already protested upon this point, the Unyamwenda men positively refused to go more to the eastward.

I found that we were still a very long way off from Tette. In a perfectly straight line the place was 157 miles distant. But in Africa mileage is not to be defined by time.

I tried to cheer John a bit; because I uncomfortably began to think that his reflections were gravely inclined towards a retreat homewards. Should we only get the men to go on with us until we came to some big chief, I still had sufficient exchange to pay for an entirely fresh lot of followers. Full of worrying thoughts and speculations I lay down to rest, rolling myself in a good blanket, in the comfortable folds of which I soon exchanged the woes of the world for the visions of sweet dreamland.

The night was much warmer than the previous one. Earwigs swarmed in the tent, but the little pests run off as soon as you begin to move about.

Before daybreak I was awakened by the usual babble of voices, which invariably began a discordant chorus about the same time; for the Mashona goes through a great deal of exertion before he springs up alert to the day's duties. First of all he will raise himself and gaze intently into the fire. Then in an absent-minded manner he will begin to sing, straining harshly the fibres of his wind-pipe in the wild effort to reach the topmost notes of his vocal register. This performance done he will get up, shake himself, and begin his morning ablutions, for which purpose a friend holds a calabash of water, pouring it into the palm of the bather's hands, so that he may wash his face, hands, and especially his mouth; for he rubs his singularly hard teeth vigorously, using his fore-finger as a tooth-brush. A morning wash is essential to the Mashona; because his eyes get full of dirt, arising from the fires, blown into them during the night.

Disputes usually begin with the awakening of the faculties. The matutinal quarrel, as a rule, is about meat; but upon this particular morning, the subject was whether the Amazuiti, as those people call the Matabeli, would or would not beat them in the next fight. Some said that they would, others that they would not; nay on the contrary that they would kill all the Matabeli the next time they came.

Evidently there was a great difference of opinion. Now and then their wild shouts of laughter would ring through the morning air, while at other times they might be seen crouching closely up to the fires, awaiting their turn of the pipe (*ikutu*), from which they would inhale the irritating fumes of the wild hemp. How curious it was to hear these borne-down people talking and laughing loudly about their prospects against inevitable conquerors! Feeble as they were, they evidently could look destiny fairly in the face.

At how many firesides, I wonder, in civilised life would laughter be heard while anticipation was rife respecting the imminent invasion of predatory and merciless foes?

The pipe of wild hemp, as it was passed from one to another, made the smokers cough with extraordinary vigour, as though they were making a strong effort to burst a blood-vessel. At the time I speak of, they had reached this coughing stage, and what with the disputation, the coughing, laughing and singing, the confusion may be better imagined than described.

Nevertheless John and I commenced to get everything ready for the advance, which it was clear was to be a formidable matter in the way of tactical difficulties.

As I could readily perceive that it would be next to impossible to set out before noon, I produced my sextant, in order to take a meridian altitude of the sun.

The awestruck astonished look on the faces of the black crowd, which surrounded me, was highly amusing; one, more bold than the others, I allowed to look through the telescope of the sextant, covered by the red sun-glass, through which he caught a glimpse of two red suns.

The sight evidently disconcerted him, for he quickly walked away, saying to his comrades: "There are two suns, two, two;" at the same time holding up two fingers, so that there should be no mistake about his "seeing double." I am sure that they thought the "white curio" was anything but "canny."

Among our numerous visitors were a few more of those old grey haired bundles of sense, whose appearance never boded good. I tried to get some recruits, but not one would consent to be engaged for more than a single day's journey. Under these conditions I could not afford to pay cloth. Shedabarume and Saiika caused more trouble than all the rest, for they were perpetually inciting quarrels, and I had a disagreeable suspicion that I would yet have a good deal more difficulty with the intractable pair.

Whatever may be the faults of these people, actual experience does not allow the accusation of theft. Very easily, and without the slightest risk of punishment, they could have helped themselves to the stores which lay about the camp; but we had no instance of larceny in that respect. On the contrary, I record with pleasure the occurrence of a simple event, which exemplifies their innate honesty. Our hatchet, a most indispensable article, was dropped on the way; and in the course of a short time it was brought back to us by a total stranger. Readers who are inclined to consider this a slight incident, must remember that an implement of that description is an exceptionally valuable acquisition for the equipment of these unarrayed children of the wild. As a matter of course, the restorer of the property was duly rewarded for his trouble.

I called up Sebaii (who was supposed to be our guide, but for some incomprehensible reason was at all times the rear man in the company), and speaking through John, informed him that we were not going in the proper direction. Sebaii was a cunning old scoundrel. Looking downwards with an amazingly knowing leer, his only answer was:

"Ahay, Ahay, Seree!"

Karemba, I suppose, had taught him this sentence, which might be supposed to comprise all that was necessary for a conversation with a white man. This, at any rate, was all I could get out of our precious *guide!* I had constantly been told that we would soon take a turn to the eastward, but now by incessant disappointment I was beginning to be stubborn.

When at length we succeeded in getting the party off in sections, crowds of Mashona followed in the wake. I was the last to leave, my companions being Karemba and the "higher ape." The latter at the time would have been a fine figure-head for a circus. His top dressing was a marvel of what was evidently considered the perfection of beauty. Feathers stuck out in all directions from his head, while down his back monkey skins hung in ample folds. He had also purchased an assegai to add to his load. Clearly the ape was imbued with a notion that in his fearful and wonderfully made body lodged the lingering spirit of some great defunct chief, so that it was his bounden duty to decorate to the utmost the abode of the ghostly genius. How he managed to buy the adornments was of course an unfathomable mystery.

Scarcely a quarter of a mile of our route had been covered when a tremendous hubbub broke out in our rear. Startled by the shouting we looked back and distinguished a number of blacks pursuing at breakneck speed. We waited until they came up, and then the disclosure was made that a great indiscretion had been committed by having passed through a country without seeing the chief to whom it belonged.

Our visitors were the slaves of Mchesa, the chief. They kept signing to me to sit down.

"You cannot go farther," said Karemba; "the chief is coming," an intimation which he repeated with great emphasis.

Concluding that the best plan would be to sit still I did so, after sending a boy ahead to stop the party.

Very soon we descried in the distance the lithe figure of a tall man, loosely robed in a large sheet half blue and half white. On he came, running and walking alternately, his great strides making him appear as though his very life depended upon every step. For a mighty chief, this hasty gait appeared a very undignified mode of locomotion. His anxiety, however, was sufficient to show that the old gentleman had a very great interest in what was before him. In his mind, of course, calculations were rife, and visions looming, regarding the quantity of cloth he was going to receive. I had previously sent up to his town a message to the effect that I wished to buy some assegais, but no response having been given for nearly two days, I had given up all hope. Now I felt that the chief might score one at least, for he had caught me. Not that I had been endeavouring to evade him, but in the anxiety to get ahead I had forgotten a strong point in savage etiquette.

I was sitting under a small bush trying to find a shade against the excessively hot sun, when Mchesa arrived, panting, and apparently excessively choleric. He at once squatted on the ground, his followers doing the same, all clapping their hands.

A cemetery-like silence prevailed for some time. Then the old gentleman having caught his second wind, began to pour forth eloquence, speaking with so much earnest volubility, that it was not difficult to perceive that he was getting rid of a superfluity of bottled rage which had generated and accumulated during his somewhat arduous journey. His town was at least twelve miles in the rear of our position.

After he had finished his expostulatory oration, Karemba and Sagwam (the latter having come back to see what was the matter) explained to me as well as they could what Mchesa had said.

"His heart was sore," it appeared, "that the white man had gone through his country without seeing him. He wanted to show assegais to the stranger, and how he could fashion them with his own hands. For the latter purpose, he had brought with him the whole paraphernalia of manufacture, bellows, iron, &c., to make them on the spot, and that he had travelled very far, and would not go farther!"

Answering the old man I said, "I had travelled much farther than he had—many, many moons—in order to see his country, and that I had sent his people to say I wished to see his assegais, but thought he was not coming; therefore I left. If he now wished me to buy some assegais, and to give him cloth in exchange, he must come with me to where my party was.

To this the chief consented, but not without a great deal of coaxing. It is very unlikely that he would have left me, but he had a hope that I would bring the cloth to him. We soon overtook the party and marched on to the Waynge river. Surrounded by rocks, trees, and rivers, we selected a sheltered spot, where we might be secure from a grass fire, which had been following pretty closely all along the march, threatening to swallow up the camp. We were in such a fix that I was on the point of ordering the party to take the things across the river, so that I was very glad of the assistance of the numbers who had followed us. To help in fighting against the advancing fire all hands turned out, breaking small branches from the trees, and moving forward in a line beat out the flames. Fortunately, the wind changed, and lulled a little, otherwise these operations would not have been successful, the grass being long and very dry.

Three skerms were made, one for the old chief Mehesa and his following, one for the people from the Grumapudze river, and one for ourselves.

A follower of Mehesa's sold me a fine assegai, for which

he received cloth in payment. But when my attention was engaged with something else, the assegai disappeared. In a short time I walked over to where the chief was talking to the interpreters. We went in and took our places in the circle that was formed.

The old man was speechless, looking as though his feelings had been unpardonably tampered with; his resentment seeming to be a powerfully concentrated essence of indignation. I thought I would take the cork out soon; for close behind him I saw, sticking in the ground, the assegai which I had bought. I gave notice that I was about to speak.

Through Sagwam, who acted as interpreter, I strongly protested against the fraud of the assegai being taken back after I had lawfully bought it; telling the chief that when a white man made a bargain he never asked his cloth back again.

Mehesa's reply was to the effect that the assegai belonged to him, and not to the man who had sold it.

On my remarking that I wished to see him work, he answered that his heart was sore, because after he had come so far I had not given him *mataka* (present). He had prepared his forge outside, but could not go to work until I had given him something.

I gave him a tolerable present of red white-eyed beads, but he said that his heart was still aching (for more), so I gave him a couple of yards of splendid striped calico showing very brilliant and pretty colours, yet he did not half appreciate its beauty.

Vulcan's face still wore the cloud of disappointed greed. I asked for the assegai, and he had the audacity to say that what I had given him was a present for his having come so far.

"You grasping old wretch!" I muttered between my

teeth; "had it not been that I know that farther down where I intend going iron in all likelihood will not be found, and consequently no native blacksmiths, I would leave you to yourself."

Though I had to pocket my pride, I was determined to see this primitive artificer at work; so I continued to give him beads, and as he called for more doled them out by degrees, thus removing gradually the symptoms of disappointment, until at length his countenance cleared, and it became apparent that his heart was healed.

I then took possession of the stolen assegai, and the old man proceeded to work. Negotiating in this fashion took up a very long time, particularly as I was becoming a more adroit trader, and although I had given him beads many times, the aggregate was not very great.

Old Mchesa's blacksmithing was really a good effort. Throwing aside his ample robe, undecked nudity was his working condition.

He burrowed a hole in the rather sandy soil close to a place where the underlying rock protruded, to form a natural anvil.

The tue "iron" was fashioned with clay baked to the hardness of firebrick. The small nozzle he had brought with him. The bellows were of a duplex pattern, consisting of the whole skins of goats made perfectly air-tight, excepting the neck and one of the legs, which respectively formed the inlet and outlet for the air. A strap was fixed across the opening at the neck, so as to facilitate the raising of the bellows after the air had been forced to fan the fire. The motive power employed to work the wind was an old man; who, seating himself between the two goat-skin bags, placed a hand upon the openings in each neck, and fell to action, pressing down one bag, and grasping tightly the

THE VULCAN OF MASHONA-LAND.

place where the hole was, so as to prevent the escape of air. As he did so he would relax his hold upon the other bag, raising it up meanwhile so as to allow it to refill. In this way a continual blast of air was kept up to the fire. This novel apparatus completed the improvised smithy.

The workman's tools consisted of two small square blocks of iron weighing about three pounds each—these were hammers—and a pair of tongs, made from the greenbark of the Machabele-tree. With these appliances at hand all was ready for operations.

Taking a piece of crude iron, which still retained some of the slag of the native smelting furnace, Mchesa heated it, and went through the regular process of "drawing it out" by means of hammering, his sledge hammer being a piece of water-polished black basalt, as hard as iron, taken from the bed of the Waynge river close by. The sledge was used by a lusty savage, who, taking two steps backwards, would then come forward with an energetic impetus, bringing down the stone on the iron like a trip hammer.

Mchesa conducted himself as a thorough tradesman (and seemed to be fully aware of the fact), knocking the dust off his hands, and watching with a knowing eye the appearance of the glowing flame. He never stood erect, but always worked in a sitting posture, and everything he did was accomplished with ease, dexterity, and I might almost say gracefulness. The tongs had to be renewed now and again.

No one could have the slightest doubt that the chief was looked upon as a remarkably clever man by all around him. He talked all the while to the old boy at the bellows, who never spoke, excepting when he gave vent to a monosyllabic negative or affirmative, and who deported himself in a wonderful manner, starting or stopping at any part of the stroke like a well-regulated engine, hanging his head to one side as though the weight of his brain when thoroughly set in motion would weigh him to the earth.

A delightful feeling came over me. Now shall I show my knowledge of character by overcoming this cantankerous old tiger, and making him perfectly good-natured, for as he is capable of being so dreadfully cross, he must also have the power of being the reverse. I must endeavour to see the other side of his face.

The assegai was fashioned, and the chief asked me if I wanted it. Knowing his character, I said I would buy it from him. He then made me some more, for all of which I gave in exchange some article that pleased his fancy.

So as to observe the effect I tried to flatter Mchesa, telling him that he was very clever, that the assegais were beautifully made, that I would take them home and show them to my white brothers, and that I did not know of any white man who could make an assegai so well.

He seemed pleased to hear all this, but was altogether too great a man to show his emotion, saying, however, that it was not his fault that he did not make me lots of assegais. I thought that at the price such a transaction would be a considerable commercial failure on my side.

It ought to be mentioned that the ironstone (a piece of which they brought to me) as found by the natives of this locality looks like a brown hæmatite.

Mchesa, when seen closely, was a man of moderate stature, about forty-five years of age. His garb consisted of the plain white and blue cotton robe of which I have spoken, but on his head he wore a wreath-like ornament of otter skin, decorated with white fossil shells found in the bed of the Zambesi. Known to be by nature rather cross, the Vulcan was in fact an exceedingly crabbed old party.

Hearing a great uproar in the camp, I hurried back, and found that Sagwam and a strange boy had been conversing, and had aroused the Unyamwenda by something they had said.

Shedabarume and Saiika were by this time very obnoxious, almost unbearable in their manner. I had observed on the road from the last river that neither had carried their loads to this place, but had transferred them to two strangers. People in those climes will impose upon each other as nefariously as any race I know of. I have watched them piling their loads upon others, and giving in return for the relief a small piece of meat or a few beads, sufficient of the latter, perhaps, to make an earring. The unfortunates continue to carry their burdens until the limit of endurance has been passed, and then down go the things and a row ensues.

The aspect of affairs clearly showed that a disturbing element was developing in the camp. Trouble of some description seemed to be imminent.

Inquiring of John about the matter, he said that a Mashona boy who had been captured during a Matabeli raid, and had been taken to Buluwayo, but had effected an escape, was in camp, and he it was who had been speaking to Sagwam, and whose remarks had aroused the trouble.

The boy had declared that they were taking the white man in a wrong direction. He had, it seemed, seen other white men when he was at Buluwayo, and as he looked rather a bright youth I told John to enlist him. He was christened "Umfana," which is the Matabeli word for boy.

I was very glad to get the recruit, if only for the reason that the merest ray of light from the outer world was most acceptable in these utterly barren life-scenes.

On that night the view of the camp was weirdlike in its

wildness, reminding one strongly of the romance pictures of the home of a horde of brigands.

Towering on every side around were great precipitous rocky cliffs, with ragged nooks and crannies vividly exposed under the blood-red light radiating from the dancing flames of our primitive fires. It was this wildly picturesque background that gave to the shelter its brigandish appearance, only the camp was perfectly open in its display of warlike appurtenances, for on every side a perfect forest of glancing spearheads reflected the light of the starlit sky. Groups of men circled round the crackling blaze, and their black skins shone so that individually they looked like wet bronze statues under the glare of an electric light.

As the darkness deepened, one could see how the instinct of clanship strengthened. The party divided into its three natural parts, each going to its especial enclosure, in the shape of a rough hedge hastily and rudely formed from branches and trunks of trees, with the coarse wild grass peeping up here and there through the crevices, and sometimes drooping gracefully to mingle with the verdant foliage, which in the daytime imparted a certain luxuriance to the romantic scene. Is it possible, amidst such a scene, that in anyone's mind there would not crop up some reflections upon the universality of the rules in Nature's guidance of man? In that diminutive and strangely placed camp the nations of the world, in a manner, were pictured.

Multitudes had been divided. Each individual assemblage had been formed into its family—its clan—and had become a body animated in itself by fraternal ties and kindred aspirations. Contrasts of content and discontent were to be found. On one hand might be seen the family which was ever ready to listen patiently to the voice, and attend humbly to the commands of its head who had risen to despotic power, and ruled his people with an inflexible hand. On the other side might be observed the nomad clan —chiefless, perhaps—wandering thriftless but thoroughly contented in a land where the necessaries of life were plentiful, and where they would sink without a thought into impotent rest. In the third place were the reckless people, destined to drift helplessly toward the darkness of anarchy and the doom of dissolution.

Not without reason, I had a strong idea that the latter was the condition of my camp.

I lay in the small tent for hours trying to gain a little sleep. Towards midnight, however, the ever-increasing hum of excited voices reached such a pitch that I turned out, being convinced that what Artemus Ward would have called "a fite" was on the verge of commencing.

So far as I could see, Shedabarume and Saiika were having the best of the trouble. The Chibero men seemed to have separated themselves entirely from the Unyamwenda, and were sitting apart at a special fire.

I walked around the crowd, sitting first at one fire and then at another, without understanding a single word of what was being spoken.

My wish was always to look utterly regardless—a feat, however, which was not at all times successful. In the present instance I wandered indifferently about for a time, and at last got alongside of John, who declared that he quite understood what all the row was about.

The people had been threatening to kill Sagwam, for having interpreted their sayings, and those of the new-comer. Very little love was lost between them and Sagwam, who, although of Makalaka origin, was born and reared in Matabeli-land, and was instinctively of Matabeli habits and notions. He was always committing the unfortunate blunder of calling the people "umtagate," which means most of things that are bad. Mayhap Sagwam was right, for their incessant and discordant chatter, and angry tones of disagreement, indicated the hatching of all sorts of schemes to lead the white man astray. Had I known all that was said, my mind might have been more perplexed than it was even then.

Shedabarume and Saiika were at length quieted, and things began to wear a more promising aspect of peace. The resistless power of sleep, too, seized the majority of the crowd, so that I took an early opportunity to crawl back to my rude shelter, and try to find the same relief.

A very restless slumber rewarded me, and I was up betimes in the morning. Getting up under the circumstances did not entail much trouble, for at night I never took off my clothes, and a rough shake was the only dress preparation for the day.

On mingling among the people I learned that the disturbance on the previous night had culminated in a separation.

Some said they would go on with me; others, including of course all the Unyamwenda, refused to go another step. Forgetting all the cloth, beads, and so forth I had given them, never to speak of such requisites as meat and meal, they were quite ready to desert in the open veldt, and of course they thought they had cornered me.

Meditating upon every contingency of the situation, I finally concluded that from these Unyamwenda I could never expect to have any peace. Besides, with my slender stock of goods, doled out at the rate I had been paying them, I could never hope to reach the Zambesi. Henceforth I decided to look upon them as strangers. I would grasp at no more straws floating upon the waters of conciliation.

We were then upon the southern bank of the Waynge river, and I was determined to get away somewhere, of course towards the north. With this resolution firmly implanted in my mind, I tore off some strips of white calico, and spread them out before me, placing upon each a small palm full of beads, and saying that I would give to each of four boys who would accompany me to the nearest chief towards the north-east, pointing at the same time in that direction, one of the separate portions of calico and beads.

Out of the numbers present four said they would go. Even these were recruited from among outsiders, and did not seem particularly anxious to proceed. Naturally I had to try to induce Karemba to come on, as it was my intention to leave all the rest with John, including Sagwam, the new boy Umfana, and the "higher ape."

Karemba, I could see, was troubled in his mind.

Up to this time, as the reader cannot have failed to notice, there had been perpetual objections on the part of the Unyamwenda to move in the direction in which I wished to proceed. The present mutiny was clearly a troublesome development of this untoward obstinacy.

Taking Karemba aside, I said I wished him to accompany me to the nearest chief, in order to try and procure boys to carry. He replied that he was tired, and, besides, the other natives had told him that the tribe living on the Ruia river would be sure to "kill the white man and all his boys."

Although I could converse with Karemba, and understand his remarks well enough, still on important occasions I would make him communicate his speech through John. I assured him that he was thoroughly safe. In fact it was a part of my diplomacy to impress upon all the men their absolute immunity from danger, so that they must have wondered what could be my concealed power of protection.

But Karemba required a great deal of suasive coaxing. A present or two, however, had more influence than words, so after a little reflection he consented.

John did not like the proceedings. He looked upon me with saddened eyes, as I packed up the few articles that it was essential we should take. When all was ready, I bade him a hearty "good-bye," telling him to keep up his spirits, and to have his eyes wide open in looking after the things.

I did not know where I was going, but I felt an undefinable confidence that the journey would be attended with success.

A few of the Unyamwenda sat sulkily beside the path which led to the water, watching as we started blithely off at a swinging gait.

Crossing upon the black polished boulders of the Waynge river, we climbed the hilly bank to the north; thence we turned in a north-easterly direction, and in a little time entered the deep recesses of the surrounding mountains.

CHAPTER VII.

FROM THE WAYNGE RIVER TO THE UMVUKWE MOUNTAINS.

Sebaii the orator—Appearance of the country—The Ruia river—"Igova, Muliliti"—The solemnity of snuffing—Fortunate shooting—"Ten thousand devils, John and Sagwam dead!"—The treacherous Unyamwenda—An early start—Effects of a sudden appearance—John in despair—Astonishing the disturbers—Lucky help—Necessity for quick progress—Visit to Muliliti, the chief—His home circle—The 'cute old dodger Sandani—Feet torments—Marshy country—New carriers and a new guide—A marrow-bone feast—Endurance of natives on the march—Signs of lions—The Umzengezi river—Discouraging news—Humours of roll-call—Splendid view from the Umvukwe mountains—Solitude.

THE advancing party consisted of Karemba, four men, and old Sebaii. The latter carried his wooden pillow, also the general utility saucepan and small kettle, which likewise served as a teapot, or anything else in the way of a drinking or liquid boiling utensil, it mattered not what.

Utterly useless as a guide, and very indifferent as a carrier, Sebaii was a fine specimen of a Mashona fireside orator, magnificent in his talk, a prince of humbugs, and an unrivalled snuffer and peacemaker. He had been enlisted at Unyamwenda, but in reality had no connection with that town. I was glad to get him, especially because I had not the faintest notion of the character of the country into which fate would lead me, nor of the monsters of the human species whom I might encounter.

As we looked back upon the route we had traversed, we

could see towards the south steep cliffs and deep shadowed cañons, forming a scene that was majestic in its grandeur. On our side of the Waynge river the country displayed a series of hills, threaded by well-watered ravines all descending towards the south-east; the rivulets draining a somewhat sterile tract, sparsely covered with a growth of low forest.

Hartebeest, roan antelopes, zebras, and other swift-footed fauna abounded in this region.

The gloamin' found us camped under the shelter of a small clump of bush in a strip of low-lying meadow-land, on the southern bank of the Ruia river and in close proximity to its head-waters. This stream is the principal tributary of the Amazoe, which drains a very large area and finally joins the Zambesi, about twenty miles south-east of Tette.

A distance of fourteen miles now lay between my two camps.

The new guide, Amenanza, was a tall and a fine man; the most picturesque specimen of a Mashona I had seen, having a costume of the most meagre description, consisting of a small skin around the loins, bracelets of buffalo hide, and large earrings of brass wire. For weapons he had a knobkerry, three assegais, and a hatchet.

That he had led us a rather roundabout way over a mountainous country was very apparent; but he now assured me that we were near a town.

Pointing to the opposite side of the river, Amenanza directed especial attention to a granite mountain; one of many which lined the northern edge of the water, and seemed to spring up abrupt and isolated from the plain, with intervening expanses of level land, then another hill, and so on as far as the eye can reach.

"Igova—Muliliti," he said, which I found to be the names of a town and its chief.

Oh, how contented I felt with these few men! There was no wrangling. Everything seemed to go on smoothly. Free from carking care I sat, until very late in the night, before the crackling blaze of an immense fire roasting pea nuts, and learning as much as possible of the Mashona tongue. Distraction of some kind was bound to turn up, and just as I was dropping off to sleep it came to my mind that I had forgotten to tell John to wind the chronometer. To-morrow, however, if I succeeded in getting boys, precautions could be taken before it had run down.

Sebaii, by stentorian shouts, was the harbinger of another dawn, as he sang, or rather shrilly screamed his morning chant, straining his voice to the utmost tension of his india-rubber windpipe.

Two boys were immediately dispatched to the chief of the town, to inform him that I desired to speak, and that if he came to the camp he would get a present.

The people of the town must have espied us on the previous night, for but a little time elapsed before the chief and a large following appeared and seated themselves in groups. Karemba welcomed the chief, and Sebaii seemed quite in his element as a courtier. The latter's grave demeanour befitted the importance of the occasion: he kept his eyes riveted upon the ground, while he clapped his hands to greet with generous warmth the new-comers.

My consequential follower then produced his snuff-box, which consisted of a small calabash ornamented with brass wire. The box was first handed to the chief and then to those who stood around. Sebaii managed his snuffing with the same silent solemnity that might be expected from a Scotch Presbyterian elder, when tapping his box at the opening up of a doctrinal question before the minister. Exactly in the same way Sebaii gravely tapped his box, and handed it round. When he had no snuff he would just as solemnly and naturally pick up a couple of pebbles, and grind some loose tobacco into a powder, of which he took a pinch and then held the rest out for the acceptance of his companions.

In the present instance, a good deal of sneezing and hard coughing followed the friendly pinch. The strangers gazed at me with keen scrutinizing glances.

Sebaii then entered upon a protracted and eloquent oration, which was followed by a long response from the chief.

After I had presented the latter with a piece of cloth, Karemba, who acted as intermediate spokesman, assumed a lofty air as if it was the chief who in reality required assistance, and not the chief's rather dissimulating supplicants. Karemba, too, made numerous promises saying that if the chief would assist by sending boys to fetch my baggage at once prompt remuneration would follow.

As was usual in all such cases there was a good deal of argument, but to my amazement the people proved friendly. They were quite ready to go, but said they wanted meat. Answering this request, I said that as soon as I saw them leave I would go and hunt. They then informed us that they knew a shorter way to the other camp than that by which we had come, and would be back as soon as possible.

Greatly gratified with the success in this matter, I started off to hunt in the best possible spirits.

Striking buffalo spoor, we tracked upon it for a considerable distance, until suddenly Amenanza, who was my only companion, pointed sharply to a small clump of trees, and following the guidance of his hand I could distinguish a moving object amid the copse. Creeping up and hugging the ground as closely as possible, I soon, by a rapid peep over the top of the grass, discerned the quarry—a fine sable antelope bull (*Hippotragus niger*), with a magnificent head, and beautiful sweeping horns.

Fortune was clearly favourable, so I could not do better than accept her offer; for were I not able to find buffalo, I might have to face the disappointment of going back empty handed to the camp, and with the knowledge that on the return of the boys with John there would be no meat, and consequently much delay.

Aware of the importance of success I took a very careful aim, fired, and managed to bag the fine beast I had been admiring.

With a few bounds Amenanza, looking like a gladiator, was soon upon the spot endeavouring to extinguish life with the assegai. But the vitality of these animals is wonderful in its endurance. Expert as this man was with his weapon, and although the shot had penetrated just behind the shoulder—a little high—it was some time before the antelope died outright.

From marks upon the body it was evident that some wild animal had attacked it. The quarters I found to be very much marked by the claws of some beast of prey, probably a leopard or lion. I soon was at work skinning the carcase, and cutting the meat into loads that might be conveniently carried. To skin and cut up so large an animal quickly, is pretty hard work.

The boy who was with me was sent back to camp to tell some of the people, who had assembled before we left, to come and carry back the meat. The inducement was effectual, for very soon a crowd of men arrived, surrounding me and showing their eagerness for meat in a most urgent manner. I gave them the "internals" of the beast (the rest having to be kept for the workers of my party), and they literally fought like fiends for the possession of the stuff, tearing the flesh into shreds; one man, perhaps, coming out of the fray with just as much as he could hold in his clenched hand, while another would have a very small length of the inward parts. Feeding hounds is the only resemblance to the scene that I can think of. Generally speaking, however, the combatants were very good-natured, and nothing untoward occurred with the exception that one man got rather badly cut.

Pleasant thoughts occupied my mind as I walked back to camp with this meat-laden party. "A lucky morning this has been," I said to myself, "for I shall work wonders with this meat."

I had sent off boys with special dispatch to fetch over the caravan. I hoped that John would come at once, as I had sent strict injunctions that he should not delay for a moment, remembering the old adage—particularly applicable to dealings with these people—"strike the iron while it is hot." I know this, from experience, to be a very sensible bit of advice, both literally and metaphorically.

It was now long after sunset, but neither John nor the boys I had sent had put in an appearance.

Eating rice and some venison stew which Karemba had occupied an afternoon in preparing, I wondered much regarding what could have happened, my vague surmises including all sorts of impending trouble.

Reflections of this nature, however, were soon disturbed by the increasing mutterings of voices coming nearer and nearer out of the darkness, until at length numerous black forms appeared, stark and distinct under the ruddy light of the evening fire. When I observed their looks, dismal thoughts and forebodings arose.

Standing before me, were the same boys whom the chief had sent out! They were without loads, and no John could be seen. Who should appear, however, but Umfana, the Matabeli boy, and his looks had sufficient scare to alarm even men who might be more than mortal. But besides facial dismay, his faltering voice was charged with terror. Describing the situation on the Waynge river, he kept continually repeating the words, "Ya hâmba, Unyamwenda, bulâle Ijân, bulâle Sâgômô!"

"Ten thousand devils," I muttered; "John and Sagwam dead, and the Unyamwenda off to their distant rocky homes! What fiends! It never can be true!"

The reader may imagine my feelings. What was to be done? I write now as I thought then of my first impression respecting the rueful news. Soon, by dint of constant repetition, and through Karemba, who could now make me understand his words well enough, I was enabled to get a better comprehension of the fearful outburst.

It appeared that the Igova boys were not friendly with the Unyamwenda, a fact which accounted for their persistent refusal to go with me towards the east, and that the Unyamwenda wanted to kill John and Sagwam, and seize the calico and beads, in order to take them back to their own country.

I would have started upon the instant to the scene of the disturbance. But to have attempted such a mission would have been to court failure, if not disaster. Not one of the boys would have gone. And how could I rely upon these Igova men? They would go home in the meantime, and probably I would not have the chance of again getting them to go on.

One thing, however, was clear. I must go to John without any delay. How, in the name of wonder, was I to get these men?

As a preliminary to inducement, I gave each of them a small piece of meat—just enough to whet their appetites—telling them at the same time that if they would proceed with me in the morning I would give them white calico and plenty of meat on the return of the party to the Ruia river. Their reply to the proposal was shrewd enough. They said that the Unyamwenda people would not give up the things. Evidently the people did not understand me, for they repeated over and over again that they would not go without the white man. Finally, I knocked the facts into their heads that, whether they went or not, before daybreak I would be on the Waynge river, and that if they chose to follow early in the morning I would be sure to fulfil my promises.

They then disappeared in the surrounding darkness, but Karemba told me that they would be sure to go.

That night, as anyone can understand, was an uneasy night for me. I kept turning over in my mind what might be the upshot if these rebellious Unyamwenda positively refused to let the things go without an exorbitant demand upon our resources, that is to say, upon the store of goods. Of course a discreet policy could be the only wise course to adopt.

With a few men, another line of action would not have cost me a moment's thought, but with a force of thirty, a mistaken act of intimidation on our part might have proved fatal.

Come what would, my mind was made up to be on the Waynge river before, or soon after, sunrise. With that resolution firmly fixed, I lay down to seek what rest might be vouchsafed to me.

Very small ants were swarming in the blankets. These little pests could even be found in the sugar; in fact, everything savoured of ant.

The spot we had chosen for the camp was damp and cold, for we were close to the river. After a long day's journey, however, it is better not to camp far from water, as distance entails a great amount of labour in carrying the indispensable support of life.

Little sleep came to refresh me during that brief night's recumbence, for my mind was in a quandary of doubts and surmises. A cold, wetting mist hugged the land when I got up. It seemed as though it could penetrate even through the skin. My garb, too, was so light that in less severe circumstances I always went through a shivering fit in the morning. As a matter of fact, it was that same feeling which usually awoke me. I seemed to become a second-grade Mashona, as it were, for I could get up early and kindle flames from the smouldering fire, to crouch over them, suffering their pungent smoke to blind and choke me.

Before the sun lit up Waynge camp a stiff fourteen miles had to be covered. I wished to appear as an apparition, a thorough stage ghost, stalking grim and gaunt out of a hidden door in the dark and massive rocks. This I knew would astonish the intractable Unyamwenda not a little.

Long before the proper time to start I sat up, meditating beside the blinding and choking fire. In this position I felt solitary, for looking at the slumbering boys as they lay together, huddled close for the sake of warmth, and snoring in blissful unconsciousness, I was loth to disturb them, genuinely unwilling, in fact, to awake their minds, just then so free from care, to the stern realities of the day's work.

But circumstances permitted little delay. A veil of darkness was still athwart the sky when I gently shook

Amenanza. He awoke without disturbing the others. He was the only man I intended to take with me. I heated some tea, and tried to make him take some, but he did not seem to care much about it.

Shouldering the small rifle (C. L. K.), and giving a few words of instruction to Karemba, telling him to hurry on the Igova men as soon as possible, I soon struck out towards the west, with Amenanza walking before me.

The air was now damp and cold, and the grass heavy with dew. After the first few steps I was soaked as much as if I had been wading through a lake or river. Blistered feet troubled me, too, until I was warmed by hard walking and forgot these grievous discomforts.

We went on at a good, rapid rate, Amenanza leading the way, his lithe and manly figure, seemingly polished by the dew, gracefully sweeping through the wet and heavy grass.

Now and then a small antelope or a wild hog would start up, and speedily move away like "will-o-the-wisp." Soon the stars began to fade, under the influence of the soft white light of dawn, showing, towards the orient, grey streaks of rain-charged clouds.

On we sped, sometimes passing through grass rising six feet above our heads, although the usual height of the grass, where it had not been burnt, was only about six feet. At length the monumental looking masses of rock stood before us, and just as the living light of day began to illumine their jagged summits, Amenanza and myself stood by the banks of the Waynge river. My mind was filled with anxious thoughts regarding the difficult question how I should manage to make a settlement with the stubborn and truculent rebels.

In a few moments I stood in the camp beside John, whose appearance was a powerful picture of abject despair.

He was evidently much relieved at seeing me again, and soon told the long and eventful story of the occurrences since I had left him, dwelling especially upon the threat of the people to kill both him and Sagwam because they refused to surrender the cloth, which I saw was stacked up behind him.

Somewhat relieved about this matter, my next thoughts were of the chronometer. Had it run down? No; to my delight I found it was still going, and had still some hours to spare.

I scanned the camp. Satisfaction? Satisfaction indeed! Old Mchesa, along with his men, had left. Only a few stragglers remained. The Unyamwenda were huddled together on the side of the skerm (pronounced *scarem*) opposite to John and Sagwam, and their assegais were stacked behind them.

I kept up an air of absolute indifference, taking not the slightest notice of the crowd of blacks, who, by the way, looked rather dismayed at my arrival: perhaps from the suddenness of my appearance, but partly, I think, because I took things so easily.

Consulting with John, he said he was sure they would ask too much cloth before they would permit us to take the things away.

After a very short time had elapsed, I saw that the Igova men had arrived. Soon they were all seated on the opposite bank of the river. I did not count their numbers, but my mind was filled with ingenious schemes for getting out of the troublesome predicament, and I relied a little upon their unfriendliness to the Unyamwenda.

My mind was soon made up as to what should be done.

First of all the guns were examined and placed in a convenient place behind. This precaution seemed necessary, because it was impossible to conjecture what might be the end of the trouble.

I then called up the head-centres of nuisance, namely, the chatterboxes, Shedabarume and Saiika; also Villum (Chirimutu), the leaders of the six Chibero men, who also of late had been making themselves as unbearable as they possibly could.

I put the following questions to them.

"Have I not been good to you?"

"Have I not fed you with meat and meal?"

"Have I not given you limbo and beads, whenever you have asked?"

A murmuring sound was all the reply which was vouchsafed to these inquiries.

"Then," I continued, drawing myself up and trying to look as imposing as possible, "what have you done? You have tried to take me the wrong road. You refuse to go farther with me, although you promised you would go with me to the big river. When I sent boys yesterday to fetch my goods, you stopped them. You threatened to kill my boys. Why did you do all this?"

A number of lies were the answers to these questions. They contradicted their own remarks in every way; so I finished by saying, "Do you think that the white man is afraid of you?"

The only effect of this conversation was the coming forward of two Chibero men, who said they would go with me. But I told them I would not have them with me on any account.

I then informed the crowd that I would give them some limbo and beads to buy food on their way home. This, I know, was an injudicious offer, because the watchful Kaffir, might look upon it as an outcome of fear. However I was more than anxious to get matters amicably arranged as my supporters were in a lamentable minority.

Taking a quick look towards the Igova men, I saw in a moment that they were a man or two short of a carrying number. We were just upon the eve of success or failure. Hesitation could not wisely be kept up.

I therefore called to Shedabarume and Saiika, whose control of the Unyamwenda was complete, and who had also incited the Chibero men to mutiny, offering each man a yard and a half of white limbo and a handful of beads, and saying with a Hobson's choice determination, "Take this, for I am going to move the things now." The pair turned off scoffing, as they shouted to the others:

"The cloth is too little, we will not take it!" At the same time they signed with their arms that they must have a fathom. Not one of the others moved an inch.

There appeared to be no course now open but to show these fellows that there was a limit to the white man's patience and forbearance. It was necessary that he should show the troublesome crowd that he was not afraid.

I pretended to be in a dreadful passion. Like an ancient Roman wrestler leaping into the arena of combat, I sprang forward, and suddenly seizing Shedabarume by the neck was lucky enough to dash him to the ground at one fell sweep, at the same time tearing off his necklaces of charms, and literally ripping the waistcloth from his loins.

These I threw into the fire, and stamped upon as they lay in the red, smouldering embers; Shedabarume by this time standing absolutely naked before his brethren.

With another bound I was upon the amazed Saiika, and was equally successful in levelling him, depriving him of his slender clothes, which I likewise consigned to the devouring flames.

Then I stood up with an air as defiant as I could possibly assume, shouting aloud to the waiting Igova boys and telling them to lift the things and let us clear out.

Here once again fate was auspicious. Strange to say the Chibero men, headed by Villum, who had mutinied with the Unyamwenda, came forward saying that they would continue to follow the white man. In a commanding tone I ordered them to proceed, pointing out the bundles they should take. They were started off at once, doubtless labouring under the happy delusion that I was conferring a gracious favour upon them, whereas they were positively essential to me; although fortunately they did not know this.

When everyone had started I took a searching look around the camp, to see that nothing had been forgotten, and then I left, the Unyamwenda meantime standing in a motionless crowd outside of the skerm, astounded at the suddenness of our quick despatch.

Not long afterwards John asked me how it was that I had not brought enough men, saying that had it not been for the Chibero men we should not have got off. With a wink of satisfaction I replied that I had managed to get the Chibero off before they had time or were smart enough to see that we were once more fairly in their clutches.

Luck like this has helped many a man, and as we marched along I felt buoyant through a sense of even slightly brightening prospects. We crossed the north-eastern slopes of the divide, passing by rivers whose waters finally mingle with those of the great Zambesi, near to Tette.

It was almost sun-down when we arrived at the Ruia river. The camp was soon enlarged. The Igova men received their meat and cloth. John said that the sable antelope head shot on the previous evening. was one of the finest he had ever seen.

A happy night was spent. Songs were sung continuously, the shrill voices of the boys ringing out right merrily in the still air of the night.

Amidst the festivities I was made a sort of small king. As I lay upon a pile of long grass, which, when at hand, I would sometimes use as a mattress, the jubilant revellers would come and dance before me one by one, while Karemba and a brother performer would tune up their musical instruments. When I saw the cheerfulness of the people I felt that my efforts had been well rewarded.

There can be no doubt that I had got out of a difficulty which had threatened to become very serious. No sooner had this been effected than thoughts arose about the succeeding day, when I would again require boys to continue the journey.

Oh, what a time it would take to reach the river at the rate we were going! Sometimes my thoughts would ponder sadly in this way; but then I would reproach myself, remembering that I was at all times in an extraordinary hurry, among people who did not care a jot whether I went on or not. Nevertheless unless I strained every nerve to push onwards the disordered caravan would inevitably become a total wreck; for if the articles of barter which kept us floating disappeared, we should at once be hard fixed in the stern straits of privation, which of course meant utter dissolution.

For the future I resolved that meal would not be regularly carried. We would try to get on with the meat which was shot. Meal was heavy to carry, and I thought it better to tell the boys that it would be bought at each town we came to. This would perhaps be an incentive towards a faster advance when they became satiated by an excess of venison. At the same time it reduced the number of carriers that were required.

The incessant payment in advance was a very bad plan, but without it no one would move. More than once I have thought that if the system was generally adopted in manufacturing Britain there would doubtless be a greater depression in trade than there has been even in these "free and independent" days.

Muliliti, the chief of this district, had now to be visited. It was advisable that we should endeavour to get a few boys from him.

Not long after Sebaii had crowed his usual salute to the peep of day, I bestirred myself to make ready for the route, but found John in one of his immovable humours, swearing that the damp and the cold had stricken him badly. This could hardly be wondered at, for the place that had been chosen for a camp could not have been more unhealthy, the fog lying low and heavy around us from a little before sunset until long after the great orb had risen again to follow its daily course.

Ultimately, however, John was induced to proceed, and taking Sagwam also, we crossed the Ruia river, and in a little time found ourselves at the gates of the town of Igova. There we waited until the powerful barriers were pulled down to enable us to enter. When we passed through the gates we were without delay ushered into the hut of Muliliti, the chief.

At a glance I could observe a great difference in the design and construction of the hut, compared with those which we had seen farther south. It seemed very comfortable, and had a fire in the centre, an abundant supply of mats made from the bark of the Machabele-tree lay around, and interwoven branches fenced off one side, where stood two very nice looking Mashona cows. A calf seemed to have the free run of the establishment, and in a ludicrously human-like manner huddled close up to the fire beside one of the tiny children, for it was evidently a veritable thoroughbred Mashona. The little child hugged the animal affectionately, and eyed me all the time, no doubt, judging by the expression of the face, thinking that the horrible white monster had come to buy his playmate.

Two of the chief's wives occupied dark recesses in the background. My impression was that the household seemed to form a very comfortable family circle, in which I was glad to find myself, as it was wretchedly cold and wet outside under the searching mist.

Allowing for a seat in the usual state of silence for a considerable time, I then made a start in negotiation, saying that I wished to pursue my journey north-east, and inquiring what boys he could give me.

Muliliti pointed towards the east, and said that his people would not go in that direction.

Well, thought I, it is useless my saying anything when there is no choice; and, following this reflection, I said aloud, "Give me boys to take me to the next town," pointing at the same time towards the north.

He said that the tribe to the north were not Mashona, but Makorikori, and they were friends of his. He also remarked that he had plenty of boys.

Informing him that if he would bring the men over I would give him a present of cloth, he said he would go at once and fetch them, so in the meantime I gave him a donation in beads as a sort of retaining fee.

We then retired to the camp. On our way a number of men asked for "mataka," which, as I have stated, is the word for present in the Mashona tongue. I engaged as many as I could get to promise to go with me, for from sad experience I found that the word of a petty chief was not of much account.

Literally the chiefs have very slight power over the people, their authority being only exerted over those who are actually their personal property, that is to say slaves. From what I saw of Muliliti, I judged that he was a very easy master.

In the meadows below the town I saw a small herd of cattle grazing; a sure sign that there was still some distance before us ere we reached the tsetse-fly country.

Everything was again ready for a start. Of the loads we kept open only one bundle of beads and one roll of calico, to be used in emergencies, and also to buy a little gold which was offered by some of the village people, women and old men principally, who all made signs that they had worked very hard in the river to get even the small quantity they possessed.

One elderly fellow, with a particularly bad squint, showed himself a remarkably smart and cute old dodger, as he tried all sorts of underhand tricks to get extra pieces of calico. No sooner did I buy one quill of gold from him than he would hand out another, but all of them had very little of the precious metal. He also tried to palm off a quill of mica, which resembles gold, and in California is called "greenhorn" gold. I set him down as one of the veritable Hebrew children, not in blood certainly, but in spirit a very Moses of the Moseses. I handed the old rascal back his base metal, along with a handful of dust, a proceeding which seemed to amuse the bystanders mightily.

The wily fellow was far too shrewd a trader to seem to be taken aback, and he simply produced some of the real article again, so that we continued to bargain. Afterwards he ran out into the grass, where he leaped in the air to show what a wonderful man he was; how warlike and how dangerous. The retreat was acted in a most natural manner, the performer immediately returning to me with the palms of both hands extended, but held together ready to receive a present in return for his exertions.

This old man, whose name proved to be Sandani, was destined to become an important agent in the expedition.

By long odds he was the greediest beggar breathing; an inveterate accumulator of gratuitous spoil. Withal, he had some good points.

One of his movable properties was a young man—his son, he said—whom he offered me at a bargain, but I declined to trade.

Sandani, however, I tried to engage, as it seemed clear that we would be short of carriers. The chief had not yet arrived, and I was beginning to conjure up grave doubts as to whether he would put in an appearance. After a great deal of preliminary wrangling, he said that he had concluded to go.

Immediately afterwards Muliliti appeared, and with him a number of men. "These, of course, are for me," I muttered; but on inquiry I found that the chief had but two men whom he could command to go, and very subdued-looking individuals they were. Their names were Chikobore and Eingatara. Neither of them were of the Mashona tribe, but I could not find out to what country they belonged. Chikobore was in future to act as guide, both being enlisted in the oddly-mixed throng which now made up the party.

To Muliliti I gave a few yards of white limbo, and left under his care the fine sable antelope head with the hide, which I had carefully prepared, telling him that it should be handed over to John whenever he passed on his homeward journey.

On advancing, we had again to pass the little town of Igova, which lay on the opposite side of the river. The spot proved too attractive for our new associates. They could not pass without going in to see their friends for a last and fond farewell. As a matter of course, two were missing when the assembly was sounded. Karemba succeeded in unearthing, in place of the deserters, two very wild-looking creatures who were sadly in need of some cloth. These were immediately enlisted, and once again we were off, striking away towards the north.

To the left of the line of march, looking up the winding course of the Ruia, and stretching far away from north to south, stood the bold Umvukwes. On the banks of the river rose those singular, isolated peaks which have been described, while interspersed among them and near to their sharp and broken crags were spherical mounds of granite seeming to swell up from the plain.

In the direction in which we travelled, and sweeping round upon our right, lay expanded a vast natural park, studded with clumps of woodland, and intersected at irregular intervals by rivers, whose forest-clad banks, luxuriantly green, contrasted gracefully with the deadened colours of the intervening wastes of sun-scorched grass.

Small herds of antelope were constantly passing, although game did not seem to me to be very abundant. Numbers of little bucks were seen starting up and rushing off at a furious pace through the long grass.

Three hours of pretty hard walking through black marshland gave a finishing touch to an increasing misery from which I suffered. A description can only give a faint idea of the personal conditions under which travelling was effected. My feet were in a horrible state, as may be imagined when I say that I had been pressing and pulling them in, out, and through the marshy land until my old boots were filled with black mud and dirty water, while cuts an inch long on each heel made their existence painfully evident at every step All the time, too, my body was bathed in pouring perspiration, while the sun cast down merciless rays of fiery heat upon my aching head. The boots were worst of all. Oh, thou sham bootmakers of London town! How heartily did I condemn thee, one and all, to perpetual torment, which could not be more bitter than that which thou mad'st me endure!

Fording the Pembe river, we continued to wade through morass and through grass saturated with water, until we gained the southern bank of the Rumabiri. There we selected a comfortable and well-sheltered spot, pitching our camp amid the rich woodland which clothed the river banks with a profusion of graceful foliage.

The waters of both these rivers—the Pembe and Rumabiri—flow to the Amazoe.

We had made but a short march, but it was better to do so perhaps for the first day, as the men would not then feel their loads so cumbersome. And such loads they were, too!

As I lay down with a thump upon my blankets I said to myself, "Old bones, this is working your passage with a vengeance!"

I scanned the map here, scaling off the distances—not without a pang, when I thought of that new experience of bad luck, my poor feet—and saw how many weary leagues had to be travelled before we would stand upon the banks of the Zambesi. Actual marching is nothing when everything goes on cheerily; fatigue never touches harshly; but the incessant brawl of beggars, groans of discontented sick niggers, and the quivering flesh of sore feet, exasperated me, a feeling which became more poignant when I found at night that we had only done ten or fifteen miles during the whole day. Towards night, under such provocation, disgust drove out all the energy of my system.

Happily, my times of depression were short-lived. A cup of tea and a short nap were comforts sufficient to make disagreeables be forgotten, and in the present instance I cheered my spirits by reflecting that during the past two days I had done two good strokes of work. First I had managed to get clear of the Unyamwenda; and second, I had succeeded in making a fresh start with a full complement of new carriers and a new guide.

While I was congratulating myself upon these matters three men came into camp from some unknown direction. They said they would carry loads for a present. It seems always so in Africa, where one either finds a feast or a famine. Here was luck, however, and I augured that all would go well for a while.

Old Sebaii as a rule appeared in camp hours after the rest of the company, a rather funny fact, considering that he was supposed to be one of the "guides." But all Sebaii's ways were amusing. With an inimitably sedate bearing he would seat himself upon the ground, and then pass round the snuff, at the same time coughing and sneezing violently. No sooner were the spasms over than he would begin one of his interminable orations, for he was one of those natural windbags who make progress with words but not with sense.

A marrow-bone feast was held that night. Those who took part in it first equipped themselves with two pieces of rock; then when the great leg-bones of antelope had been broiled on the blazing fire they cracked them with the lumps of rock, and sucked out the marrow. The bits or drops which fell upon their bodies were rubbed thoroughly into the skin, which they are delighted to have soft and glossy.

Now and again, sharp above the din of many strident voices, might be heard what one might call a half-subdued shriek. It was John trumpeting shrill and sharp for Windvogel to get a light for his pipe, his tones being of the same nature as those which oft in the stilly night infuriated man employs to disperse the serenading cats on a London roof. John's shouts were marvellously successful in getting a response instanter. They seemed to awaken acute and suggestive memories of numerous bitter chastisements; for John never forgot that the poor bushman was his absolute property.

Our natives were by far the grossest feeders that I had encountered in my travels. Their staying powers are not very great when they are gorged. As an instance of an opposite nature, John, who had lived all his life among the Matabeli people, informed me that the endurance of the latter is very remarkable. On the war-trail they will stand ten days without any food, all the while travelling immense distances.

At that time my diet consisted entirely of boiled rice, meat, and tea. Some hard crackers, or rusks, which had been brought on were almost finished, there being only about three pounds of crumbs, as black as gunpowder, which I was reserving for use in the event of sickness.

Lions were here; but it was impossible to get a shot on account of the high grass, great portions of which stood up unburnt and in its natural vigour. I suppose it never will be burnt, as that part of the country seemed to be very sparsely inhabited, and the long belt of marsh which ran through the land would soon kill the fires.

Soon after leaving the Rumabiri river I was astonished to find that our course was not changed, and that we were ascending the eastern slopes of the Umvukwe range of mountains. I should have to await results. We were moving northwards, and I could only hope that circumstances would be favourably changed, so that I should be able to see the way more clearly, in order to choose and shape my course whither observation directed. Protestations at that time would have been foolish, nay, perhaps disastrous to the whole scheme.

The head waters of the Umzengezi river were shortly reached. This stream forms one of the chief tributaries of the Zambesi. Springing from the very heart of the rugged Umvukwe mountains, it runs in a northerly direction, and, increased by numerous and not inconsiderable affluents, grows steadily larger, until from a small burn with a rocky bed—at the spot where we stood—similar to those which leap and play down the sides of the Scottish hills, it swells to the proportions of a large river, with a channel some hundred yards in width at its confluence with the Zambesi, near which the bed of the stream is composed of sand and shingle. The Umzengezi cannot be characterised as an immense river: it is broad, but not deep, and becomes shallow in the dry season. Its volume during the rainy season, however, must have an enormous force, when the water rises to an extraordinary height, as could be seen in the torn and rugged banks.

Continuing to pursue the same course, our ascent of the heights was so gradual that we could not realise the fact that the summit of the range was near at hand.

We made our mid-day halt upon the borders of Mashonaland and the country of the Makorikori tribe.

While we rested under the shade of the scrub forest three

strange men came into the camp, and, much to my disgust, evidently frightened the Mashona by the news which they brought, to the effect that the Makorikori people would not let the white man pass through their country, as they were fighting with the Portuguese of the Zambesi valley.

The chief, whose name was Chuzu, they said was a very bad man, and would be sure to kill the white man. The long and the short of their story was that it would not be safe to go on there.

I bought some assegais from them; not that I wished to be encumbered with any more than I had, but with the hope that when they had a piece of cloth they would leave. Not they. They remained, snuffing, smoking, and talking, what I then innocently considered to be nonsense.

With these timid people it is not advisable to talk about what the way is to this or to that place. John whispered to me what was going on. The three unwelcome visitors had started a very promising scare. All through the ranks could be heard the muttered sound of the word mataka (present); oh, that endless refrain!

Above all things it was certain that I should have to give them mataka that evening, and that it would be necessary to go through the usual farce of telling them that under my wing they would be perfectly safe.

Fourteen miles formed the extent of our march for that day, and we halted at the highest point that we would cross on the range.

On stopping for the night the first thing to be done was the construction of an impenetrable barrier, in a circular form, without which we might have the chance of losing some of our delightful company, any of whom might become the prey of the voracious carnivora of the country.

Roll-call was the next duty, and was a ceremony that

seemed to afford infinite fun to my simple followers. Seeing and hearing me read their names out of a book gave immense delight, although they evidently pitied me, and placed me in the category of the very much demented. The few things I had were distributed so generally that this was the only plan of finding out whether all were in. Sebaii, the peace-maker and unfailing guide to laziness, was found to be the only absentee, such was his aversion to making camp.

My feet were in a deplorably painful condition, and bound to become worse, because the boots were getting more tattered and torn at every step I took. Despite this, however, curiosity prompted me to wander forth to see what was to be seen from the summit of these rarely-visited mountains, upon which the light of the evening sun still shone bright, and would continue to gleam for another hour and a half.

Just before sundown it was my custom to make up the few lines in my journal, which was kept in very small notebooks, and easily recorded with an indelible pencil.

Walking quietly through the low forest I emerged upon the heights. The journey filled a longer time than I had anticipated, the distance being deceptive to the view. When upon the spot, however, I climbed one of the moss-clad rocks, and turned my eyes upon the surrounding country.

A study of nature in its sublimest forms and of wonderful wildness lay outstretched before me. I stood upon the dividing-line of the Umvukwe range, where the waters of the Zambesi zone parted to flow east and west.

Turning towards the south-west the boldly characteristic feature of the mountains is the peculiar baldness of their crowns; they resemble a succession of great grass-covered cones—with here and there a few isolated rocks piercing the air—extending as far as the eye can reach.

Towards the north can be distinguished the horse-shoe band, running to the right, and then curving to the left. Almost due north the distant mountain-tops are barely visible, being lost in the gloom of departing day. The crescent thus formed is filled with luxuriant forest.

Between my standpoint and the darkening and distant summits rises a heavy slate-coloured mountain, which has the appearance of a dense cloud overhanging the dim waving line of forest.

Eastward the picture becomes wild indeed. Rocky mountains can be seen spurring outwards, and breaking into a wild and indescribable confusion of gigantic blocks and obelisks, rent, torn, tilted and turned in every direction, or piled one above the other in a chaotic grandeur of fantastic and grotesque disorder. One fire-formed tower* especially exalts itself hundreds of feet above the others, like a giant amid the giant sentinels of the mountains, a crowning effort in Nature's convulsion when she made valleys sink and mountains rise long ages ago in the unrecorded past.

The landscape towards the south descends in long, winding, wave-like lines of forest, shaded by the deepest green. Through the woodland belt the meanderings of numerous small rivers can be distinctly traced.

Late though it is, there is still an unspoken charm to rivet my gaze upon this lovely scene. The sun is fast sinking on its way to light other regions and other worlds, casting the while its farewell rays of warm red light upon the veil of mist that soft and glowing hangs gently round the foot-hills, and clings to the umbrageous forest stretching far beneath. The molten gold of the sun itself

* The natives call this singular pinnacle the Barré.

seems to gild with glowing beams the rugged peaks of the higher crags.

What an indescribably strange sensation it is to find that you are utterly alone in a savage land, and that do what you might it would take months of arduous travel to enable you to exchange a word freely in your own tongue! As I sit watching the hushing hand of Nature gradually calming the world to rest, the solitude and silence seem to release the springs of thought and prompt the mind to ponder on the hidden mysteries of creation and their unfathomable problems.

At such moments how grand are the ideas that course through the mind—to die as soon as they are born! How could any one help being struck with the vain nothingness of his personality, as a veritable dot of dust sitting remote and alone amidst a vastness of an almost audible stillness?

Outstretched before me were those grand natural monuments of granite, on whose adamantine sides were inscribed the evidences of numberless epochs of the primeval world. Comparison is one of the privileges, or perhaps weaknesses, of man. Let us compare our lives to these rocks. What can be said of the short span of human existence when considered in relation to the age of those hoary heaps of solid stone? Such a question must overwhelm the littleness of the greatest mind.

It matters not how high may be the pitch of culture to which the intellect may have been elevated, it cannot approach any nearer to the infinite than the crudest conception of the aboriginal mind.

And what is the endurance of these mountains in their present form compared with the physical history of the Universe? Not more than a flash of light which twinkles for an instant upon a transient wave. Time has here given one of its most unanswerable challenges to man. The attempt at definition would be as fruitless as the ponderings of a mortal mind upon the boundless infinity of space, through which, as I gaze, the sun is spreading far-reaching gleams of its dying glories.

I watch the orb of day as it sinks slowly to rest and leaves the blackness of night. As I look my eyelids seem to stretch wider and wider, and I feel as if I could, without a sigh, sink to rest in sympathy with silent Nature. Suddenly, with the gathering gloom, the spell is broken. I awake from this trance-like reverie. Higher thoughts vanish like the fleeting phantoms of a dream. I find myself once again an atom of ordinary mortality, and under the faint light of the friendly stars sparkling in the firmament, with difficulty wend my way back to the busy camp.

CHAPTER VIII.

CHUZU'S.

Soothing of the followers—Names of trees—The Karue river—Warnings of danger—Rocks alive with people—The Makorikori people—Fear to approach the white man—Alarm in the camp—" Geeve it um, master, geeve it um!"—Surrounded by armed warriors—Forebodings of danger—Chuzu, the chief—An unsatisfactory interview—Demands for powder—" Master, mas'er, the people are coming to kill us!"—The bag of sovereigns—Anxious moments—" You are M'zungo"—Tricks of intimidation—The party is threatened with massacre—An old woman's friendly warning—Ominous signs—Our midnight retreat—An awkward bridge—Out of the difficulty—The disappointing check—" Ho, for northern Matabeli-land!"—Shall I return?

ALTHOUGH he knew I was given to fits of wandering, John had been speculating about what had become of me.

After a frugal supper was over I anticipated the demands of the men by giving them each a present. Then in solemnly weighty tones I made a declaration (which had to be interpreted) that all the men under my care were absolutely free from danger. John's opinion was that if we could get them through the Makorikori town our difficulties with them individually would cease. The chances of rebellion would then be held in check by dependence. I watched the demeanour of the higher ape with some amusement, for he was perfectly insensible to everything except head ornaments, and now appeared in a complete ostrich feather cap, which made him tremendously proud of himself. I had a painful consciousness that all these feather purchases were seriously reducing the contents of the sugar bag.

The succeeding morning was piercingly cold, and all vegetation was bright with the glistening dew. Very little sleep could be found, as it was impossible to keep warm, so that we were glad when the time arrived when we should quit the cheerless spot.

Those who wore clothes – that is to say John and myself —were soon literally saturated as we tramped over the flooded marsh and through the dwarfed forest.

Innumerable small streams were passed. They coursed through the soft morass and evidently were fed by mountain springs. Now these rivulets all flowed swiftly westward, for we had crossed the backbone of this country and were moving over the western slopes of the great divide.

I found it difficult to obtain correct native names for the trees in the forest. Whenever the question was asked, it was productive of a dispute among the boys, indicating that there was a grave probability that they might be wrong. The larger trees, however, were similar to those I had seen in Matabeli-land called Gonté.

Close to the banks of the Karue river we halted. An impenetrable thicket of the luxuriant foliage of wild fruit-trees sheltered us. Dotted here and there amid the entanglement of rich vegetation was a species of date-palm, whose long leaves of the most delicate green drooped gracefully over the confused undergrowth.

Human miseries, however, almost on every hand prevented me from making as many practical observations of the natural features of the country as I should have liked to have done. At that time, for example, I was sadly perplexed by an evident reluctance on the part of my men to advance. To hurry the movement I told John to bring up the rear of the party, and that in the meantime I would go on.

So constant had been the warnings of danger, that I treated them lightly; but I now began to think I had perhaps been unwise in paying so little heed to the dismal foreboding of my apprehensive followers.

Karemba, two other boys, and myself in advance of the rest, proceeded on the journey, and after limping, for it could not be called walking, we in four hours covered about eight miles from our last halting place.

As we emerged from the forest flats we observed, gradually rising into view, the great grey mountain which had been seen from afar on the previous night, when it had the appearance of a motionless cloud hanging over the dense darkness of the covered plain. Now it stood boldly out in all the grandeur of its massive and lofty immobility, with its noble outline clearly shown against the beauty of the soft blue sky, while the sunshine gleamed brightly upon its time-worn sides.

For the last five miles the footpaths had been good and hard, only broken here and there by belts of long grass. The path showed signs of a considerable traffic; only men, no cattle. I saw a good deal of buffalo and eland spoor, but of course in our present miserable circumstances hunting was out of the question.

When we had reached a point within half a mile of the mountain stronghold, we sat down to rest, as we were very far ahead of the party.

Karemba was uneasy. He said I ought to have sent a present to the king before approaching near to his town; adding that it would not be well to walk past the place and camp. I must own that I was very wrong in ignoring what Karemba had said; but then it should be borne in mind that I was spoilt through hearing so many false reports of danger. Hitherto the chiefs, without exception, had treated me well: at any rate they could not be accused of being hostile. Our troubles all arose from friction among our own little party.

"Karemba," I said, "the chief will be all right. I will give him a present in the morning."

"But this is a very big man," he replied, "we should camp here until he allows us to pass through his country."

The speaker seemed much frightened. But I was loth to imagine that anything could be wrong. As we neared the stronghold Karemba kept repeating the advice, "Stop here, and let two men go on."

Under ordinary circumstances this proposal would not have been unreasonable, but I was fearful of the main body of the party, the members of which would assuredly beat a quick retreat on the appearance of the slightest excuse to do so.

The main body soon arrived. With four men beside me I kept the lead about four hundred yards ahead of the rest. Soon we arrived at the foot of the mountain fastness. The path which led to it made many circuitous windings, and ran across a little rivulet which was spanned by two rough poles.

With the wildest shouts telling that we wished to buy food (the customary cry of the Mashona as they advance to a town—it is equivalent to the sentinel's assurance of "friends") we kept moving on. The shouts echoed and re-echoed amidst the recesses of the great rocks, as we continued skirting round the mountain.

I looked upwards. There, as though in the dark haunt of a demon, I could see wild-like black forms ranged in rows along the tops of the rude Cyclopean rocks, while lower down, close to where the pathway led, human forms seemed to spring from every rock.

Our cries had "garrisoned the glen" with a vengeance! Devil-like the creatures leaped from stone to stone as they hastened towards us.

No sooner did they see me than they were off with a bound. Some ran ahead of us at breakneck speed, as if bent upon carrying quick tidings to their chiefs and headmen of the arrival of a white man. Then I inwardly said: "Fool! these people do look alarmed. I ought to have taken Karemba's advice." Now it was too late.

As we trended our way the natives sprung from all sides. Whenever they would pass me they would give me a wide berth. They seemed frightened and very much astonished.

Many, I noticed, carried flint-lock rifles, but the majority had the assegai, and the bow and arrows similar to the weapons of the Mashona.

In appearance they at first sight might be said to resemble the Mashona. Unlike the Mashona, however, they do not file the teeth. Their tribal distinction is seen in the manner in which they tatoo their faces, which are marked by little incisions cut around the temples and upon the forehead down as far as the bridge of the nose, I think making them very hideous.

By the time that we had crossed the little stream of clear water on the farther side of the town, the crowd had assumed very large proportions. We immediately commenced the work of making a strong camp. How long we were to be here could not be foreseen. Our camp was situated in the small belt of thick forest which covered the bank of the stream.

I at once deputed Karemba and some of the boys to go and buy some food, thinking that the timidity of the people would in this way be allayed.

As the Southern Cross was nearing its zenith I was much

tempted to take an observation, but from the inside of the skerm this was impracticable, owing to the boughs of a tree which were just in the line of sight, so that it would have been necessary to take all the paraphernalia out to some barer spot. Therefore it was more judicious to defer the matter to another day, when I might be better acquainted with the feelings of the people. In the meantime astronomical studies might only aggravate them, by creating an impression that I was exercising some subtle and evil influence over the crops.

In the bush I could distinguish numbers of women who had brought bunches of corn on the cob, &c. They were trading freely with the boys, but they would not approach me upon any account, keeping well clear of the skerm in which I stood.

The boys soon returned with a good supply of provisions, which were wanted seriously, for we had not been shooting for three days.

John was not very long in letting me know that the boys were very frightened. They would go no farther on any account or for any present. Of course my first thought returned to the question how I could get some boys here to proceed? The prospect was hardly a pleasant one, for the people were evidently mistrustful.

Weariness soon made me oblivious to surrounding troubles. I turned into the small tent which occupied the centre of the enclosure, and, after writing up the journal, almost immediately dropped off into a sound slumber. But the repose was not of long duration. Karemba soon came to arouse me saying that a brother of the chief had come bringing with him a tusk of ivory in order to purchase powder. Karemba suggested that the tusk should be bought seeing that the owner was the chief's brother. I was unwilling to accede to this, because although I had plenty of cartridges my supply of loose powder was scant.

The case seeming to be urgent, however, I gave one flask, knowing that he would ask for more. This, of course, he did, and then I repeated the donation. Then I lay down again, but in a little while Karemba returned, declaring that the chief's brother must get cloth, and signing with his arms that he asked for five fathoms.

I felt that this was not a matter of trading, but was a concession to satisfy a branch of royalty; so I tore off the cloth, thinking, with a sigh of relief, how glad I was to get rid of the grasping nocturnal nuisance.

But there was no rest for me! I had hardly lain down when I felt a sharp tug at my blanket. This time both John and Karemba stood before me. John was evidently very much disturbed and said:

"Geeve it um, master, geeve it um! De boys is all frightened; dese people is fighting wid us. De boys will run, master!"

This fairly awoke me. Looking out I could see all our boys sitting up, not one of them being asleep. The news was then repeated that all the boys were afraid: the people they said would fight with us, if I did not yield to their requests. Consequently I gave out four yards more.

I then went over to the fire and sat there, my object being to endeavour to instil a little confidence into the wavering men. Things were beginning to look serious. I told John as a last chance, to try and find out quietly whether the boys would go forward early in the morning, and we would soon pass out of the country. This proposal I need hardly say was *not* a success.

They were going *home* in the morning! If they went in

the direction I wished them to go they would surely be killed by the tribes near the river.

A heavy dew had been falling. I could see the reputed brother of the chief clearly by the light of the fire. He had a very numerous following of armed men, whose weapons, all wet with the globules of dew, glistened jewel like in the moonlight rays.

I would have liked very much to have entered into a conversation with this man; but considering his hostile attitude, and the peremptory tone he adopted when asking for more cloth, a demand which was repeated *ad nauseam*, I kept aloof. After coming out of the tent I had to give him more, and from these frequent concessions it might be construed that the white man was afraid. Again and again he asked for powder, but this demand was refused point blank.

Morning dawned beautiful, clear, and calm, contrasting strongly with the distracting tumult of our camp during the night. Meat was very scarce, so it was necessary that some should be had. Therefore I started in pursuit of game, although I did not like the idea of leaving the camp in the present crisis. One of the Makorikori stragglers, who were outside the skerm, was picked up through his having been in conversation with Sagwam. Taking him with us we soon came upon eland spoor. The boy said he saw a big bull eland close to us; but the forest was very thick, and it was impossible to get a shot.

My guide was in a great state of excitement as we stalked along. Unfortunately the eland must have sighted us, for a rushing sound and a crashing of the bushes quickly told us that all chances of bagging were gone like the wind. I would have continued hunting, even after this disappointment, but was doubtful about the expediency of leaving camp for any length of time. There was a great danger of my party deserting at any moment through fear.

During the little hunting trip, however, I was enabled through the medium of Sagwam to find out through our young guide the direction in which Tette lay; the information convincing me that I had been perfectly right in what I had told the Mashona all along.

He also gave the information that the tribe which occupied the land lying immediately to the north were called the Bazurke. From our position at the time, as near as I could make out, Tette lay almost due east. Therefore as the Mashona refused to proceed, I determined that they should no longer lead me by the nose. I could have pioneered the way quite easily, but in that case the course would have been easterly, and they would not go in that direction. They had repeatedly refused to do so.

The young Makorikori promised to go with me, if the chief would allow him. All the signs, however, went to show that the king was of a very different type, in the power of his ruling, from the others whom I had encountered in recent wanderings.

On going back to the camp, I looked towards the great mountain, and my impression was that the scene was by far the wildest that I had ever witnessed as a position for a town. It completely defied attack from without; the huge rocky mass standing nearly a thousand feet above the level of the fields of gently waving corn which spread out from its stupendous base.

Whispered reports of various kinds—but all unsatisfactory —urged me to expedite the sending of a present to the king. Between the Chibero men, and the men I had enlisted at Igova, there now seemed to be a great difference of opinion. This made the relations of the party more disagreeable, certainly far from being a pleasant experience after the night's lugubrious incidents. Thoughts, too, which were anything but cheering began to disturb my mind. If our new acquaintances were hostile, and refused to give me boys, what then? How was I to proceed under those circumstances?

As I meditated upon such contingencies, there arose a new cause for speculation if not alarm; for, from the chief's kraal I could hear the sounds of the firing of guns, the beating of drums, and a general howl of many human voices. What the uproar meant I could not divine.

Selecting some calico of the strongest texture and of the most seductive pattern I could choose, I gave it to Karemba along with a message to the effect that I would like to see the chief.*

I also said that I wished the chief to give me boys, to escort me through his country to the next town in the direction of the Zambesi. As I was anxious to see the entrance to the seemingly impregnable stronghold I accompanied my ambassador for some distance on his way.

As we were nearing the town two boys from the camp overtook us. John had despatched them in hot haste to say that the chief was in the camp, and that we were to come back.

On returning to the camp I soon distinguished the chief, who, supported by a considerable following, was seated close to our skerm. He was a young man with an evil countenance. Minute tattoo marks described jagged lines down his forehead, and circled around his temples, while his body, all over, was decorated with little stars, very

---

* Regarding cloth, it may be interesting to note that the Africans I have met are not in any way particular about colours; they prefer pure white.

neatly made. A number of slave girls had accompanied him to answer his beck and call with due humility. Everything he required, tobacco and so forth, was handed to his highness by these girls, who in doing so, assumed a kneeling posture, and held their hands together palms upwards.

I was inclined to be very friendly with Chuzu, the chief, but did not get an opportunity, for he said immediately that "his heart was sore because the white man had come into his country without asking his permission, or sending him a present to let him know he was coming."

The cloth already referred to was then presented by Karemba through one of the chief courtiers, as it is not regal etiquette among these tribes for a chief to receive a present into his own hands. When it is given he looks at it and hands it back to his *attaché*.

It was very apparent now that a very big mistake had been made in not taking Karemba's advice. The interview with the chief was brief and unsatisfactory. He soon retired, and again in the night-time drums were heard rolling in the distance, and the wild shouts of his people rang out clear in the silence of the forest.

Bodies of armed men made fires around the camp. They were evidently watching our movements. What were we to do? John said that it would never do to leave while all these watchful warriors kept their eyes upon us.

A most uneasy night was spent, and there were no signs of relief when another morning dawned. The Makorikori people had repeatedly made demands for my possessions. They especially would have powder, but that I was determined not to give.

By the time that the sun was well up over the Umvukwe mountains, our position began to assume even a more serious aspect. Nearer and clearer could be heard the fiendish yells of approaching savages. I do not wish the reader to think that such shouts invariably had a warlike meaning, because I have on many occasions heard sounds of a similar nature which were simply the result of an exuberance of animal spirits. Now, however, the noises created awful surmises. But there was little time to let them take shape. While I was writing a few lines in my journal, John rushed up in a thrilling state of excitement.

"Master, master," he exclaimed, "the people are coming to kill us! Oh, what shall us do? They want to know what the white man wants in their country, and de old boys will run, master."

"Keep cool, John," was my reply, "how many of the boys know of this?"

"All de boys knows. Oh, look at Villum, sir! He is shaking all over. My Gaut, ouh, my Gaut, here is de people coming!"

Sure enough the Makorikori were crowding upon us. Seeing that everything was known to my men, I assumed an attitude and expression of unabashed confidence. Walking to the entrance of the skerm; I looked back at the boys, and shouted to John to tell them that, as I had said before, they were perfectly safe with me, and that I would nave no running. If an attack was intended, John, Sagwam, Karemba, and myself would defend them with the guns. In order to impress this promise, I told John and Sagwam to sit close to the guns, while I strolled unconcernedly about the camp, as if I were perfectly comfortable, and dwelt in conscious safety.

Inwardly, as the reader may imagine, I felt anything but happy, or even indifferent. Very soon we were surrounded by warriors, who piled their assegais and flint-locks against the sombre looking trees, which closely environed the skerm.

If the worst should come, could any thing be saved? Hardly, I reasoned; for, threatened by such overwhelming numbers, it would be folly to expect my quivering household to stand firmly in the face of hostility. I therefore went to my tent, and taking the money—all in sovereigns —I had been carrying in a small bag, to meet natural requirements on the sea-coast, I rolled it up carefully, and tied it firmly round John's waist, telling him that the contents were to be handed to Mr. Selous, to Mr. Fairbairn, or to Mr. Thomas, at Buluwayo.

John's chances of escape were infinitely better than mine; for I knew that my body would naturally be the chief target for the enemy. As any man would, or should, do in a similar position, I had made up my mind to keep my men well together.

A whole multitude had by this time assembled in our vicinity; and soon the chief himself appeared upon the scene, accompanied by a number of endunas or headmen. An ominous sign was that the women and children, who had followed the crowd, were sent home.

The chief seated himself at a considerable distance from where I stood. He did not come near, or even look at me, but now and then would eye me askance.

One remark he addressed to me was: "You are Mzungo" (meaning Portuguese), an assertion which I straightway denied. Evidently the suspicious monarch imagined that John was a white man too, and indeed the sallow complexion of the latter was very like that of some Portuguese: his skin was even lighter than that of many of the same nationality whom I have seen. John and myself, too, were almost always sitting or standing together.

Chuzu's every action revealed his excess of uneasiness, caused by the sudden advent of the white man, and he kept up a constant iteration of the question:

"What does the white man want in my country?"

Karemba's services were here invaluable as an interpreter. I felt certain that so long as we could keep the chief in close proximity, there would be no active demonstrations of hostility. He would be afraid he might fall a victim to the deadliness of our rifles. His uneasiness was remarkable; he evidently had the greatest difficulty in sitting still, and restlessly walked about, seating himself sometimes, but almost immediately rising to his feet.

Like many other travellers, I tried a little tacit intimidation. I especially showed how quickly C. L. K. could be manipulated, pantomimically going through all the manœuvres of firing. I also told Karemba to tell him what an awful weapon my eight-bore was, the cartridge of which was exhibited. Personally it was, perhaps, better to say little. Nothing that we said would be believed; so a little dissembling was advisable.

What I was literally endeavouring to do, was to prolong the inactivity until darkness had fallen. Then I resolved to beat a retreat at all hazards. Of course I could not find out anything from Karemba, until the chief had departed, and I knew not a word of what had been said. At night in a predicament of this description, one feels quite a host in himself; for experience among the wild races I have encountered has taught that while one is awake at night, and on the alert,. they do not like to begin the attack.

Sitting in our camp, I saw the boy whom we had met when hunting during the previous day. He was busily engaged in talking with Sagwam; but he soon left, and

John then informed me what he had said. The boy's mother it seems had overheard in the chief's kraal that we were all to be killed that very night. The old woman had sent the boy to warn us of the danger.

I will not attempt to describe the troubles of the camp after this intelligence had been diffused. Moments seemed to be hours; and it was with the utmost difficulty that a complete stampede was checked: although at times it appeared to be imminent, even inevitable. The position I was in was very peculiar, for I could not know a word of what was being said, except through interpretation. Therefore I waited anxiously for the current of events.

Farewell to thee, oh, setting sun, which a thousand times hast gladdened my wearied eyes! Never before, nor with greater joy, have I watched the golden glow of thy glorious light, than I now do when thy far reaching gleams sweep over the deepening shades of rock and forest, until the last faint tints linger over the heights of the darkening earth.

Welcome, welcome, night! Ere that sun again silvers the eastern sky, many miles will lay between us and this inhospitable spot.

By nightfall the chief had departed, but his warriors still remained, keeping up their hostile vigil. Then I had an opportunity of hearing from Karemba what were the fears of Chuzu. It seemed that the chief thought that I had come as a spy into his country: and would not believe that John and myself were other than Portuguese. That night we were to be surrounded. Karemba was to leave the camp, as they would not hurt him.

Chuzu's men, Karemba also stated, would all leave about sundown. This was actually the case, for just after the sun had sunk, they one by one disappeared with bounds into the bushes; some saying that they were going to stake out their nets for game on the flats beneath, through which our road ran, so that their proximity was a cause of additional apprehension.

Numbers of people must still have remained in the town, for when the chief returned, the beating of drums was again heard vibrating through the air.

After the main body had departed, two headmen of the chief remained, and were seated at the entrance to the enclosure. The fires were still kept burning brightly, so as to make those watching from a distance understand that we were still awake. At the last moment even, I was afraid that the Mashona would leave their loads.

I told them to go slowly round the town—on no account to hurry—while I would remain in camp until all had left. By that time only one of Chuzu's men remained, and he seemed to be immovable. I took hold of his arm, and told him through Karemba that he could not leave, but must remain until the camp was cleared; if he attempted to raise an alarm he would at once be despatched.

The distant sounds of shouts and of beating drums had almost died away when the word was given, and the boys shouldered their loads. It would have been a grand *coup*, for Chuzu had he got all the rifles, cartridges, powder, and trading articles, but on this occasion such was not his fortune.

Keeping Karemba with me, I remained until we thought that John and the party had reached the most westerly point of the mountain's base, for the path we had to follow ran close beneath the mighty boulders, at the back of which the chief's town was situated.

Cursing Chuzu and our bad luck, we took leave of the astounded prisoner, gladly bidding adieu to our dangerous camping ground, and overtaking the party under the vast shadow of the mournful rocks at the nearest point to the town.

On that memorable retreat the Mashona marched faster than they had ever done before, and all in close order, one treading upon the other's heels. Once, just at the point where the path took a bend, the bark of a dog was heard, immediately causing the men to push on at an extraordinarily rapid rate.

A small river that ran past the southern end of the town, beside the maize gardens, and close to a number of stake nets set for game, had to be crossed. This was a much to be dreaded point in the event of hostile action. There were only two small poles to cross over.

Excepting the accident of two men falling in, we soon got well over to the other side. Before penetrating the forest we made a short halt for rest, and it was with slight satisfaction that I looked back. True, we had come successfully out of a difficulty; but then we had worked so hard to get here, and what a disappointment! We had yet a long distance to go before we were out of this wretched country. A feeling of relief had just cheered us when we knew that we were within a few days' journey of the Zambesi, and now we were turned relentlessly back. Deeply and strongly did I invoke all the chastising gods to visit condign punishment upon the suspicious and stubborn Chuzu.

I said just now "this wretched country." Experience certainly made it so to us. Yet even under the pall of disappointment, as I looked back upon the landscape I could not help being struck with its boundless beauty, expanding silent, varied, and lovely under the pearl-like light of the cloudless moon, and showing the great moun-

MOONLIGHT RETREAT FROM OHUZUS.

tain like a mighty sphinx, which overlooked for all eternity the western wilderness.

We stepped with a swinging gait into the depths of the luxuriant forest "It's an ill wind that blows nobody good," and my disappointment brought joy to others. While visions of grave probabilities and graver possibilities filled my mind, the household were singing—O happy day! They thought they were *en route* towards the waggon. Roaming was over. Soon they would revel in luxury in the hunter's home, in the balmy land of the honey bird.

Ho, for northern Matabeli-land! There all was sunshine and plenty. Meat, meat, meat, was to be eaten during the intervals of long oblivious hours of happy sleep!

Ho, for Buluwayo, the kraal of the great black king! Home! Home again, in time for the merry dance at the opening of another year!

Shall it be so? Has the journey failed? Am I to retrace my steps, desponding and disappointed, back to the home of the white man?

CHAPTER IX.

RECONNOITRING.

"Ah, master! I tink of me leetle wife."—Negotiating with Sandaui—He tells of Negomo—Chibero dread and mistrust—The valley of the Etsatse—The Grumapudzi river—An uninviting country—Gold finding possible—A friendly welcome—"Gughle, gughle seree!"—Curing a fit—My first present—Frightening the white man—Native drums—Gold—Products of the country—Mode of life—Chibabura presents me with an ox—Friendly people—Assegai practice—A successful shot—Cobbling shoes—Appearance of the people—Adornments of the women and men—Absence of gold ornaments—Smoking customs—Entertainments—Weapons and implements—The "look out"—A strange musician—Anxiety about John—Powder of native manufacture—Reflections on the retreat from Chuzu's—Startled by a baboon—Retrospect.

A SOFT refreshing breeze swept up the Etsatse valley on the night of the 10th of July, fanning into lively flames the fires which we had made from the wind-fallen timber. Around the flickering blaze unhappy groups sat in a sulky silence, which was broken only by the melancholy sound of the wind as it bent the trees, and made them creak a doleful and depressing dirge.

"What makes you so fearfully despondent, John?"

"Ah, master! I tink of me leetle wife."

"Never mind, John, we will yet get to the Zambesi. Then just think of the lot of elephants we may come across; there are plenty on the river."

"But, master, de Igova men is gone, and dese Chibero say dey will leave all de tings here. De meal is done,

My Gaut! what shall us do wid dese peoples? Karem, he say he is very tired now, and want to go home."

After a long confabulation of this kind John's spirits rose, and I was by no means sorry when I heard him say:

"I like to see de beeg town on the rafeer (river)."

The old man Sandani, whom we had recruited on our journey northwards, sat opposite me, for he never went far from the source of the bead supply. Sandani was evidently on a foraging expedition, and was bent upon being able to give a good account of himself on his return home.

The Igova men who had left had each received a small present. Although they left rather awkwardly, they had done all I could expect them to do, as they had said they would only go to the Makorikori country. Their desertion rather suited my views, too, because it prevented the possibility of a further and immediate falling back towards the waggon.

I had left the payment of Sandani until the last. When his turn came, I said that I wished him to wait for a little, and I would pay him more than the rest, assuming that his absorbing love of calico would yet be the means of our getting valuable information. As it was clear he was to take all he could from me, I was determined to get all I could from him, so that the thoughts of both lay in similar directions.

Besides, I was impressed with the belief that the old boy had not lived and roved amidst these rocks for nearly half a century without knowing something of the eastern country. Sandani, however, evidently judged me with a suspicious mind, being apparently under the impression that I meant to cheat him and his son out of their honest emoluments. All the morning he had been in a storming rage, which had gradually exhausted itself, for he was then paying strict attention to replenishing the inner man, while at intervals he would look at me with a comical reproachfulness in his squinting eyes.

During the evening I revealed to John my determination to endeavour to skirt Chuzu's country. Seeing that the Mashona would not go to the east, I said I would try to get old Sandani and his son to go with me, along with Karemba and Sagwam, so that we should see what luck or loss lay in store for us in the mistrusted direction. All ideas, however slight, of returning to the waggon were now wholly abandoned.

The worst of the position was that there was no way of getting up a reliable party. The only plan was to work as we had been doing, from one chief to another

At this juncture all the household's happy thoughts of home were mercilessly annihilated. One and all became very sulky, and there was a marked disinclination to move except in a southerly direction.

I had a few cotton blankets left, and of these I offered one to Sandani, at the same time holding my palms out, and explaining as best I could that he should also have that quantity of beads if he guided me to the next chief. At that critical point of the journey not one of the interpreters could be implicity trusted; they were too anxious to get home.

A great deal of questioning drew the information from Sandani that there was a very big chief whose country was about two days' journey to the east. His name was Negomo.

At the sound of this name the Chibero men cocked up their ears. They had been giving old Sandani the cold shoulder during the journey, and they now began a vigorous protestation to the effect that the Negomo people were not their friends, and would be sure to kill the white man and his boys. As a matter of course, this had the result of sending Karemba and Sagwam nearly out of their wits with fright. Fortunately old Sandani was so much interested about his blanket and his pretty beads of red porcelain, that he answered all expostulations with scowls, declaring that he was a personal friend of the great chief.

I had then to go through the ever-recurring routine of giving assurances of safety, backed up by presents, and promises to my two faithfuls.

Intending to travel as lightly and as fast as practicable—because it was impossible to say what was ahead of us—we only carried a blanket, a few yards of cloth, a small cooking-pot, and a tiny bag of rice and tea. For the rest we trusted to the rifle, and we were ready for an early start on the following morning.

Early perhaps, but hardly easy. The Chibero men delayed us seriously through their continued remonstrances. They declared that the white man would surely be killed by the Negomo people. Old Sandani and his son were ready, but the two faithfuls had weakened in spirit at the last moment. Finally, however, I succeeded as on former occasions in getting their objections removed, and we were ready for the road. Karemba was the most stubborn and the most difficult to satisfy, but ultimately urgent assurances of absolute safety brought him to acquiescence in the beginning of our new venture.

"Good-bye, John; keep your spirits up. We will soon see the big river and the great town."

"My Gaut, master! look out! Look out, sir!"

"Never fear, John; we will soon return. Good-bye!"

A handful of beads were passed to each of the Chibero men, and then we were off, *en route* eastwards to the unknown.

Wending our way down the valley of the Etsatse, we

crossed some very marshy strips of land, and two hours' journey brought us to the verge of the great plateau through which we had marched. On the south-east, at no great distance, the Rusaka, or Uakania mountains, to which I have already alluded, were clearly visible. These mountains hem in the Grumapudzi river on its southern side. A large portion of this country could, with little difficulty, be reached in waggons.

Rough as these hills are, with their immense huddled heaps of broken rock, their recesses are rich with mines of wealth, going to feed the gold-producing rivers, which year after year are accumulating the precious metal as it is moved by atmospheric influences, or washed by the action of the rains.

Some Mashona gardens were passed, in which we came across numbers of youngsters, who fled in all directions as soon as they saw us.

A short walk in a direct line brought us to a point where we would be compelled to descend rapidly into what seemed to be a boundless expanse, broken by chains of sharp mountain ridges, shrouded in sombre blue, and whose outlines resembled the tempest-hurled billows of a far-stretching sea, lessening as they receded, until both form and colour mingled with and were lost in the leaden hue of the horizon.

Through these mountains, descending to their rugged ravines, and winding up the tortuous paths of their roughened sides, lay the line of our journey.

Uninviting as the country was, the sensation of peering into the midst of a wild unexplored region was not devoid of charm. All this land through which the Waynge and the Grumapudzi rivers flow, is called Whata.

The appearance of the country seems to indicate the

likelihood of gold being found. But it is impossible to say whether the working would pay; a surmise that could only be decided by systematic prospecting by adepts in the art of gold finding.

Sandani soon pointed out a massive square rock, which towered up high, far away amidst the mountained sea of stone. As he pointed, he said, in sonorous and commanding tones, "Negomo." Taking our opinion from the imposing solemnity of his style, it was clear that this great chief must be given all the deference due to the species of mortal gods who are to be found in every part of the world.

Old Sandani here caused considerable delay. He said he had a wife living in a village close to the adjacent rocks. Karemba said, with no slight emulative pride, that Sandani had many women. The troublesome old fellow had to be wheedled with all manner of strategic tricks before he could be induced to move. He would stop for the night; his wife would make meal, and so forth.

At five o'clock in the afternoon we had covered seventeen miles. Then old Sandani sat down in a determined way, and positively refused to go another step. He looked at me in a most comical fashion, his squint eye seeming to say, "Oh, no you don't! No more 'next water' for me. I'm run down for to-day."

I had been saying, "camp at next water," but now my anxiety to get forward had touched Sandani's wakeful fancy, and he meant that I should pay for my too-evident weakness in disclosing my wishes.

Our diminutive camp was soon ship-shape, and a good supper of pea-nuts was a welcome close for the day. Our resting-place lay beside a small marshy piece of land; a most unhealthy, as well as uncomfortable, spot, I should say, during the rainy season.

Sandani informed me that by noon on the following day we should arrive at a town ruled by a headman (enduna) of Negomo, and that it was probable that the chief would give me boys. He indicated the probable time of our arrival by pointing vertically towards the sky, showing the position of the sun, whose path across the heavens he graduated with considerable accuracy, an accomplishment which was peculiarly well manifested among the natives generally: they would in this way rapidly indicate any particular time of the day.

During the night a hyena came very close to the skerm. The brute had evidently sniffed the odour of the frugal evening meal, and in our small assemblage his appearance caused quite a thrill of excitement.

Lovely weather prevailed. The nights were not hot, neither were they cold, although a chill was apt to be felt in the morning, especially when the camp was pitched on the bank of a river or near a swamp.

The sun had hardly peeped above the tops of the trees when we were again on the move, without making any deviation from our course of the previous day. The old guide led us through dismal-looking stretches of morass and belts of woodland and plain until we crossed the Waynge river, the same water we had encamped upon higher up, when eventful times were upon us.

When the sun had almost touched meridian we were still holding on our course. Towering in front of us were the great rocks which we had gazed at from the distant west.

The old man said that close by was an outlying village, and that the chief's headquarters were at least a mile beyond. Gazing upwards towards the rocks, which stood out clear against an almost steel-blue sky, we could distinguish the heads of many men, also the naked figures of children.

They had seen us moving slowly along the winding footpath beneath, and again and again they shouted to us from their coigne of vantage, than which I could not conceive of a finer position for a town or a stronghold, offering safety to a small tribe.

Determined not to be led into a trap like the last one, and showing that I had profited by former experience, I now positively refused to go any farther. Sandani here turned the tables upon me, proving himself to be a "dark horse." He said that with him all was right.

Numbers of men, armed with assegais and knobkerries, came running down the steep pathway to meet us. I was glad to find that Sandani had spoken the truth in the old camp. The people evidently knew him. Doubtless the sad reprobate had another wife stowed away amidst these cheerless rocks.

The news of our arrival must have spread like forked lightning. For no sooner had we ascended the mountain than we were surrounded by crowds of the descendants of Ham, of all sizes and ages, from the crowing infant in arms to the mumified savage who might be marching along with the century. One and all seemed very friendly, but they were much impressed with the novelty of my colour.

We halted in a grotto of rock. Sandani, after accepting snuff from the surrounding sightseers, gave forth a heavily-charged harangue, which utterly eclipsed all former orations, and seemed to fill his audience with an intensity of admiration at the marvellous range of his rhetorical power. Poor Karemba was now completely silenced, for in the older man he had found a decided rival, bursting with a greatness of eloquence which would brook no opposition, as Karemba himself was forced to admit.

Both Sandani and Karemba, our natural orators, were

despatched with presents for the king. They consisted of a fine piece of strong cotton cloth, of many brilliant colours, and some "flashy" porcelains.

Once they were off, I sat comfortably amid the rocks, with the wondering crowd perched around on every side. As I looked at the naked ones sitting on their haunches, with their heels well tucked in beneath their bodies, and nearly all eating roots or cracking nuts, I could not help thinking how much the scene resembled one which I had witnessed, at which a family of baboons were all posed in similar attitudes. The human beings did not, perhaps, make so much noise, but their movements in eating and in acting, as well as their posture when at rest, were all of the same character as those of the lower animal.

After a very long wait, during which I was speculating seriously upon the likelihood of our being favourably received, or contumeliously ejected from the territory—we might be sent off without having even the satisfaction of an indignation meeting—Karemba returned. His face was lightened by a half-suppressed smile of satisfaction as he said:

"Gughle, gughle, seree!"

The whole meaning was that the king was good, was glad that the white man had come to see him, and would be able to give boys to go and fetch the valuables. Nothing further, of course, was said regarding my intended journey towards the north.

Here I was, then, at the outskirts of a Makorikori town, in the country where the Chibero men had declared I would surely be killed. I had only four followers, but we were perfectly happy, and fairly contented, with every indication of receiving good treatment at last.

I was requested to show my rifle. Just as the exhibition

was about to begin one of the audience suddenly went into a fit; and immediately, as if thoroughly conversant with such affairs, the old men gathered round the sufferer. They quickly placed a blanket over his quivering form, reminding me of the fire-extinguishing plan. Under the blanket he kicked violently, "squirming" all the time like a dying hare.

A grave-looking old fellow advanced, and in a sitting posture took up his place close to the afflicted one's head. Apparently he was concentrating his thoughts, for in a little time he began to talk slowly and solemnly, and in a most methodical manner going through a long and evidently, to the bystanders, an interesting incantation, in the course of which he told what manner of man the victim was, and where he had lived. It was difficult for me to find out anything intelligible about this peculiar ceremony; even Karemba looked solemn when I inquired as to its meaning.

This incantation, or mayhap the revival of nature, had the desired effect of driving the evil spirit out of the unfortunate man, and leaving him in his normal condition. The wild contortions and upheavals which had been going on under the blanket gradually subsided, until the figure resembled an ant heap, with a blanket over it, drying in the sun. After a short pause, the man sat up, looked about, and immediately took snuff. A dead silence ensued—Richard was himself again!

The reader may imagine that it was with the greatest difficulty that I was enabled to keep my countenance straight when witnessing this funny ceremony, but fortunately I did succeed in keeping up a stolid expression.

The weather being of the brightest and best description, I was induced to take many a solitary walk through the silent ways and by-ways which threaded among the rough rocks. These were the times for reflection, and often there, as elsewhere, did I meditate in solitude upon the plans and prospects of my enterprise.

At the camp a man brought a deep wooden plate containing hot roasted pea-nuts, the first present I had received from the natives in Africa. Of course the gift was conferred with a keen view to future reward. Women and girls came to sell rice, millet, corn and native beer. With a few beads I had I amused myself by trading, as provisions would be much needed when the whole of the party arrived.

I was impressed with the idea that the Makorikori must be very much given to feasting, for the beating of the tom-tom and the firing of guns were loudly audible all the afternoon; and now as I reclined, rolled up in a blanket, on a bed of wild grass, with nothing above but the clear starlit vault of heaven, their distant drumming and singing were the last sounds I heard as I dropped wearily off to sleep

A lovely morning ushered in the day. All nature was cheerful, according ill with my mind, which was filled with restlessness, until I had sent Sandani and Karemba to the king to intimate that I would like the men to be sent to-day, and that one of my boys would accompany them to show where John was encamped on the Etsatse river. Etiquette forbade my accompanying the messengers. I had to wait a visit from His Majesty first.

As the day advanced numbers of people collected around, watching my every action, and highly entertained when they saw me use tools for eating.

Occasionally some wild-looking characters, no doubt endeavouring to tease, or to see if they could frighten the white man, would run with a swift spurt close up to me, stamping with their feet, whooping and whistling a short, shrill, and very piercing note, while their clubs were used with threatening gestures more ominous certainly, but very like lungeing in fencing.

Exhibitions of the rifle were a great success. The novel way of removing the front catch, and disconnecting the rifle from the stock, gave these simple people intense delight. In return they showed us some articles of their own manufacture, notably drums made from the trunks of trees, which were hollowed, and on one end covered with tightly stretched hide. These drums were played upon with the naked hands, and also with sticks.

Some of the people brought gold. It was carried in the customary fashion, *i.e.*, in the large quills of birds. The sellers had come from the Grumapudzi river; some from the Amazoe, where in hollow wooden trays they wash the alluvial deposits in the water in order to extract the gold. The people will carry their small treasure great distances so as to exchange it for an ornament or a piece of cloth. I was unable to discover whether these primitive miners understood anything about the method of extracting gold by pulverising auriferous quartz.

The country produces both iron and copper, and the people manufacture beads from these metals.

Lemons, citrons and sweet potatoes are grown.

Like the Mashona, the people live in a most simple manner. Nevertheless they are readily distinguished from their neighbours by the tattoo marks on the face and body. They seemed to have a good supply of Tower muskets—flintlocks—decorated in a wonderfully ornamental manner by means of brass-headed tacks which thickly stud the butts, while the grip of the stocks as well as the barrels are bound at regular distances with brass wire, sometimes very neatly plaited.

Soon a number of young warriors appeared upon the scene, evidently anxious to show their agility, and how gracefully they could " burn powder." Two or three of them in a body would take a short run forward, dancing from side to side, aiming, and looking up, down, and around in all directions as though searching for the hidden enemy. When through with their varied manœuvres, they, with a " whoop ! " and a wild spring, would dart into the air, turning round and round with top-like rapidity, and not ungracefully, while they pointed with their guns towards the four quarters of the globe.

The people were very friendly, bringing an abundant supply of sweet potatoes, which I continued to buy, as our only substitute for bread or biscuit. When rice and potatoes could be had I was perfectly satisfied. The potatoes, when baked beneath a heap of cinders, were very good, but not nearly so sweet as the American bulb.

In a little time I saw some slaves leading a young ox towards me. When the party, which proved to be a deputation, arrived, they addressed me, saying that the ox was a present from the chief Chibabura, enduna of Negomo. Not one of the boys being in camp at the time, it was not without difficulty that this gift was intimated.

I was quite amazed at the occurrence, the kindness of the treatment contrasting very strongly with the rough experiences of the past. Had I alighted upon a land flowing with milk and honey ?

These friendly exchanges were extremely gratifying. Sagwam soon arrived in camp, and then I was able to make myself understood, while he informed me that the young man who had brought the ox was the king's son, and would like very much to see my rifle.

Crowds of little boys congregated in our neighbourhood, and were playing all day long. Their game was throwing the assegai at moving objects, a feat which required a great deal of practice. The targets were round roots, about the size of ostrich eggs. These they would hurl along the ground, and as they rolled would stick them with assegais in a most dexterous manner.

The assegais were made of hard wood, burnt at the points, or tipped with bone. Probably similar weapons were used by their ancestors, in ages that are shrouded by the gloom of unwritten centuries. Even the sight of an assegai can arouse a curious train of thoughts, which reach far back to those remote times when the first race of mankind—undoubtedly hunters—roamed free in the primeval forest: when, according to Lucretius—

"Men's earliest arms were fingers, teeth and nails,
And stones and fragments from the branching woods."

The surrounding crowd was now very large. As the king's son was a unit in the assemblage, I determined to waste a cartridge in order to show what the white man could do with an assegai propelled by powder. A reputation as a shot was undoubtedly a desideratum under the circumstances. So I took up a position as an exhibitor of wizard marksmanship, one of the round roots, such as the boys used, being the target. It was sent flying through the air; and as it sped I sent a bullet after it from "C. L. K.," fortunately shattering the thing into fragments, which flew in all directions. Then I quickly disconnected the weapon, holding the stock in one hand and the barrel in the other. The appreciative audience greeted the performance with a shouting chorus of applause, such as would have thrilled the heart of an acting manager.

Amid exclamations of astonishment, looks of surprise, clapping of hands, and the dancing of little boys, I presented the empty case of the cartridge and some beads to the king's son. Altogether the very ordinary performance had brought a reputation to the marksman. The trifles I presented to the king's son were all I possessed until John should arrive.

Greatly to my delight, Karemba and sixteen men soon appeared, the latter having been sent by the king. They were dispatched at once, Sagwam being charged with full instructions to bring John, and to tell him that he should act well with the Chibero men, giving them each a present, and letting them go home. Sagwam's parting desire was that I should not kill the ox until John and he had returned. Sagwam invariably had a memory of his inward cravings, and was by this time by far the fattest man in the company.

I would have gone myself, but since the time when my feet first began to give trouble, I had covered over 129 miles of marsh, hill, and plain, and during most of the time my feet were soaking wet. So I determined to remain where I was, and try to cure my suffering extremities, besides exercising some ingenuity in the handicraft of the cobbler. This neglected, I should be soon unfitted, despite the best determination, to proceed.

Leisure gave opportunities for observing something of the character and customs of the happy, or properly speaking, contented race among whom I was placed. The women and children flocked around, and appeared to consider my writing as an occupation of amusement. But even to Karemba, who had been a great traveller, writing was an impenetrable mystery. On a previous occasion I had asked John whether a Mashona could be induced to carry a letter to the Hanyane river to deliver to any hunters who might be there. John said that the people did not understand letters, and would not carry one; the idea being that it was better to have nothing to do with what they did not understand.

Some of the younger women here were pretty, possessing neat, slim figures. Obesity was evidently an indication of mature development. Hair-dressing was clearly an operation demanding not a little time. In fact it must have been very laborious work. The most popular fashion at this time was the stringing of divers-hued beads on the hair, thus making the head look like a mop of many colours. Married women shaved their heads.

The tattoo marks on the faces, when neatly done, are far from being repulsive. The women simply pierce the upper lip, through which a thin wire ring, sometimes ornamented with a few beads, is passed. Pendant from their necks hang numerous charms of ivory and wood, also the claws of wild animals strung together on lines of gut and bark. Their bracelets are of brass wire, the plaiting of which is ingenious; while thick wire of brass or iron form the anklets.

The men in some cases wear ear-rings and bracelets. The latter are rings cut from the solid hide of the buffalo, or some other thick-skinned animal. A very prevalent custom among the men is the wearing on their necklaces of a small sheath-knife and snuff-box.

Men have also many ways of decorating their heads. In the woolly hair some will shave partings an inch wide, turning them into circular patterns. Others who have an objection to the curly crop will straighten it with the finest threads of bark, so that when it is finished it looks like a mat of twisted silk thread, as it literally shines with oil. On the loins they wear, before and behind, a strip of leather, which drops in front nearly to the feet, and is always garnished with beads of iron, brass, or copper. On the march they tuck this long pendant up to the belt. Little bags made from the whole skin of the tiny and woolly ground squirrel hang from the neck as a store place for tobacco, snuff, and light articles of use. Trinkets are made from bone, and belts from the white fossiliferous stones found in the bed of the Zambesi.

It was a gold-producing country, yet I did not see a single ornament made from the precious metal.

The men, generally speaking, had very bad teeth, covered with a yellow-looking tartar, which seemed to be due to the practice of incessantly smoking hemp or tobacco. They produce the latter commodity. Perhaps the eating of hot pap, and hot roasted nuts, which are devoured to a great extent, may also contribute to destroy the appearance of the teeth, as they are taken like hot cinders.

In physique they are by no means a fine race. I did not see a really finely-formed man among them. Nevertheless the Makorikori are physically a better looking people than the Mashona.

They were unceasing in their efforts to give entertainment, coming frequently to the spot where I was sitting in order to perform some wonderfully energetic evolutions, some of which I have already described. Now and then I have seen them jumping into the air with their guns, and while off the ground they would fire, making two revolutions with the agility and dexterity of acrobats. My impression was that these displays were in honour of the white man, or it may have been to test the extent of his generosity. When they saluted a stranger they did not shake hands. That custom seemed to be unknown. They clapped their hands instead, which was likewise a sign for thanks.

Weapons and implements such as assegais, arrows and bows were formed on Nature's crude anvil. The bows are of a heart shape, very heavy, and made of good iron, much valued among the tribes in the Zambesi valley.

These days were the happiest I had spent for a very long time, having almost perfect repose. Whenever it could be managed, I would escape from the crowd of visitors and saunter in solitude through the sinuous tracks in the rocks, until I came upon some sequestered nook where I would sit down and occupy the passing hours by writing up the journal, and silently meditating as I looked upon the tranquil scene of forest landscape.

The serenity was delightful. A selected favourite spot was the top of a stupendous boulder, from which a magnificent view could be obtained, stretching far over the western wilderness. With the aid of the telescope I could see any object of the size of man which might appear in an opening of the forest, for the path led out to a clear spot beneath my "look out." Here I watched for John, for it was now a week since we had left him and the party.

Sagwam had gone, but no word from him had yet arrived. What had befallen them that they should be so long? Would I again have to go over all that weary road to settle matters with the discontented Chibero men in the same way as I had to do with the Unyamwenda? A day or two of delay must decide the question.

Every evening I watched the daylight dying, and bade an anxious farewell to the sun as it sunk beyond the landscape, and bathed with glowing shades the wilderness of vegetation. But darkness fell, and hopes for another day were crushed. Ah! those sunsets. What reveries, what hopes, what fears filled my mind as I gazed upon them in solitude from the recesses of those highland rocks! I had been thwarted on all sides, although I was always ahead endeavouring with might and main to get on.

Now the question seemed to be, seeing that I had left my party behind, Shall I ever see them again? and if so, How many will there be? How philosophic we should become under this system of cogitation, in which patience becomes a second nature as annoyance finds no home in the mind!

After these periods of reflection I would return to camp, and wile away the evenings by eating nuts, and listening to Karemba playing upon his piano, with variations of begging from old Sandani, who never left me except upon urgent occasions.

During the daytime I had to give constant exhibitions of shooting, varied by feat-like tricks of different kinds, which aroused and sustained a regular flow of merriment.

One man, whether sent by the chief or not I could not say, was in constant attendance with his piano, set inside a hollow calabash, which wonderfully improved the resonance of the instrument. The calabash was decorated with dry shells of fruit and various chips of hard substances, which gave a sharp rattling accompaniment. This fellow would dance and over and over again repeat the strange native melody, which was grievously jerky in its modulations. His position was directly in front of me. There he remained, stamping upon the ground, and with spasmodic energy advancing and retiring.

By this time I was beginning to feel thoroughly uneasy about John, and had fully made up my mind to start in search of him on the following day; for I had cobbled my old shoes of zebra-skin until they were strong, and, although yet a trifle bottle-nosed, my feet were also better. Anxiety was certainly not allayed by Karemba's doleful shaking of the head as he remarked that John wanted to go back to Buluwayo.

The people of this district, although belonging to the

Makorikori tribe, were in no way connected with the few of the same name whom we had encountered at Chuzu's. Like the Mashona they live in detached bodies. One chief, however, sometimes ruled over a number of towns. Chibabura is the enduna of Negomo, whose chief town, as I said before, lay to the east of our position.

Negomo had immediately been informed of my arrival, and Karemba said he would be sure to come over, although I earnestly prayed that he would not, knowing that his appearance would mean a heavy call on the bank.

Four men came into the skerm to sell gold. Judging from their costume they were evidently hunters. They wanted powder for the gold. I think their desire was to find out whether I had powder suitable for their muskets. I asked them to show me the kind of powder they had. They said they made it themselves, and I offered to give them some of mine in exchange for some of theirs, as I had a curiosity to see what kind of stuff they used. On examination I found it to be very similar to a powder I had seen made by the Mexicans. Taking the efflorescence of saltpetre they mix it with the charcoal made from the bark of the mufati tree : it is baked in an earthen pot for five or six hours, until caked, after which it is finely pulverised, and exposed for some time to the sun's rays. The powder burns very slowly, and its explosive force is insignificant compared with the strength of ours.

I hardly know who was the first to teach these people how to manufacture this mighty agent of the chase and of warfare. Perhaps the earliest knowledge arose among people who had been the slaves of the Portuguese, or from those who had some connection with slave caravans belonging to the east coast.

I had become so used to evening musings, that whenever

the sun reached the well-known downward point I would gladly, with lithe steps and a light heart, hurry off to one of the favourite retreats. At such times I was as lively as anyone could be when going to witness some remarkable novelty or some grand spectacle in the artificial institutions of civilized life. I would talk to myself, all the time whittling a piece of wood like a thoroughbred "down-easter" from the state of Maine. Again and again in lightning thoughts I would re-enact the moments of excitement passed in bygone days.

Upon that evening I thought of our retreat from Chuzu's. Even now the memory of that night, and the weary days which followed, arises vividly in my mind. It was a strange affair. The vindictive and suspicious monarch must have thought me very ambitious if he imagined that I wanted his barren land of rocks. How I would have liked to have seen his face next morning when he found that the bird had flown! Worse than all, too, that the valuables had also disappeared! Those crotchety Mashona folk had given trouble during the forced retreat. They would insist upon halting and making fires, which I was equally determined they should not do; no sooner did they fan the dry dung and grass into a flame than I would put it out. Sometimes, when they thought it for their own good, they would hurry on, but after crossing the river they had stopped and said: "What would the white man do if we were to leave him and all his things now?"

I remember that the chief at Igova was indignant when he heard of my treatment by Chuzu.

On our return to the Waynge river (where I had walked miles ahead of the party), I was very familiar with the features of the old landscape hemming in the river with rugged masses of towering cliff and half-tumbling crag, through which the waters, in a crystal stream, went merrily on, dancing, glancing, and singing on its course. The silent pool, too, I remember, as a mirror which on many occasions gave a reflection of a wild-looking man with a rough-like beard and tattered clothes.

Then there was the old camp, the arena of excited and feverish actions. The deserted spot had been swept completely by fierce flames of fire since we had gone, and around it blackened embers and bones were strewn by the cheerless wind, until it reminded one of a deserted abode of wild beasts rather than a habitation of human beings.

What a start I got there! Awful sounds, indescribable perhaps, but something between a bark and a cry, came from a cave within a few yards of where I was. Breathless with curiosity, I went up to the place, and there found an old baboon, whose vocalisation had been the cause of the start; but on my appearance the screeching creature darted quickly off, stricken with fright.

Then after the severe fifty miles had been retraced there was the wildly exciting eland hunt on the Etsatse river, when the victims to our rifles fell just as the last rays of sunlight flashed out from the west.

Thoughts such as these recalled the chief events of the journey. They do so distinctly even now as I write after a longer lapse of time. I traverse the old ground again, grapple once more with old difficulties, and almost revive the old relief that was felt about troubles overcome, finding in the whole retrospect a meditation that is not without its generous gift of pleasure.

CHAPTER X.

INYOTA'S TRANQUIL LAND.

Camp fires in the distance—Reappearance of John—His miserable looks—
Sandani is gratified—Camp before Inyota—Karemba's eccentricities—
John's troub'es—Kaffir ingratitude—The Bushman lost—A vain search
—My terrified companion—The numerous wives of Sandani—The
"oracle" sings the praises of the white man—Chibabura's reception—
A palaver—Wonders of the mirror—Physicing the crowd—Settling
Sandani's claims—The Rock of Wisdom—Chibabura's town—Native
workmanship — Bark blankets — Pottery — A favoured land and
people — Makorikori songs — Character of the people — Customs—
Knowledge of agriculture—Contentment—Freedom from crime—Their
life compared with civilised poverty—A peaceful scene—Oh, happy
and favoured Inyota!

PEERING into the darkness, for some time, I thought I could discern far away the flames of what might be large camp fires. The distance was so great, however, that even with the telescope I could not be sure of the sight. But the sign gave me a ray of hope. By noon next day John might appear.

When I returned I found that our small camp was garnished with the beef of the ox which the king had sent. It was not advisable to keep it longer. In passing, I may say that the breed of cattle is small, but the beef is as good as any that I have tasted. To me it seemed far superior to any antelope meat.

The morning came and passed without event. I looked out for John continuously, but he did not appear. About four o'clock in the afternoon I was watching Karemba broiling a piece of steak, and turning it round before the fire with his filthy fingers, when a thrill of excitement moved the camp to activity. What could it be that roused this lazy band of loiterers? My eyes did not deceive me— John, by Jove!

Yes, John truly! But he looked like the proverbial shadow of death! Undoubtedly something was wrong: I was accustomed, unfortunately, to receive more tidings of evil than of good. I welcomed him as heartily as possible. He spoke little in reply, only murmuring a few words.

My intention was to make a move the moment the party had arrived: I wanted to get nearer to the king's town. After John's appearance hardly a minute was lost. Old Sandani was longing for a fresh opportunity to roll out sonorous sentences which otherwise would have had no chance of being left upon the sands of time; but I knew that acceding to this persuasive delay by allowing him to commence his harangue would mean that the sheet anchor had been cast.

We proceeded until we reached a point within a few hundred yards of the gates of Inyota. Few events, no matter how serious, have not their ridiculous side. Here old Sandani squinted at me with a gleam of satisfaction inspired by the arrival of the *shop*. The expression on his odd looking physiognomy, told, as clearly as visage could tell, "You see what I have done! Didn't I say so?" Great, however, was the satisfaction of knowing that now the camp was moved to a point where there was every reason to hope that a new and a well organised start might be effected with an entirely fresh set of carriers. Now that the loads were lightening, still fewer numbers were required.

The new camping ground was a distinct improvement

upon the last: it was more open, besides being in close proximity to the town.

The men who had escorted John and the valuables were upon the eve of leaving for the town; so I deputed Sandani to go with them, carrying a fine present for the chief.

Among the household who were left, every one of course shirked most studiously anything approaching work of a more arduous nature than roasting meat or broiling bones. This they would do *ad libitum*.

Karemba now budded and flourished as a tremendous swell. He condescended to give meat to his poor brothers, and held long consultations with Sandani. He frequently smoked "ikutu," and acquired a specially affected cough, which by vocal application became his undeniable and exclusive right. The cough might remind the hearer either of a steam whistle or the crowing of a cock; but to Karemba's *confrères* it seemed to be very comical, much hilarity being caused whenever his lordship deigned to agitate his breezy windpipe. Above all, he would order others about, sometimes showing a good deal of sense and often force.

Sagwam had gained an air of very fashionable delicacy, and was out and out the fattest Kaffir I had. He was not to be crowded at the fire, and could only carry a little medicine. His last load was two bottles of castor oil, and latterly the sight of it was enough to provoke serious results to him without even a taste.

Old Sandani liked very much to assume the coveted position of being unburdened. My mind, however, was made up that not another of the staff should be knighted unless they would declare their intention to follow me to Tette, and accept payment on arriving.

The absence of the indispensable ape began to be a source of wonder here—he was not in camp.

After supper, Sandani returned from the chief, whom he said would visit me on the next day. Negomo, the king, he said, would come in a few days. On another occasion the former had put off coming to my camp at the time he had appointed; therefore I decided that if he did not appear by noon on the following day I would go to him, and try to refresh his memory.

Now to John and his troubles. Calling him up, I inquired what had happened during my absence. The poor fellow was looking very ill.

"Ah, master, I came veree bad, veree seek, and veree tired!" He continued his complaint in most lugubrious tones, relating the vicissitudes through which he had passed, especially the hard, hard time he had spent while settling matters with the Chibero men, who seemed to have kept up their notoriety for unreasonableness.

Ungrateful for the numerous presents I had given them, they had even refused to carry back the fine eland head which I had taken so much care to preserve. Facts like these, coupled with other experiences, however trifling they may appear, prove conclusively that absolute ingratitude is one of the leading traits in the Kaffir mind. John, it seems, had given these Chibero men two fathoms of white calico and a quantity of beads. This was far to much. But my troubled squire told me that the people would have been fighting with him had it not been for the presence of the men I had sent over.

The Chibero people it seems were very much frightened by the Negomo men, and were greatly surprised at the sudden appearance of such a force.

"For, master," continued John, "after you left, dese Chibero men often say, 'Oh! the white man will be killed by dese peoples: he will never come back here again!'"

Their anger was not allayed even by the presents which John gave them, and they showed their annoyance by telling him that when they returned to the Hanyane river, they would break open the box which had been left in the waggon, and take away all the things. They would fight with us, too, on our return to the waggon.

"Empty words and foolish threats, John," I said, "let them speak; they haven't the backbone to carry out their words."

"Ah, master," replied John, "but dese is a bad people."

John was quite right. The frightful examples of humanity had not a redeeming feature in their evil character. Release them from judicious restraint and you let loose the tiger; but its heart is in the wrong place: mischief, not valour, is in its breast, and its threatening cries are vain. Not being a believer in the existence of totally consuming depravity in any human soul, I have tried to find some good point to recommend the Chibero, but utter failure has been the result.

John went on with his story, and his eyes were almost tearful. He told how the poor Bushman was lost. I asked if the Bushman had been fighting with any of the men.

"No," was the answer; "de day after de master leave us, I loose um; and I never see um again."

Every rock in the kopjie beside the old camping-ground had been searched. Alas! the Bushman had disappeared; where, no one could say. Probably not one of the company would ever know. I, for one, never saw his face again.

Poor Windvogel! Whatever may have been his fate, I will pay him a parting tribute, by saying that, although the weight of bad in his composition would in all likelihood have brought the moral scale, balanced upon the sensitive fulcrum of human judgment, down with a thump, yet he had little for which, like a Briton, he could "thank his stars!" From his earliest days his surroundings were far from conducing towards the birth, not to speak of the perfecting, of moral excellence; yet certainly his tiny egg-cup-full of brains were not devoid of some enlivening elements of good nature, his face being always radiant with smiles.

John's sorrow about Windvogel's disappearance was not, I am afraid, due to any fear regarding what had overtaken him. It was caused by the thought that he personally had lost a piece of valuable movable property.

Immediately after sunrise on the following morning I started on a hunting expedition, taking with me from among the bystanders a man who reported eland close by. The occasion proved an exception to the general rule, because only one man followed me. The hour was too early for the others. It was an exception too in another way.

On descending the hill towards the hunting grounds, my solitary companion halted, and then, looking furtively back towards the town, he began to walk quickly, gradually increasing his pace until it became a run, when he disappeared at full speed. I could not imagine what was the matter with the man. On returning to the camp I found that the boys were highly amused. Karemba said that a man had passed, saying during his flight, that he was afraid of the white man, because he thought he would kill him. I could not help thinking that I must be growing very fierce-looking, when my aspect could instil so much terror into simple minds.

Game was scarce. Eland and roan antelope were the most plentiful. The people are constantly out hunting in large parties.

Sandani, apparently, was growing great in the eyes of the

household. Even John, who had a well-developed dislike for anyone who in the least degree resembled a Mashona, said of Sandani : "He say plenty of good things of de master, and Karem say he is a beeg man, in dis contree, and has got lots of wife!"

Quite a number of Sandani's properties in the shape of growing girls, came and knelt before me, offering various kinds of native produce; the old man all the while looking upon his live stock with an expression of genuine pride.

"Are all these yours?" I asked.

"Yes," was the emphatic answer; "mine, all mine, every one of them!"

Among the number was one very nice looking young girl, who had her hair bedecked with white and red porcelains: her necklace of plaited wild-grass was studded here and there with a species of white shell ; around her waist was a belt of beads of all colours. I bought some wares from the girls, and amused them by showing my watch. As I did so, I pulled the girl I speak of close up, so that she might have a better chance of seeing, and was highly amused at her signs of alarm.

As yet I had been unable to get the avaricious lord of many wives to divulge the news whether he would or would not proceed with me farther.

About noon a considerable group of men were seen coming through the wood on our right. Among them was Chibabura the chief. Soon they were seated in a circle close to our camp.

After the usual salute by the clapping of hands, I walked over to the select circle, and seated myself opposite the chief, with the oracle Sandani on my left, and the rest of the household extending beyond.

Softly the oracle began to speak, at first in broken sentences.

Then warming to his work he increased his volume of tone and length of expression, laying great emphasis upon the words at the end of each sentence, and all the while shaking his head more and more as he proceeded.

Thus he sang my praises. He told how the white man had come from afar across salt water; and as he narrated the facts he kept up the general custom of counting with his fingers, at the end of the sum bringing the finger which terminated the calculation quickly to his mouth, and throwing the hand forward in the direction of the person whom he addressed. This gave the number of the party, and likewise intimated how many many moons I had been upon the journey from distant lands.

They were informed what a wonderful hunter the white man was: how he had shot the running deer, and how they had eaten abundantly of the meat of the eland and the koodoo. With the white man all was plenty. He had bought beer with cloth. He had been treated badly by Chuzu, the great chief, upon the threshold of whose home he had trodden with a fearless step, although the chief wanted to kill him. They were told of the long marches of the party, and how, when the white man returned to his own land, he would speak to his pale brothers of the countries he had seen, and how Chibabura had treated him. Last, and far from least, the white man had an inexhaustible supply of blankets and charms which he had brought with him; in fact he was a dry goods bank.

Some clapping of hands, succeeded by a pause, followed. An all-round snuff was indulged in, and then came the chief's turn to speak.

His tone and words were very friendly. He said that he liked the white man to come and visit his country, and hoped that more would come bringing cloth and beads with them. As to journeying through his country, I could proceed, and he would give me boys to take me to Kunyungwi (Tette).

The last promise gave me marked satisfaction. That, I thought, would be a stage farther. The goods still in hand would just be sufficient to buy food, and perhaps allow a present to be made to some of the chiefs. There was not enough left to make payments in full to more than one lot of carriers, and this would have to be done in advance before leaving the spot where we were.

As on other occasions, I went through various rifle performances, which highly delighted the chief, whose admiration was greatly excited by the ingenious construction of the weapons. When he saw the elephant-rifle, he was fairly amazed. I did not show him the white man's gods in the shape of watch, and so forth; but during the afternoon entertainment, a great novelty was produced—never before exhibited by the company—with immense success.

The novelty was a looking-glass. The astonishment and amusement it afforded were unbounded. Now and then one of the crowd might be found who did not seem to think that the reflection of his physiognomy was altogether flattering; and the glass would therefore be quickly handed on to others. Some would vainly try to get ahead of the reflection, by making wild and rapidly changing contortions of the face, only to be sadly put out by the discovery that there was no motion swift enough to defeat the glass.

The chief had a good look at his mirrored face, and smiled as though he were tolerably well satisfied.

Handing the glass to some of the petrified parties who were sitting around, and who might, judging from appearances, have been dug out of the strata of some deep geological epoch, they examined their fearful and wonderful countenances in a very scrutinising fashion, clearly bent upon discovering some deception. After a careful examination some of them seemed quite frightened at their ugliness, which evidently had never before been brought so forcibly under their notice.

Chibabura suggested that I might shoot some meat, so that the boys whom he would send with me might be able to leave some for their wives and families.

The chief was rather tall and slender in figure. In colour he was a shade lighter than his *confrères*, and had an expression that might almost be called meek. The lips were very thick, and the *white* of the eye—as is characteristic of the negro—was blurred with streaky shades of deep brown.

John had been out hunting, and it was long after sunset when he returned. He had shot an eland cow, but reported game to be very scarce.

At this period the household were nearly all sick. Dysentery had set in. So I physicked the whole crowd— all in order—giving to the shamming ones a mighty dose of the ever-fateful podophyllin powder.

Sandani now divulged the intelligence that he could not leave to go on with the white man " much as he loved him," and so forth. The old fellow had certainly talked with us to such an extent that he had almost wholly lost the use of his voice. His presence had enabled us to reach a turning point in the fortunes of the expedition, and I really felt very grateful to the old man. As to the question of his not coming with us, the decision was not to be wondered at. Old Sandani had far too much to attend to, even in relation to his domestic affairs. What with his numerous family, and a wife or two at every rock about the country, his hands were pretty full; especially as he was always endeavouring to be everywhere at one and the same time, and had many loves besides the multitude of recipients of his lawful affection. His heart in love affairs was of a very elastic description.

Considering all this, I proceeded to cash his demands on the dry-goods bank, although every strip I gave him was like parting with an eye-tooth. John, who knew the close state of affairs, would now and again give vent to a gentle reminder.

"Ouh!" he would exclaim; "he want all de tings. And de master is geev um dat fine cloth what I like to take back to my leetle wife!"

"Never mind, John, keep up a light heart, there's plenty more cloth on the Zambesi."

About eight o'clock on the next morning, accompanied by Karemba and Sandani, I climbed up to the town, which occupies a half-hidden position on the northern slopes of the mountains, amid a huge agglomeration of rock comprising masses of granite, some rounded and showing a few seams, but mostly jagged, broken and angular. Overhanging boulders of gigantic size frown threateningly above the small clusters of rudely-formed huts, which dot the open spaces to the north.

Small shrubs, thorny trees, creepers, and long tufted grass spring out from the crevices in this wild and natural rockery. Upon the bare spots which intervene are to be found the huts of the artless, but contented and happy inhabitants.

We soon found ourselves at the "Rock of Wisdom," an immense slab of hard, slippery rock, polished doubtless by the feet of many thousands of assemblies; for here it is that the chief holds his court, and where the pipe of peace is passed, while the hoarse cough of the hemp smoker may be heard from dawn to sunset. This hemp-smoking produces a most violent irritation of the mucous membrane, and the continuance of the practice brings on hæmorrhage, ultimately causing death.

The chief invited us to his hut, where beer made from maize was produced. From the numerous huts which were dotted closely around, I could infer that Chibabura had numerous wives. The huts were irregularly scattered here and there, but all in close proximity to that of the chief.

Chibabura showed me what a large stock of beads he had, telling me that the beads and cloth that they had in their neighbourhood came from the Zambesi by way of Negomo's town. He likewise stated that the Portuguese sent black men out with trading articles to buy gold. One of these parties I afterwards met on my journey northwards.

Escorted by Chibabura we all walked to the "Rock of Wisdom," and from that position the chief pointed out the direction in which we were about to travel.

Our "coigne of vantage" commanded from its altitude a panoramic view of the whole of the outlying country. Expanding from left to right lay a vast forest-clad park, girded upon every side by towering precipitous mountains. Over the distant hills away to the north, in the direction we were to travel, twin peaks of basaltic rock spired heavenward in clearest grandeur, like the steeples of some gigantic structure, not fashioned by the hand of man, but suddenly reared by some wild convulsive throb of puissant nature. Beneath these natural spires was situated the town of Zingabila, which we were destined to pass.

Chibabura assured me that his boys would go with me to Kunyungwi.

There is but little difference in the people's mode of

living compared with the Mashona. The difference in dialect also seems to be slight. Chibabura's town was exceedingly dirty. The accumulation of years was seen in the heaps of rubbish of all descriptions which were strewn along the winding streets, and covered the ground on every hand.

The women and children eagerly crowded out of their huts to get a view of the white curiosity which had appeared. The thin wire ring which they wore in their upper lip was by no means ornamental. It must be uncomfortably in the way when they are eating. Numbers of Mashona people could be distinguished among the population.

Some of the women made a rapid retreat into their huts when I approached. Doubt and fear were clearly seen in their ebony faces.

But the little boys seemed to have the same instinctive curiosity which is to be found among white urchins. They gambolled about, and stalked and dodged me from behind the stones and huts.

Goats, hens, and in some instances cows, find room in the huts. Neither horses, pigs, nor donkeys were to be seen. The people have no idea that such animals exist.

Their blankets are manufactured from bark, which is also used for string and rope netting employed in the pursuit of game. It has many other purposes, however, for it is very strong, and the fibre can be used without preparation.

The pottery is of the commonest description, closely resembling that which I have seen in Mexico used for similar purposes. I also observed numbers of troughs and other vessels hollowed out of solid blocks of wood. None of the examples of their handicraft, however, showed the existence of taste; although now and then some rude attempts in the direction of decoration might be seen in carving and in brass wire-work.

"A favoured land and people!" was my mental exclamation, as we left the town of Chibabura. Ambition was wanting and glory was unknown. Contentment, the object of most of the aspirations of civilised life, reigned supreme in these heedless people's minds. Through the labyrinth of life, their path was clear, thoughtless and happy.

Their time was occupied in supplying daily wants, in herding their cattle, and in building their huts. Their short-lived hopes and fears referred only to the prospects of the crops and the possibilities of attack. They seemed to have no ideal god: no thought nor hankering after life immortal. From careful observation I might call them, Primitive Materialists, for they cannot conceive the existence of a soul life, nor believe in the maintenance of individuality after the breath has passed away from the earthly frame.

The dead are buried in an upright position, the bodies being wrapped with pliable branches, and the head near the surface of the earth. Some of the contiguous tribes, I have heard, bury their dead in a sitting posture, or rather with the body doubled-up.

There is music in their strange and weird-sounding songs, which they never seemed to tire of singing to the accompaniment of that odd-looking tinkling instrument, resembling a block of wood fitted with iron sliding keys. There is also a peculiar and by no means disagreeable rhythm in the expression of their long-worded and weighty speeches.

Necessity has been the mother of their invention of the hoe for husbandry, and the assegai for defence or defiance. The natural state of man it is said is a state of indolence, and in the rapid and deafening whirl of civilised life everybody aims at the acquisition of relief from the burdens of care, and peace amidst the turmoils of mankind. The Makorikori live and move in this coveted simplicity; and in some respects they are to be envied.

> "Earth hath been a peaceful place!
> Free from folly, free from jars,
> Were the simple, early race
> That could look upon the stars."

"What a character!" Cynical travellers might say, "Where is the redeeming feature?"

I will allow that they are an aggravating lot, through their indifference to the lapse of time. But we cannot be severe. Even the Government of this exemplary country of ours has let time slip away quite as heedlessly, when the sacrifice of thousands of human lives was the penalty for the indifference, and until the appeals and remonstrances of the martyr Gordon were heard only from his remote and mysterious grave.

What can the simple Makorikori know of the wide world in which he moves? What can he know of the mental greatness of cultured man, or the mighty influence and meaning of the Christian faith?

After all these ages of his forefathers' lives, he does not know how to cook his food decently. He throws his great handful of meal into an earthen pot, until it is too thick to stir, and he does not give it time to cook: he broils his meat, when he can get it, upon the embers. From an English point of view he is a filthy creature and smells like a badger. He has no idea of cleanliness; for the matutinal washing of face and hands is necessary in order to remove the soot and smoky filth which has gathered about his eyes during his sleep close to the edge of the fire.

What can he make? His assegais and hatchets are inferior articles at best, and it is not every Kaffir who can make these implements. The work is in the hands of the tradesman who has inherited the tools, which have been in use for ages, without an advance of skill. He displays not the slightest sign of ingenuity; his iron is found in a particularly favourable condition for working; his wire-work is of a very ordinary character, being either plain twist, three plait, or something equally as simple. Scratching the fertile earth is his only knowledge of agriculture.

His habitation in the rocks is not half as neat as the nest of the most careless of birds. He devours nuts, roots, and fruits like his brother the ape, the only superiority over his relative being that he has learned how to use fire in order to weld iron and to cook, or rather heat, his food. He is as easily amused as a child. In a human sense his life is a failure; he has no ideal; he is akin to the brutes of the field and the forest.

Against all these features we must remember, while admitting his backward state, how slow is the tide of progress where adversity has never been known.

Above everything, their contentment—a feeling quite unknown in civilised brains—is great! Of course I refer to this particular people, and not to all of the dark denizens of Africa.

I say that the progress of the Makorikori is nowhere, but contentment is seen everywhere. Where is vice? Where is crime? A domestic quarrel is of rare occurrence; murders are almost unknown.

The laws of the people are evidently effective as they stand. There are no jails. Murder is punished by death in some cases. The chiefs, however, seldom kill their people. Asylums are unknown, for in this country madmen are extremely rare. With clubs and sticks the thief is driven away from his home and from his tribe; in short, he is drummed out. Thus, or rather let me say, by natural instinct, good behaviour is a typical distinction of the people.

The traveller cannot help being impressed by the air of freedom which these primitive men and women breathe. They have a total want of anxiety; their children are as plump and round as distended bladders, no matter whether they are the offspring of a chief or of a slave.*

Suppose, for the time being, that the cultured blessings of civilisation give place to matters material, how infinitely preferable does the life of a Makorikori appear when compared with the struggle of a poor man in a crowded city of Christendom! The children of the latter are penned in narrow slums; they grow up stunted in body and depraved in mind, and anon the deep lines of care or crime appear prematurely upon their youthful brows.

The civilised poor man is not half so happy as the untutored savage, although the latter lives far beyond the sound of church bells. Can it be that heathen freedom and plenty in the wind-swept wilderness are preferable to civilised starvation in the polluted atmosphere of a rotten hovel? The subject is worthy of consideration.

* * * * * * *

The light of day is becoming dim. I look upon the peaceful and interesting scene of this sequestered retreat of the aborigine. Excepting the careless hand of chance, no influence has changed the even routine of the people's lives for generations past.

The naked herd-boys, with spears and "kerries," are

---

* I have, however, seen children from Mashona villages, after a Matabeli raid, so thin as to remind one of living skeletons.

driving the crowding cattle, which emerge from the gloom of the forest, into the rolling meadow beneath, and up the steep ascent towards the town. Long lines of women-folk are carrying in the produce of the gardens; happy children romp about, with a thick coating of dust upon their tiny but plump bodies, which makes them look like animated pods of clay. Slowly, and with a wearied gait, far behind the rest, older women follow, their shrunk and feeble forms denoting that their sun has nearly set. They still strain, however, under heavy loads of wood, their bodies covered with dust, and their ancient noses coloured with snuff.

One by one the crowd enter the narrow portals, and soon all are within the rock-girt citadel. No sound is heard save the lowing of the cattle, varied sometimes by the merry ripple of careless voices, and even these die away with the fading light.

Oh, happy and favoured Inyota! Long may the gentle winds of peace and freedom caress your mountain home!

Darkness quietly steals over the scene. Once more the town is hushed in sleep. The short day is again spent, and is a cypher in the illimitable numbers of the past. Soothed by the silence of the surroundings I sink to rest. Before the morning dawns we must be up and away, bidding a long farewell to Inyota's tranquil land.

CHAPTER XI.

AMONG THE MAKORIKORI PEOPLE.

Tedious marching—Magombegombe mountains—John is "varee seek".—Our comical goat—Baboons—Lubola mountains—Zingabila—Mode of making bark blankets—M'jela, the chief—Kunyungwi still far off—Desertions—Method of securing an ox—Difficulty in getting boys—Presents from M'jela—Umfana's eating powers—The Dorah river—Camping places selected by natives—A lioness in the way—Lost chances of a shot—John's lion experiences—A fearful position—A wild forest scene—Hovering vultures—Adventure with a lioness—Native scramble for the lion's prey—Happy natives—The Mutua river—The Ruiana river—The Makomwe mountains—An amusing old fossil—Long fasting—poor diet—The "dry goods bank" nearly empty—"How many moon's is dat since we leave Buluwayo?"—Miseries of travel—Native houses—The "Three Brothers"—The great basin of the Zambesi—Tropical forests.

A SILENT and lovely evening followed one of the hottest days which had been experienced during our long journey. Now the party was somewhat weary, for the march had been long and tedious. The many miles we had covered had carried us through tracts of marshy country, the deep black soil being intersected by numerous muddy rivulets. We had crossed the Ruia river, beside the headwaters of which we had encamped during the eventful journey to Chuzu's.

We were now holding upon a more easterly course. Chuzu's inhospitable country would, therefore, be left far to the south-west. We had to cross streams which had swollen to the proportions of goodly-sized rivers, and remembered that we had seen their original waters trickling in tiny rills in their rough and rocky birthplaces on the slopes of the Umvukwe mountains.

Our first camp was pitched in a cosy spot under the frowning shades of the Magombegombe mountains, consisting of gigantic rocks, which were as bare of verdure as blocks of well-hewn stone, and whose yawning, cavernous gaps had for ages been the trumpets of the storm, shrieking aloud or groaning dismally through the riven nooks.

Where, oh where! was that much longed-for Zambesi? I was beginning to think that it was a mirage of the map-makers. The fact was clear that my party would soon break up. There was but one course left for me, and that was to press on with all possible speed. The aspect of affairs was daily becoming more serious.

John's conversation was far from being inspiriting.

"Master, I am varee seek. I feel all de life" [he meant his body], "and dese peoples say that dey don't go to the rafeer. De town is long way dis side! Den I tink of my wife. My Gaut, I tink there is wanting in de house at home now! My heart is varee sore dis night."

"John, John!" I exclaimed, knowing his weak point; "elephants ahead, my boy. Never mind to-day—onwards!"

This chat occurred upon one of those nights when I had to cheer the man in his despondency. But now he proved to be inconsolable; therefore I told him that if he would go to the town to which our new guides would take us, he might afterwards return homewards. I would not ask him to go any farther; I would try and get Karemba to go with me. After this declaration I retired to my blankets.

When attempting to find repose, I found the old goat in an uncomfortably playful mood. It is curious what a lot of amusement may be found in observing the antics even of a goat, especially of such a truly comical one as ours. It had evidently a very hard day of it; stealing the bunches of corn which the Inyota had hung upon their spears, and being chased around the camp in a very lively manner by the owners. Our goat was an inveterate thief, and a wonderfully advanced animal of its kind. It was so tame that it became a nuisance, for its nose was never out of such pots and pans as we possessed, in spite of frequent singeing and burning. One of its tricks was to upset the baskets of rice, and run off with as much as it could.

But we were near the tsetse-fly country then, so that we should soon have to bury the poor old goat; and, perhaps, some others of the party, judging from the general expression in the features of the followers. One, especially, complained that his throat was swelling. There are times when one feels for men who struggle hard a sympathy as warm as though they were near of kin; but the indolent and the discontented are repelled with a heart colder than the drifting snow.

A chilly morning with a heavy dew awaited us after our night's repose. All the vegetation was wet, so that our legs were soon drenched to the knees; luckily no farther, because the grass was not long enough.

As we passed through the forest, or over winding, grassy belts, which run in and out between the sugar-loaf monuments of rock, and, at short intervals where vegetation is more abundant, amid rocky grottoes, we saw and heard numerous baboons (*Cynocephalus porcarius*), whose strange bark echoed and re-echoed as if they were inviting us to pay them a visit.

Upon one evening during our march I had watched a family of these creatures as they went to drink in regular lines, one before the other. Through the grass they had steadily beaten tracks to their drinking fountains, and back to their town sites, high up, encircled by rocks and small trees.

Moving along the foot-hills of this riven region of old volcanic forms, we gradually ascended until we reached the backbone of a high ridge, running in an easterly direction, and called Lubola mountains. Towards the west the great rock, which crowns the Barré mountain, was clearly visible. This we had first observed when we were upon the Umvukwe range. This igneous region is very striking. We passed a spot where the natives had evidently been reducing iron ore, for there were large heaps of slag from the furnace. But although I hunted diligently for the kiln, it could not be discovered. The iron ore had been brought from the neighbourhood of Negomo, near the Amazoe river.

Changing direction towards the east, we soon distinguished the twin peaks which had been seen from Inyota. We moved rapidly on, and shortly descended into a deep gorge, through which we passed to emerge upon a small plain clothed with a growth of low forest, and encircled by a slightly elevated chain of pointed mountains.

Here we halted, our position being close to the town which boasts of the peculiarly musical name of Zingabila.

As we approached the place, I had an opportunity of seeing the *modus operandi* of an important native industry. Bark blankets were being made close to our camp. Two boys had felled a tree, the bark of which they cut round about eight feet above the root. They then commenced to peel off the bark by means of two wooden adzes, removing it much in the same way as we would take off a long stocking, which is turned inside out during the operation, thus forming as it were a seamless kilt. The splitting down the sides is a subsequent piece of work. Considering the diligent manner in which they worked, the boys would certainly be able to turn out two or three blankets a day.

The stripping must be done while the tree is fresh. If it is allowed to lay even for a very short time the bark becomes too hard. After being taken off the tree, the bark is soaked, until the outer and harder surface is removed, leaving a blanket of wood-bark fibre of great durability;

MAKING BARK BLANKETS.

but I cannot say of extraordinary warmth. The women use these blankets as waist cloths.

The Zingabila people had seen us coming, and it was clearly apparent that our appearance had caused great excitement. They ran in every direction. To avoid any disagreeable event, and without losing time, I sent a message to the chief, to the effect that I would visit him, and bring him a present.

On the route we found the spoor of the rhinoceros, eland, and lion; but on the whole game was far from being abundant.

When going to the chief, I took with me the Matabeli boy, who was bright and intelligent, and even aspired to the position of our friend Sandani. I found it an easier task to make him understand me than the others. On such occasions John was not good at interpreting, saying that he could not well comprehend the Mashona tongue.

We were well received by a middle-aged man of moderate height, and of a type similar to Chibabura, whom we had lately left. The resemblance was so marked, that I need not tire the reader with a new description.

His town was literally, as I had been told, placed under the two great peaks; for just where we stood addressing the chief Mjela, their basaltic forms—needle like—tapered their points hundreds of feet above the group of dwellings.

The inhabitants, who pushed and eagerly crowded forward to see me, said that they had never seen a white man before.

Much to the satisfaction of the bystanders, I presented to the chief, through Umfana, a fine coloured blanket, of a yellow and red pattern, in alternate squares. It was very amusing to see the gratification he evinced when he received this present. He made one of his slaves stand on a rock in front and hold the blanket before him, stretched from hand to hand, so that we had an exhibition of a square curtain, with a black knob topping over the centre.

Mjela seemed to be a pretty good sort of fellow. I put a few questions to him about the distance between his town and Tette, or Kunyungwi, as these natives termed it.

He proceeded to describe a town which lay upon this side of the river. He had not been to Kunyungwi, but knew that it was very far away, pointing vaguely towards the east, in such a manner that we might be directed even beyond the rising sun.

According to his statements the town which lay ahead, away down in the great valley of the Zambesi, was called Chibinga, and was three days' journey from Zingabila. At Chibinga, he remarked, was a man who had bought gold from him.

"Ah!" thought I, "he must be Portuguese. We will soon be at the river, although still very far from Tette."

Mjela began to talk with great volubility, saying that he had been badly treated by the Chibinga people, whom he called Mzungo (white). He said that they had promised him rifles for gold, and when in good faith he had sent the gold, they had only sent him some cloth. The bearers of the cloth, therefore, he had kept as hostages, or rather prisoners, and would not release them until the promised rifles were sent. All this he wished me to say when I got to Chibinga.

I asked him if the people were white. His reply was, that they were not like me, but they called them Mzungo. Then he continued, at intervals, to count with his fingers, showing me, with three extended, the others closed, how long it would take to reach Chibinga.

At that time I thought, according to a hasty reckoning, which afterwards turned out to be correct, that we were still over seventy-three miles, in a straight line, from the river. Without including the natural deviations of travelling, this distance would mean twenty-four miles' journey every day. These men of mine could not do the distance in less than a week. Then I asked how long it would take to reach Kunyungwi by water. Could I get canoes, &c.?

The chief replied that Kunyungwi was on the other side of the water, and that we should have to go eight days on the river. From that assertion, I could see plainly that this worthy knew nothing about Tette. Notwithstanding this, however, I bargained with him to let me have the boys I required, as I anticipated desertion.

In return, he asked me how far it was to my home. I showed, by counting on my fingers, that it was ten full moons distant, a statement which called forth the loudest exclamations of astonishment, at what was to them an incalculable distance.

After rather a long conversation, much clapping of hands took place. I found, on my return to camp, that the chief had sent me a present of a goat.

I related to John the result of the interview, trying to make the distance look as short as possible. On being informed that we would have to canoe on the river, he said:

"Master, I don't go on de water. I frightened for dat!"

I saw immense numbers of the large crow with white collar, and some very pretty birds. The specimens I took were destroyed, so that, unfortunately, I am unable to classify them. Numbers of spoonbills and jays were seen, also shaft-tailed whydah birds breasting and fighting the wind.

A delay of several days occurred, owing to the desertion of seven boys who had been enlisted, in addition to those who were given me by Chibabura of Inyota. Desertion caused frequent trips to the town. During my last visit I had sat for hours awaiting the boys whom the chief had promised. My diversion, while wearily waiting, was watching the manner in which the people secured an ox. Two men, one on each side, held the beast, while another pierced the partition of the nose with an iron needle, about eighteen inches long, threading a thin rope of bark through the nostrils. Thus secured the animal was led down with me, accompanied by the chief, to the camp, where, over an earthen jar of beer, M'jela talked himself to utter fatigue.

He said that our old enemy Chuzu had many people, and was a very bad man. But he was a powerful chief. Mjela was not at all surprised at the way we had been treated. Had we stayed much longer, he said, we should certainly have been killed.

Beer was brought to the camp in large quantities by the women. Very reluctantly I bought it for the boys, giving away the last piece of white calico I had. Therefore I was compelled to stand and deliver some of our few remaining pieces of striped cloth.

The night was exceptionally cold, the camp lying low in the valley. At six o'clock in the morning the thermometer registered 42° Fahrenheit. The elevation was 3425 feet. At the same hour the most intense cold I have observed, in Mashona-land, was 35°.

The party was despatched on the route as soon as possible. I knew the lying proclivities of the chiefs, and did not expect the boys he promised early, or until I had actually gone personally to the town, and ferreted out the contingent.

John was far from being pleased at starting without me; but off he went, leaving behind three loads, and the ox which the chief had presented. The idea occurred to me that, if all plans failed in the effort to wrench boys from amongst these stubborn dwellers in the rocks, I would tie the loads on the back of the ox and advance, an operation, however, which might have required greater powers of persuasion than I possessed.

The fact of my not having killed the animal on the spot defeated the old chief's purpose. His evident intention was to keep me a longer time in his country.

When the party was off I, taking with me Karemba and

Umfana, repaired to the town with all haste. We found the old chief seated, as usual, in the calmest of attitudes, "sunning" himself upon a rock.

A picturesque looking figure was old Mjela's. The finely-decorated battle-axe, which he always carried, had a hard wood handle wrapped with a profusion of brass wire plaiting, besides which he had two very fine large knives. Asking him for what purpose he required so much knife power, he assumed a warlike pose and made a few passes, which he intended to have the effect of showing that with these weapons he was not only invulnerable, but unconquerable. From his movements, however, I judged that his gifts were more in the direction of ripping than thrusting.

As my things were all gone I began to beg, saying that I wished a knife to remember him by, but he shook his head, and said that he could not sell them without asking his women. To me such an answer from a Kaffir chief seemed wonderful. I was determined to have a keepsake from the old chief, so finally he presented me with a small brass-bladed knife which he carried in his necklace.

Mjela did not appear to be in a hurry, so I told him that the boys he had promised must come with me at once. His reply was that he liked me, and would be glad if I would stay longer in his country; to which I replied that at present such a delay would be impossible. When he was informed that the party had started, he seemed astounded. To Umfana he gave a present of a hoe, for having interpreted and spoken so well.

By that time Umfana had become a flourishing orator, and his capacity for eating was unrivalled. The chief's women gave him a large wooden bowl of corn-meal pap, which he wiped beautifully clean in a very few moments.

This feat accomplished, we made a start. Being one man short, I led the ox myself.

Starting off at a jog-trot, our path led us through a low, mountainous region. When we overtook the advance party, we proceeded six miles on our journey, arriving at the Dorah river, which was crossed, our camp being pitched on the northern bank. The Dorah has a rocky bed. Where we then were it was about fifty yards wide, and its look was that of a clear crystal stream. Twelve miles had been the length of our day's march.

I saw out-croppings of quartz, but none showed even the slightest traces of gold.

The night was bitterly cold. The camp was in a most unfavourable position, being much too low in the valley of the river, where a heavy vapour enveloped us. It was useless attempting to go on to higher ground. The Makorikori were not a whit better than the Mashona in that respect. They would not go far from water.

I have heard it stated that natives never camp where the fog hangs. Yet it has been my experience to learn that they do not give consideration to anything of the kind. They camp in a regardless way, provided water and wood for fires is close at hand. I have seen them even camp upon rocks in the very centre of a river.

These instances are cited merely to show the absolute indifference of the people to their surroundings. A traveller is helpless among them. While he is in their hands their chief aim is to get as much as possible out of him. We were seldom able to make an early start on account of all sorts of extortionate and dilatory schemes on the part of the natives.

More beads—oh, these eternal demands!—had to be given before a new start could be made. A promise had also to be given that if a really good march was effected the ox would surely be killed, at which announcement Karemba's joy was unbounded. The slaughtering was to be his privilege, and the hide his property.

Our advance led us through an undulating, or rather a hilly country, the shallow valleys of which were threaded by numerous tiny rivulets. Low forest growth, thicket and high grass, covered the rolling land. The vegetation seemed to be a first-class cover for wild animals.

And so it was. Just then my rather awkward line, which, like the poet's wounded snake, "dragged its low length along," received a check. The head suddenly swerved. The boys, in great alarm, threw down their loads, and fled towards the rear. What was the matter? Looking ahead I saw, much to my annoyance, a lioness leap into the thicket, after dropping a duiker which she had been carrying in her mouth. As usual I had been in the rear, endeavouring to push the men on—a duty I heartily disliked, but to which unfortunately I was becoming habituated. Oh, how many capital shots were missed in this manner!

The men did not condescend to proceed again until they had divided the lioness's spoil of duiker meat amongst them. We had not marched far when I saw agitated clouds of vultures hovering in the air, and winging their way above the trees directly before us. Where these were I felt sure there must be more meat, and probably lions.

I was afraid to call to John, who was ahead, to stop, because I was conscious of the fact that any extra noise might frighten the lions away should they be there.

As quickly as possible, therefore, I dashed past the carriers onward to the spot. Too late! John had gone blundering along without paying any attention to my strict orders that, should there be any signs of lions, he was to be sure and halt, in order to give me the chance of a shot; for it must be remembered that in this country, no matter how numerous these animals may be, success in "potting" one is not only mere chance, but also the reward of very careful stalking. The undergrowth is so thick, that their retreat is made sure by a single bound.

Through the leafy branches of the trees standing immediately in front of us, I could see a lion and a lioness. Evidently startled by the noise made by our party, they for a moment stood at attention to see what was the appearance and character of the bold intruders who dared to interrupt their sumptuous meal, consisting of two zebras, which lay dead beside them.

I saw we had been detected, so I bounded on as quickly as possible, trying to get round the trees in order to have a shot. Too late again, but just in time to get a very good view of both, although there was not the slightest chance of a shot, for they were off in the high grass, over which I could just discern the top of the head of the male. I continued to entertain a hope that he would stop, but he was soon out of sight; and so another chance was gone.

As I had rushed past John, I called out to him to come along, thinking that his experience would be of some assistance in raising the beasts. His only response was the confession, "Master, I am very frightened thes day."

On consideration I thought that I might not have been so ardent in the chase had I possessed his experience of lion hunting, for on a previous occasion John had been treated in a very rough manner by one of the kings of beasts.

While out hunting with a number of boys he had shot at a fine lion and wounded him. Reloading as quickly as he could, he had looked for his game in order to give the *coup de grâce*, when to his surprise he found that the first shot had had no effect beyond firing the fury of the animal, which now ran with great speed towards its enemy.

John at once threw down his gun, and bolted for dear life. But in speed the lion was too much for him. Poor John was overtaken in an instant, seized at the small of the back, the brute's fangs piercing the two large muscles which are situated beside the vertebræ. The unfortunate man was thrown violently to the ground. The lion then literally tore the flesh off his legs and thighs. It was only the continued shouts and yells of the whole party, none of whom had guns, that finally made the lion run off. Wonderful to relate, John rapidly recovered from his wounds.

But never afterwards did he yearn for lion hunting. As Mr. Selous hinted to me at Buluwayo, this horrible experience had shaken John's nerve in such circumstances.

I determined not to abandon the spot where the meat was, thinking that its attractions would soon bring the lions back again, when I would try my luck. Going on with the carriers for about half a mile, we arrived at a small watercourse, and I said that there we would camp, while to the immense delight of the company I also agreed that the ox might be killed.

With "C. L. K." in my hands, I asked Karemba to go with me, but he said he did not like to go. Force would be of little use under the circumstances, so I departed on the doubtful venture without a companion. I waded through high grass and plunged through thorn and thicket until the spot where the lions had been seen feasting upon the zebras was reached. The bodies were quite fresh, evidently lately killed. The lions had been hungry, for they had made away with the greater portion of the flesh.

What a wild forest scene this was! Low in the air the

vultures were flying above the bodies of the lions' prey. I crept into a small bush which stood within three yards of the dead zebras, so that if the lions came back to their interrupted meal, I might be able to get a good shot, late in the evening though it was. Certainly under the silvery light of the moon a deadly shot might have been made at this close range, and when first I took up my position the wind was blowing favourably, that is to say if the lions came from the direction in which I had last seen them.

It is difficult to describe how such a scene as this delights the heart. Thoroughly wild it was, and exciting as well; for there seems to be a charm in reclining in and watching the forest homes of wild beasts, looking upon the struggle that the animals have for their rough subsistence, and noting their various grades of strength lessening, in this case, until the smaller crows might be seen pouncing upon the morsels dropped by the voracious vultures in their determined fight for food.

The vultures seemed to darken the air. They hovered about the place, and were quick to detect the slightest movement I might make. Getting into a comfortable position, I remained motionless, and the birds came down in flocks.

The variety was remarkable. Some were very large, with a dark brown plumage; others, slightly smaller, perhaps, had grey feathers. I lay so quietly that they perched upon the branches just above my head, even within a couple of feet of me. Here was a splendid opportunity for an observant naturalist. The heads of the birds varied very much, some being wholly white; some having white faces and black caps falling over the back of the head; and some with white and pink hoods, and with naked flesh, coloured heads and necks. Great numbers of crows—white-collared

"WITH A LOW GROWL SHE STALKED THROUGH THE TALL GRASS."

crows and ravens—formed a large circle outside the scene of operations filled by their death-loving kin.

Soon my attention was otherwise engaged. A rustling was apparent in the high, rank grass directly in front of my position. I waited and watched attentively.

The lioness! Yes; but unfortunately now there was no wind, except an occasional and very gentle breath. With a low growl she stalked through the tall grass. Had she got my wind? Something must have been wrong, for I was motionless, and held my very breath in my anxiety to bag a fine leonine specimen.

At shady sundown I still lay in the same position, and the lioness came again. But she would not venture out upon the little open patch where lay the zebras. She assuredly must have winded me. I waited until late in the night, when clouds were coursing across and obscuring the friendly moon, and the gathering darkness urged me to retreat in case I might be no longer the hunter but the hunted.

I had some difficulty in finding my way back to the camp, but by listening attentively I distinctly heard the chatter of many voices becoming nearer and clearer in the pulseless air, and suddenly, when the lost light of the moon flashed out from a rift of the darkening clouds, I could distinguish in the open glade numbers of boys armed with assegais advancing quickly. They were my own Inyota lads, come forth in search of me.

After hearing the particulars about the lions, the Inyota said they would like to go and take the meat which the lions had left. By no means reluctant to see the scramble, I went back with them. We were soon on the spot, and they at once began operations under the restless gleams of the moon, for no fire was made—they were too impatient for that. Little delay occurred in their attack upon the abandoned prey. An animated scene was the onslaught; for spears, axes, and knives, were quick at their gory work of chopping, cutting, and stabbing, while the greedy horde tore at the flesh, squabbling and even fighting over leg bones and other tit-bits which stirred their gluttonous desires. The scene baffles description. Over the carcases human blood even was spilt, for two men were severely wounded in the combat. To me it was a wonder that some of the flesh-loving belligerents were not killed outright.

"Let him take who has the power, and let him keep who can," was the order of the time; and at last Might again was Right, and every bit of meat found its way to a successful fighter. Even the unclean ribs of one of the zebras which the lions had gnawed, and the vultures pecked, had been gladly seized.

Lions were evidently numerous here. Shortly after we were in camp we heard their roars; and after the chorus had subsided, and slowly died away, there arose the wild, screaming laughter of hyenas, making the dismal hours of night more melancholy, until the grey dawn appeared bringing light and peace.

Sleep was, to me at least, impossible amidst those hideous sounds. Every now and then I would awake startled by the inharmonious howls of the hyenas. On that occasion they were too much for me. I sat up and looked around. Smoke rose from the smouldering fires, and sinuously swept around the strings of meat which hung upon the rude aboriginal spits.

On every hand lay the Kaffirs, their heads resting upon their wooden pillows, and their bodies—as stiff as sticks—stretched out like leathery corpses, exposed to the cold and the heavy dew, with nothing between their nakedness and the stars which sparkled in the far-off heavens.

"Ah!" thought I; "wonderful men, happy men! Your physical miseries are still in the dim future side by side with your mental enlightenment. With civilisation strange troubles will fall upon you. Oh, marvellous men! natural beasts, but happy mortals! Will your blight come with the advent of the white man's boasted institutions? Will civilisation fetter your freedom, and rob you of health? Now you move in abject ignorance. The dome of heaven is your covering, and the wild prairie grass your only bed. And yet you are contented beasts, happy mortals, and, perhaps, although you do not know it, favoured immortals."

Almost wishing I was a savage, I again lay down to rest. Bad luck had disappointed me. Had it not been for the difficulties with the men, which were every day, almost hourly, thrust in my path, I would certainly have waited longer in a country which was so favourable for hunting lions.

But three moons had grown old and vanished since we left Matabeli-land, and even now there were no signs of the Zambesi. According to my reckoning, a week must elapse before we could reach the river under our present conditions.

The old chief at Zingabila had talked with great volubility, and if they did nothing else, his speeches had the good effect of elevating the falling spirits of the household, which had been sadly in need of active stimulants. In reality, however, his talk had helped very little.

He had spoken of Mzungo, which is the name the natives in that quarter have given to the Portuguese; but I was unable to learn from him whether or not, from the town in our line of march, we should be able to canoe down some river flowing to the Zambesi.

Surmises, however, were unavailing. Many a mile had still to be traversed, and nothing could be done, except pushing onward in whatever way we could until they were accumulated in our wake.

A northerly course was pursued on the following day. We soon left the light forest, and moved into a country clad with very thick bush, affording a thoroughly good shelter for wild animals.

A large stream, called the Mutua river, flows here, on its course to the Amazoe, passing through a bed of rough shingle. High reeds line the banks. Leaving here, we penetrated into thick, low forest, through which we tramped for about seven miles, and reached the banks of another large affluent of the Amazoe river. This was the Ruiana, and if a safe opinion may be formed from the appearance of the rotting reeds, which had evidently been laid low by the wild waters of the angry autumnal floods—although now the reeds were twenty feet above the bed of the stream—the inference was clear that during high waters, or periodical inundations, the stream is at least 200 feet in breadth, and of a very considerable depth.

We ascended its northern bank. From its elevations we could look back upon the land through which we had passed. The Lubola mountains, which had been climbed, stood clearly out, and high in the distance rose the bold heights of Zingabila, with the tall twin beacons glistening like silvered granite under the glare of an African noonday sun. Following the course of the same chain of mountains towards the left, we saw a prominent eminence which had the name Sakare, the chief of the place being Umgezi. Farther on, in the same direction, the ridge is terminated by a pyramidal mountain called Vura. The chief of this district is named Makomo.

The Makomwe mountains were our next ascent. By the time that the dark shadow of the Dingamombe mountain, a broad-based, isolated pyramid on our left, was thrown upon us by the lowering western sun, I was influenced to make a camp, partly through the fact that numbers of very excited, and even terror-stricken individuals, were darting past us, and disappearing as quickly as they came to view.

No town was visible, but notwithstanding this I made up my mind to camp where we were.

In a harvested field Karemba and myself took a seat upon a log; where around us the crisp and parched corn-stalks lay scattered upon the ground.

Karemba I soon despatched to try and find some water. He succeeded in unearthing a very old and foxy fossil of humanity from the cover of the neighbouring mealy stalks, and this ancient showed us a very stagnant-looking pool. We tried to make him understand that we wanted a purer water; but when the old boy got a fair look at me—he was so blear-eyed that he could not see until I was close up—he, in a most comical fashion, turned his back and marched away, heedless of our shouts, until his figure was slowly lost in the thicket. Apparently he had got a proper fright, thinking, doubtless, that I was the ugliest living thing that had ever been seen, according to the memory of the oldest inhabitant.

No human habitation was visible. I lay under a tree to await the arrival of the party, which loitered far behind. I had had nothing to eat or drink since seven o'clock in the morning—eleven hours' fasting. My mode of life had been akin to this for some time. Two meals a day were revelry under the circumstances. And the rations were

plain, decidedly plain, for they could not go beyond rice
and meat, and porridge made from maize meal. I have
mentioned meal and rice, but, now that I remember, both
were exhausted by that time. Coffee, tea, and sugar were
luxuries belonging to bygone days.

Notwithstanding all these drawbacks I was well in health
and lively in spirits, although my feet were in a terrible
condition, badly blistered and literally torn, through the
working of the old boots as they were wearily drawn through
wet and heavy land which was almost morass.

Aggravation came from other sources as well. The "dry
goods bank," for example, was now on the shoals of in-
solvency. Lately some unexpected calls had been made
upon it, and with one or two more of the same kind a
suspension of payment would be inevitable. Meal was
scarce for the men, and it would be expected that I should
buy some at this unlooked-for town. Of course I should be
compelled to refuse, and to put off the purchase until we
reached the town of the Mzungo.

Amidst these reflections I fell asleep. Some time afterwards Karemba awoke me, bringing some rice and meat
stew. I must have slept very soundly, for before me the
camp fires were now blazing cheerily, and the skerm was
made. On such occasions, and not unfrequently, it would
have required the heavy report of an elephant rifle, fired at
close quarters, to rouse me from the arms of the all powerful
son of sleep and god of dreams.

At the first waking glance poor John was not to be seen.
Looking about, I ultimately discovered him beneath a large
tree close to the skerm, his hat pulled over his eyes, while
his attitude and features formed a living picture of unutter-
able woe.

The thin and ever delicately graceful crescent of the new

moon shone clear amid the stars. Nights like this had all the enchantment of absolute loveliness, but in John's melancholy mind they opened a vein of thought trending in the direction of home.

"Master," he would say, "how many moons is dat since we leave Buluwayo?"

After telling him the number of moons, I changed the subject. This time I said:

"Ah! well, John, we shall have to kill the poor old goat now, for we shall be into fly country before we know it."

"No, sir; we shall not him keel. I wants to take him back to my wife, and let him stop mit me ther."

The goat, however, had to be left behind at this point of our journey. Truly I felt sorry for John, because I knew he hated this wandering life. Regarding the latter part of the route, I too had good cause to be sick of it. Therefore I had fully intended to release him at the next town, whatever might be the circumstances or the consequences.

The name of the mysterious contiguous town was said to be Shitimba. At sunrise on the following morning I was up and away on a reconnoitring expedition, for it would be necessary to say a word or two to the chief before proceeding farther.

Having found out that the chief was at another town, I, without further inquiries, cleared out, journeying on as rapidly as possible in the hope that before night our eyes and hearts would be gladdened by a change of scene. At that time the elevation of the land through which we were travelling was so great that it was impossible to think that we could be near the big river.

My heart, like the hearts of so many of the natives who were refused presents, was "sore." A catastrophe would have been welcome, and even a hissing shell ready to burst in our midst might not find me thankless for its appearance. The spirits of the household were frozen far below zero. A sad plight truly! To the African traveller a light heart is as indispensable as a savourless palate. Contented, indeed, is he who can see a comical side even to misery! Not a soul at that time had any interest in or sympathy towards my movements. Sulks were in the ascendant, and not one of the party cared a straw about the doings of his neighbour.

A northward line of march led us past the town of Shitimba. On our right and also on our left the flat crowns of the low mountains were dotted with the houses, which in form differed greatly from those we had been accustomed to see in the rocky regions of the south. They were actually houses on stilts, being fixed upon poles at a distance of about six feet from the ground. In this manner, also, the corn bins are protected from the ravages of the white ant, a destructive creature which we had seen but little of since we left Matabeli-land.

When we had proceeded a little farther, three detached mountains of solid rock in the shape of cones broke upon our view towards the west. Not being able to find out a native name, I called them the Three Brothers.

The beginning of our descent of the northern side of the tree-mantled mountains of Makomwe was almost imperceptible, because, although broken by rough ravines and rounded ridges, the actual slope was very gentle. Shortly I distinguished in the distance a small blue spot in the forest. It told that the northern limit of the range had at last been reached. As we advanced the spot grew larger, expanding quickly before our gaze, until the dead monotony of the trees which had hemmed us in formed the background of our position. Wearied eyes were then freed from the long-continued and dismally-contracted view of mountain, hill and dale, and looked forward with refreshing clearness upon a vast expanse of varied land stretching far and wide, bright under the powerful silvery rays of a vertical sun.

There could be no mistake. At last outstretched before us we saw, a thousand feet beneath, and reaching far to the hazy horizon, the great basin of the Zambesi!

A tropical forest, in all the luxuriance of its beautiful foliage, and its varied shades of green, with here and there the light and fainter tints of sun-parched leaves, lay extended almost boundlessly before us. Gigantic trunks of the baobab were dotted here and there, reminding one of the towers of many lighthouses rising from a vast ocean of leaves. Not a sound broke the stillness. The appearance conveyed to my mind a strong idea that we should soon plunge into a zone of excessive heat.

CHAPTER XII.

ENTERING THE "FLY COUNTRY."

A descent into heat—Tea the best drink—Drinking generally—Rhinoceros—Symptoms of another strike—Intense heat—Msingua river—Suru—"Dar is the tsetse fly now, master!"—The "Fly Country" at last—An odd hue and cry—Mysterious words—Strange conduct of the guides—Unravelling the mystery.

THE country of the Makorikori, in which we had spent so long and so eventful a time, was now left behind, and it was not without satisfaction that we began the abrupt descent to the foot-hills of the Makomwe mountains.

Night was rapidly darkening our way, and as water was scarce, and the day had been a thorough "scorcher," we pitched camp in a sag on the breast of the mountains in proximity to a rocky gulch. The position was some distance from water, and there was little pleasantness in the general state of affairs, for we were short of provisions, and for some days had been living upon unvarying meat.

I felt as though I had an absorbing craving for tea. Living upon meat alone is a nauseating experience. What a powerful effect is felt by any one who after acquiring a strong predilection for, and becoming habituated to, any special kind of diet or drink, is suddenly deprived of the means of gratifying his appetite! It seems as though the article lost was the only thing that could make life bearable, or even desirable.

Speaking only for myself, although it may be mentioned

that I have noticed the same with others similarly situated, I say that as a thoroughly refreshing drink during fatigue, or for quenching violent thirst, HOT TEA is the best; for I cannot acquiesce to the common belief in the desirability of carrying bottles of cold tea, coffee, or any other beverage intended to be quaffed during the march, or when hunting, while the body is heated. Experience has taught, not only in Africa, but in other lands where I have had by no means an inconsiderable share of fatigue, that the human system is never invigorated, not to speak of benefited, by drinking anything cold or spirituous while the body is exposed to the fiery rays of a tropical sun. It is a good plan to do as the animals do—wait till sundown. Then when cooled off, or even before cooling, a small drink, so long as it is warm, will refresh the system besides assuaging the thirst. Provided any one begins to drink drops of water or cold tea, or tipples on something else, nothing less than absolute immersion and partial asphyxiation will check the craving, and that only temporarily.

I have heard people urging strongly the axiom that it is well to follow the habits of the natives as the proper system to adopt when travelling in their country. Had I followed the practices of the Kaffirs in regard to their water libations and ablutions I am positive that I never would have crossed the Orange river. A Kaffir is a wonderful creature in that way. He never thinks of what is beneficial or hurtful. Even when perspiration is flowing from every pore in his skin, he will plunge headlong into any cold and crystal water that may be near, disporting himself merrily in its refreshing coolness, and gulping at the same time big mouthsful of the welcome draught. This I have seen on many occasions.

For some time before we camped, the roars of lions were

heard, the result being that we were almost deprived of water for the night, for nothing would induce the Kaffirs to go and fetch it, unless they were supported by a rifle. I went with them, and they carried their assegais and firebrands. We had a good deal of searching before we found the spring, which was hidden in a deep rent in the rocks, which were exposed to the action of the torrents during the rainy season.

After this, the temper of the company, which was mercurial in its sensitiveness, pointed to fairer weather; for the Inyota men said: "To-morrow, we will be sure to reach the town."

During the night a black rhinoceros ran past at a great speed, breaking the brushwood, and creating much nervous excitement in camp.

Morning brought the old and familiar cries for a "strike," which, however anxious I might be, I could not then compromise in the way that these black cormorants would like; because I had no white calico left, not even a single yard. White calico they *would* have, and failing that, they expected me to tear up my red blankets and divide the pieces among them. The innocent audacity of the last demand was very amusing.

The gift of a few beads gave them but slight gratification. It was highly diverting to watch these big men stringing their precious beads, the sight carrying the thoughts back to the very early days of childhood.

About eleven o'clock we were again on our way, diving into the heated forest. Henceforth the fresh climate of the highlands was also to be numbered among the comparative comforts which had been left behind. As we descended, the heat became intense and oppressive, it being now the hottest time of the day. The sensation reminded me of the feeling of going from the cool to the hottest room in a

Turkish bath. The men were pouring with perspiration, and their bronzed bodies shone as though they had just emerged from the vasty deep.

In time we reached the bottom of the steep descent, and struck away into the torrid belt. Not a breath of air moved. The forest seemed actually to hold the heat. Thorny acacias were abundant, but they afforded no shelter. The only shelter that could be found from the resistless burning sun was in the lee of the baobab (native name *mulambo*), some of which were of gigantic dimensions, although, comparatively speaking, their branches seemed to be very small. The only sign of life was the winging of some grey plantain eaters (*Chizæris concolor*), which constantly took their short flights from tree to tree as our advance disturbed their silent or sequestered retreat.

A couple of hours of a melting walk brought us to the banks of the Msingua river, where we found a small town called Suru. The headman soon put in an appearance, for quite a stir was caused by the arrival of the white man and his escort.

The headman was a fat and far from unintelligent looking man. Around his loins he wore a cloth, and he stood before me in a position of attention. Then he drew back his right foot, scraping it upon the ground as he did so, a proceeding which was repeated with the left foot, while he clapped his hands and saluted me. I could see at a glance that this man had been trained by the Portuguese, or perhaps by their offspring, or dependents.

The people appeared to be friendly, but very much amazed. Although I am able to speak Spanish pretty fluently, my Portuguese is rather questionable; still, I tried to discover if any of our new friends could speak the latter tongue, but not a word could be extracted.

A large baobab-tree stood in the centre of the village, and the chief led me to its shade. The village consisted of circular huts with roofs like Japanese umbrellas, made of cane, and thatched with grass. Some of the huts were enclosed by cane fences, and, as a whole, the village had a very tidy appearance.

A cane mat was given me to sit upon, and unaccustomed to such attentions, I felt as if I had been given a bounce upwards in rank and consequence.

Beer was produced, and then I determined to start a conversation.

All at once I felt a sharp sting at the back of my neck. At the same time John made a wild clutch at something, as he exclaimed :—

"Dar is de tsetse fly now, master; we have leave de old gout in time!"

It did not take long to become painfully accustomed to the sharp reminders of these little pests, whose presence showed that we were in the "fly country," as the infested land is termed. At that time a few fowls were the only domesticated live stock that could be seen.

"Who is the chief who owns or rules this country?" was my first question.

"The name of the king," was the reply, "is Sakanii. He is Mzungo [white man]."

"Then," I responded, "his colour is something like mine."

"Oh, no!" said the chief, "I never saw a man like you before; he is something like him," pointing to John.

"How far is it to the town?" I asked.

"Not far," he said, showing by the sun how long the journey would take.

"Will you give me a guide?"

The answer to this question was that he, himself, would

guide me; but we should in the meantime have to wait until word was sent to the king that I was in the country. I should have to stay where I was until an answer had been received.

This, I thought, was a strange decision. If his majesty was a Portuguese then he had evidently become acclimatised in mind, and had also adopted the customs of the natural sons of the soil. Nevertheless I felt that a great weight had been lifted from my shoulders. After all our dreary and fatiguing marches, and our harassing wrangles with the different tribes, we stood at last in the basin of the Zambesi. Only a short time ago we had been upon the eve of failure, but now I felt assured that we would obtain fresh supplies and strike off direct to the Lakes.

Just after sunset two of my assegais were stolen. Informing the chief of the theft, he immediately went through a most amusing procedure. As he walked through the small streets of the town, he stormed and raved furiously, letting the people hear what was doubtless very strong language, but the real drift of which was:

"Bring back the assegais! Bring back the assegais of the white man! If Sakanii hears that we have robbed the white man he will kill us."

The excited walk of the chief gradually became a run, in which some others joined as supporters, and before midnight he appeared with the assegais, much to my delight, for they had a history, and of course were all the more valuable to me on that account.

The chief likewise brought the news that Sakanii was away at his town on the Zambesi river, and it was not known when he would return. Consulting my map, I found that from where we were to the river, the distance, in an air-line, was about fifty-three miles.

A long palaver ensued. Mystery seemed to cloud its words. Why should I stay here, as the chief desired, until Sakanii was informed of my arrival? Could I not, in any case, go on to his town, and hear what his people said; he must surely have subordinates?

No satisfactory reply could be had. I concluded therefore that to go ahead was the only plan to adopt. To be left at this spot would indeed be an awkward position, for how could I get out of it with sufficient goods to pay my way?

The night was warm, and the first blush of morning presaged a day of scorching heat. The indescribable glow of coloured light which heralded the advent of the sun told me clearly what was before us and made me anxious to hurry the men towards making a start.

The approach to the king's town was not made without a series of not only mysterious, but actually nervous signs on the part of our guides, who numbered about a dozen. Halts were repeatedly made and consultations held. I was quite unable to learn from John what it all meant. He was as much puzzled as I was.

This position was very trying to the temper, for I understood that we were approaching the town of a Portuguese.

Six miles were traversed, during which we crossed and recrossed the winding course of the Msingua river. The guides then said that it would be well that my party should now remain where they were, and that I should go on and see the man who was in charge of the town.

I lost no time. Taking Karemba with me, and armed with a small rifle in case we should meet game, we set out to unmask the strange mystery. Only one man accompanied us as a guide.

CHAPTER XIII.

CHIBINGA.

Skulls on gate-posts—Black but *not* comely—Meaning of Mzungo—A dubious reception—Karemba's *nonchalance*—Marching into the town—Confusion of tongues—Undesirable quarters—A waterless river—Hungry retainers—Absence of King Sakanii—Hunting, a last resource —The mother of the monarch—Rats swarming—A mutilating wolf—Inyota *versus* women—"Satan" is bibulous—Flies in myriads—Signs of disaffection—Negotiations with the "faithfuls"—Truculent Inyota —The monarch's mother commands my attendance—Curious reception—Hopes revived—Deplorable servility—Comparison with Mexican peone—The palmero punishment—" Us shall die from de hunger " —I start in search of the King—Bringing down a boar—Game on the route—The Mkumbura river—Spoor of wild animals—The busy tsetse—Description of the tsetse—A lion adventure—Fierceness of heat—The Umzengaizi river—Msenza—Meeting with Sakanii—Courteous greeting—Civilised comforts—The king's mode of travelling —His Portuguese connection—Returning to Chibinga—The king's bearers—Rapid progress—Prospects of relief—Noisy welcome to Chibinga.

WE soon arrived at the outskirts of the town, which was situated on the north bank of the Msingua, and was encircled by a high pole fence. As we approached the entrance, great numbers of people flocked to witness our arrival. I observed that a human skull was fixed upon the top of each post at the entrance gate.

We pushed our way through the surging throng and reached the centre of the town. There we found a sort of plastered divan, under a thatched roof, serving as a shade from the sun, and supported by a number of poles.

Beneath this shade stood a man blacker than ebony,

the proverbial black of blackness. The figure was dressed in a suit of coarse white cotton. Head-dress there was none.

I had been on the look out for somebody a little whiter, so I turned and said—

"Where is Mzungo?"

They intimated that the black object under the shade was Mzungo (white man).

Merciful powers! Had my vision been deceived for a lifetime? If this was white, where under the heavens could black be found? The fact was clear that if these so-called Mzungo were all like this man they had been called white because their clothes were white.

I walked up and shook hands with him, an act which it was only too clear was most repugnant to his feelings. At the time I remember being much impressed with the idea that never in my life had it fallen to my lot to see a worse physiognomy than his. He could not speak Portuguese, and looked very much annoyed about my arrival.

The crowd pressed round the house, listening with evident amusement to what the chief said. I could see that the people shuffled their feet as they approached the jet-like figure. One by one, before seating themselves upon the ground, would go through the formality of raising dust.

It was very amusing to note Karemba, who evidently wanted to show that he was no commoner. No shuffling of feet for him; he was a free son of the mountains, to whom such a silly ceremony had no meaning. With an air of great superiority, he walked in front of this black and earthly deity and requested a light for his pipe, which he wore as a pendent ornament when he was not smoking. The fact, too, of his having a hat and shirt gave impressive effect to his *tout ensemble*.

The dark enigma utterly ignored my presence. Worse

than that, none of us could understand a word that these people said. Although I continued to speak in my very best mixture of Portuguese and Spanish, I signally failed to create the slightest impression. He was the most uncouth being whom I had yet encountered.

Among the motley crowd which stood around was one old man who kept saying Guerra, guerra! Under the impression that I might be able to gather some hints from this old fellow, I abruptly left the inhospitable circle, signing to him to follow as I took my departure.

"*Elle tem mêdo de guerra!*" (he is afraid of war) the old boy continued to repeat. This, of course, was to me very ridiculous. He could not comprehend any question I put to him, so I proceeded towards where my party had been left, leaving him standing in silent solitude.

En passant, I may say that afterwards I discovered that these tribes have reason to be timid, through the petty wars which are being continually waged amongst themselves.

Despite the discouraging reception, I thought it would be as well to bring forward the party. We were soon within the skull-bedecked portals of the town; into which we marched with all the pomp of a conquering army. Everybody seemed to be frightened; not excepting the double-dyed, black-looking rascal I had previously addressed. Not a trace of him could be seen. We halted in front of what had the appearance of being the lounging place of the monarch—whoever he might be—during the heat of the day.

By this time we were a thoroughly mixed crowd. Few could understand what their neighbours said, so that we had all the confusion of a modern tower of Babel

Strange to say, Umfana, whom we had always termed the Matabeli boy—although I am convinced that he was a

Mashona—could get on better with the language spoken here than any of the others. Therefore I sent him off as an ambassador to anyone who might appear inclined to listen to the proclamation that I was going to the Zambesi; that I wished to have a hut for my boys and for myself; and that it was my desire to see the great king Sakanii.

Who should appear but the veritable black man in the white cloth! Umfana had clearly succeeded in persuading him that our mission was not one of war, and that we were not bent upon demolishing the town.

John, who looked as if he were listening to the thunders of the Last Day, rapidly approached.

"Master," said he, "dat black man is asking Umfana what for de master walk up to him mit de assegai, and Karem mit de gun and all de cartridges. Master, dese Portuguese is olful black."

Of course, I told John, that so far I had not seen a Portuguese. Regarding what he said about my approaching the chief with an assegai in my hand, it was simply the way I had always travelled—that is to say either with a gun or an assegai. It never occurred to me that I was warlike; but no doubt the assegai gave me a bellicose or sanguinary aspect.

After a good deal of meditation and deliberation, the white man with the black knob sent some slaves to show us the huts. One which was circular, and 15 feet in diameter, I gave to the boys. The other, which I retained for my own use, was a small oblong building, evidently very old and very much off the straight. Its walls and floor were smeared with mud; the roof was a network of cobwebs, among which hung pendants of soot, like jet-black icicles; a window about the size of a family Bible admitted the struggling light; and mingled with all these appearances was the olfactory perception of a diabolical odour, which would have suffocated an attic lodger in the Seven Dials.

A filthy abode, sure enough! But within its walls all our goods were stored. The thought often crossed my mind: "How infinitely preferable it would be to camp in the woods." And yet I had good reasons for taking quarters at this filthy place. I well knew that my party was bound to break up very soon, and that I should have to proceed alone; therefore a repository in which to leave my goods—what little there was left—was essential.

Every observation tended to show that my calculations with regard to our geographical position had been correct. Notwithstanding this, all dreams of canoeing had to be utterly abandoned when I looked upon the river on whose bosom we were to float to the Zambesi. Before us was the waterway's silent bed cut deeply down through sandy, alluvial strata, leaving steep banks on the sides bearing the marks of places where wild currents had played with the greatest force. Where was the water? Certainly not here; for nothing but sand, interminable sand, could be seen. We had traced it for miles, but had not seen even a solitary pool that might lead one to hope that water would be found a little farther down its arid course!

Canoeing indeed! What did Chief Mjela mean? There, before us, were the women digging holes in the heated sand in order to procure a supply of drinking water.

Above all things in my mind was the predominating thought: "Where are the beads and the cloth which will enable me to satisfy my men?" This was no white man's town: it was a regular Kaffir kraal! I had inquired if cloth could be purchased. There was none. All I had left were a few pounds of beads and four blankets, besides the two or three yards of striped cloth which I had promised to John for his "leetle wife."

The men came forward in a body, and, patting their bellies, which certainly did look rather baggy, declared—

"We are hungry; give us cloth, and we will buy some meal." What was to be done? Before anything, it was necessary that the individual who ruled the town during the absence of Sakanii should be unearthed.

By a bit of good fortune a man turned up who could talk well with Karemba. He offered his services to show where game was to be found. I was determined not to rest or wander until I had cleared up the situation; so I made use of the man by persuading him to procure a messenger who would convey to Sakanii the intelligence that I was in the town. The people of the town would not do anything for me until they received orders from the king. The letter I sent to Sakanii was written in the best Portuguese at my command, and the man who took it said that he might be back in five days. The town of the king was on the Zambesi, and was called Chigurindi.

With the first streak of dawn John and myself were up and away in search of the much-longed-for meat. We moved out in different directions. Game was found to be very shy; but by noon we had both returned, I having bagged a very fat bush-pig and a fine specimen of the wart-hog with good tusks; while John had shot two Koodoo bulls (*Strepsiceros Kudu*), although he was able to secure only one of them. I had seen a big herd of eland, but could not get within range, as they had seen me. The spoor of white rhinoceros was discerned; but these animals are remarkably scarce in this neighbourhood. Black rhinoceros are more plentiful.

Having been informed that the mother of Sakanii lived

in a big round hut, enclosed by a thatch fence of high grass, and as it was hinted that she was the supreme dictator during the absence of her son, I sent her a large supply of meat, an act of courtesy and diplomacy which brought forth in return two baskets of tomatoes and one large basket of meal. The exchange was a considerable help to us.

The night which we had spent in the hut had been almost unbearable, to us who had been so long accustomed to the fanning of the freshest winds during the time of rest. Confinement was suffocating; but John remarked that we had better sleep inside, as the house had been given us. From whence its horrible effluvium arose I could not conceive; but apparently the dwelling (save the mark!) had not been used for years. Throughout the dismal night the swarming rats squealed and fought. The ends of two candles were still to the fore, so we lit them, and so long as they burned we had a little rest.

On the second night, however, I was determined to try a change, so I cleared the rubbish from beneath a neighbouring tree, and enveloping myself in a blanket lay down with much satisfaction. Mental congratulations, however, were soon disturbed by some of the townspeople who came and intimated that we should go into the hut, to avoid the ferocity of a wolf which came to the town at night, and was very dangerous owing to the freedom of its habits in the way of carrying off bites from the face, such as the nose, chin, and so forth.

In spite of this warning we remained outside; although the protestations of the people were very impressive. I felt, however, that it was better to take our chances in the open air than spend another miserable night in our filthy den overrun with vermin, which seemed to be its natural inhabitants. It is fair to say that next morning I saw a woman who had one eye wholly destroyed, while several other women were very much disfigured in the face, the result of attacks by the wolf spoken of.

A complaint was here made to me that the Inyota men had been causing a disturbance among the young women. Should such conduct be continued there would be fighting between them and the men of the town. It was the satanically black man who made the complaint, which he did in a vehemently expostulatory oration, intended for all whom his voice could reach.

I had no copy of the Mutiny Act to read; but, assembling the Inyota men before me, I said that if they expected either cloth or beads they would have to behave themselves. Failing to do so they would get nothing, and would be sent away without meat or meal. This impressive address was concluded by a few very decided words and penetrating looks, after which the meeting dispersed. I gave the ebony fiend a bottle of brandy to sooth his indignation, and another day was numbered with the past.

During the middle of the night our friend, his satanic majesty, appeared, much under the influence of the medicine which he had evidently partaken of very freely, so that his system had received a violent shock. He thoroughly appreciated the "liquid encouragement" which had upset him so completely, and said, as a matter of course, that he wanted more, more. I told him I had no more; for I was not going to give away the only bottle I had left. After that he succeeded in making himself a successful nuisance, and effectually stopped our sleep for the main portion of the night by his tipsy uproar, although not another drop did he get from my canteen.

Days of hard work, followed by hideous nights, passed

slowly away. Throughout the day work was very hard, for we had to keep the town in meat. At this duty, John and I took turns. Sometimes we spent nights in the forest, which was in every way preferable to the usual resting place. The game was exceedingly shy, and so far from the town, that pursuit entailed long stalks under the burning sun, which glowed through the heated atmosphere, lying like a steam-cloud over the labyrinthine, tropical forest.

Whenever we shot anything, swarms of human vultures crowded around, so that the meat was soon exhausted. As a matter of fact, it would not keep for two days, as it rapidly became offensive.

Flies were literally in myriads. Fortunately the tsetse fly—although swarming in the neighbourhood, and, in fact, throughout all this belt of country between the foothills of the Makomwe mountains and the Zambesi—did not trouble us. In the town it was by no means constant in its attendance; in one place they might be innumerable, but a mile farther east, few could be seen.

It was at this stage that John came to me with rueful tidings for which I was not wholly unprepared. He said that Sagwam, Karemba, and himself were all " veree tired ; they had wandered far from home, and wanted to go back."

"I not want to leave de master," continued John, speaking for himself; " but I must go. I tink of my leetle wife."

" You must stay," was my response to the so-far faithful trio, " at least, until I am able to get boys or to see the king. I can't give you the present I would like to give, because I have but little left."

" But," remonstrated, John, " will the master not come back wid us to Buluwayo ? "

"No, John, I have made up my mind to get to the lakes. I would like to go back and hunt; but I want to see the Zambesi River and the great lake beyond. Besides I think I will shoot more elephants there."

The mention of the coveted animals evidently touched the heart of John, but he said sadly:

"Ah! master, I like to see dat contree var dey say dar es lots of olifant. But I must go back to my leetle wife. Master, I tink I am fighting wid dose dam Mashona when I get to de waggon!"

Trouble was not confined to the "faithfuls." The Inyota men now said that they were tired; that the rains would soon be upon us; that they must get back to their gardens to sow; and above all, that they wished to get back to their women folk. In short, they desired immediately to retrace their steps.

My answer was, that I had sent a messenger to Sakanii, and if they could show a little patience, I would hunt for their meat, and otherwise take care of them until Sakanii should arrive. All I had promised them would assuredly be paid, and they would go back to their wives with cloth. Numerous reports regarding the return of the king, who was sure to have plenty of cloth, were current; so that the belief that I would be able to pay the men was natural.

Fifteen days, however, had elapsed since the messenger had left for the king, and as no reply had come, the spirits of the household were at zero.

John was a pitiful sight. His face reminded me of the seaside-bather's expression when he emerged from the water and found his clothes gone, while some watchful imps of humanity were witnessing his distress with ecstasies of joy. Sagwam, dissolved in tears, drearily prophesied that he would starve, and surely be killed on the way back by the Inyota men, who had threatened many times to carry our hut by assault, as they declared they well knew that the white man had plenty of cloth, although he would not pay. The white man, they said, wanted to keep them until the chief came, and force them to go on to the Zambesi.

Their manner of protesting was curious; one would walk up and down the street in front of the hut, looking very much excited, with his eyes protruding, and all the time haranguing his brothers to the effect that he was going home, that they all must go in fact. For the white man would yet make them go to Kunyungwi. If they refused they would get nothing, and if they went they would get nothing—in fact, they would get nothing anyhow!

They also said that the endunas had lied to me; the king would never come.

Simple as they are, these people never give credit for any good; all are judged as being bad and unworthy of trust, or, like themselves, only actuated by fear or hunger.

Had I shown them the inside of my sacks, I should have been considered weak, so I declared that if they would not take my word, I would not satisfy their demands; especially as I had given them no cause for doubt by any previous dealings.

"Satan" had proclaimed that if disturbances took place the inhabitants would drive the whole party outside the town. These emergencies were met by my reading a special Riot Act, adapted exclusively for the purpose.

One evening, on my return from a hunting excursion—a tolerably successful one, for I was laden with koodoo-meat— Karemba came to meet me, with a face radiant with smiles. Of course I at once thought that Sakanii had arrived. Hurrah! now our troubles would soon be at rest. I would tempt the ruler with glittering English sovereigns. Alas! the king had not arrived; but John had a long story to tell. A number of strangers—messengers from the king—had come to the town.

"And," continued John, "de beeg woman, de moder of de king wants to see de master."

Consequently I followed two men, who took me to the large hut. It was very dark inside, but I was told to go in. As there are no windows in these abodes, I could see nothing on entering. Gradually, however, I could dimly discern the figure of a very old woman, wearing no garments save a waist-cloth, and whose horny skin resembled a bad cigar, when the outer leaf has been removed. The shrivelled old "anatomy" greeted me with some words which I could not understand. She was evidently a native.

"So, ho!" was my half-uttered ejaculation; "if Sakanii's father was like Sakanii's mother, there must have been precious little of the Portuguese about him."

The miserable hut was almost filled with baskets of an immense size, for holding provisions. Two men were sitting beside the old woman. She said they had just arrived from the Zambesi, and that her son would follow on the next day. He was on the road, and as a token of the truth of this statement, she showed me an immense knife, which the men had brought with them; the only way she could tell he was coming, for the old lady's education indicated more of the exercise of the hoe than the wielding of the pen. Her bump of understanding was agricultural to a degree.

While the interview was proceeding, I could not help giving place to the impression that the whole affair was a trick designed to keep me in the town, so that more goods could be had from the too slender store; the people thinking of course that my supply was inexhaustible, and that every word I spoke was utterly untrue. Moreover, they might think that by detaining me they would ensure their supply of meat. If this in reality was their plan, it was not a bad one; but I could not afford to fall out with the old lady.

Returning from her majesty's presence, I found all the boys in a happier frame of mind, Karemba declaring he was so glad that he could hardly keep still. Poor Karemba was the man who had assisted me most during this arduous trip. When I saw his mirthful mood, I could not help thinking what an easy matter it is to be jolly when all around is sunshine.

This faint glimmer of hope and excitement was soon past, and I wandered down to the sandy bed of the Msingua River, where I dug a deep hole, and had a bath. Thus ended another day's proceedings.

I now discovered that "Satan's" real name (by the way not half so appropriate as that which I bestowed upon him) was Vitrine Usigingome. Along with others of his caste, he appeared dawdling in the streets, inviting me to go and drink beer, under the impression, doubtless, that this would keep me in a humour to part with goods more readily. Accompanying the crowd, we soon arrived at the lounging place of these peculiarly lazy men, consisting of a circular grass roof raised upon poles, and a very good dried mud floor, on which a cane mat was placed, where the company lay or squatted to drink pombe for the livelong day. Such is the *dolce far niente* of these half-castes—a life of most repulsive indolence.

And yet they are the progeny of conquerors. As such they must be given due deference by the sons of the conquered, who, when they approach to address them, or to sit in their presence, must go through the odd shuffling of feet, which I have already described.

It disgusted me immensely to see natives who were quite as good intellectually, and physically excelling these creatures, shuffling their feet before their assumed superiors, who are called white men, although it would defy an anthropological wizard to guess their origin, and a nineteenth century Socrates to ferret out the usefulness of their existence. Sometimes, as the poor people would pass them in the street, a shuffling of feet took place, and a clapping of hands, after which salutation the humbler mortals would pass on.

This pitiful servility reminded me of the fawning of the poor Mexican peone (who in every sense of the word is a slave), whom I have seen as he cringed before his lord and master, especially when working for his own countrymen. How the miserable peone kneels to the ground to beg forgiveness for every trivial offence! The sight is enough to make one's hair singe with the heat of the head; it is so abhorrent to see a man kneel before you, or before any other mortal. Bending low the knee to mankind, or to any material form, seems to be the depth of dishonourable humiliation. How infinitely superior is the man who stands erect, and speaks freely, knowing that at best he is only confronting a fellow-being!

On some occasions, by the way, in the valley of the Zambesi, I have witnessed chastisement by the use of the *palmero*. This is an instrument of torture infinitely more effective than our barbarous cat-o'-nine-tails, and an equally important relic of savagery.

The man receiving punishment is made to hold out his hands alternately, so that the operator is enabled to give blows as hard as he can upon the open palms. When the stroke is given, the flesh is drawn into the small apertures of the weapon, so that an excruciatingly painful effect is produced. As soon as the assigned number of strokes has been delivered the victim rolls on the ground cringing before this emblem of Christian authority, to show how thankful he is that his life at least has been spared. Curiously enough, the first cat-o'-nine-tails I saw in Africa was among the furnishings of a Mission station.

But to resume my story. Days passed, and hopes of Sakanii ever coming were dying away. I felt that more active steps would have to be taken. There was positively nothing left even to buy a chicken. Notwithstanding my promises of payment as soon as the king should arrive, the people would not give me anything.

One old man brought me beer, doubtless expecting a great reward in days to come. But we led a wretched life. Misfortunes, however, had a certain quieting effect upon the nerves. The old enduna—Kaparam by name—was a constant visitor, and an irrepressible beggar to boot, although he was earnest as well as arduous in his endeavours to gain a reward in this world, by constantly bringing pombe, with the evident purpose of thawing my heart, so as to draw forth the beautiful flannel blanket I had *not* got. He could not be induced to believe in my absolute want, but had a firm faith in the fancy that copious supplies of pombe would bring out the material truth. Latterly he too turned away his face, probably thinking that I was the closest man he had ever met.

"Satan" and Co. by this time had ceased to invite me to drink beer with them. They also had found out that the "bank was broken."

The Inyota men came and said they were hungry. Forty-eight hours had passed since John had left to hunt, and just after dark he appeared, and I at once saw by his unhappy expression and jaded bearing that he had had bad luck.

Here was a perplexing situation! The people showed they thought that now I would be forced to give them some of the cloth (which it was fondly thought was stored away) to buy some food, although the fact was that I had parted with the last blanket for a basket of meal for them. I felt sure they were hungry, for the meal had been finished three days before. Now there was absolutely nothing left to buy meal or sweet potatoes.

In the afternoon I had sent to "Satan" to say that I wished some chickens, for which I would pay on the chief's arrival; but his answer was that he wished payment on the spot. This is exactly the Kaffir character.

Being now completely at a loss to know what plan to adopt, I went forth to meditate and resolve; but my reflections were disturbed by a very wrathful woman, who happened to be telling her husband something about his character in very trenchant and searching tones. Troubled and despondent, I took up my gun and wandered into the forest, where I managed to shoot some guinea-fowl and francolins, both very shy, being close to the town and hard to get a shot at.

I indulged in a brief meditation, for while in pursuit of the birds I had not ceased to turn over in my mind the most feasible plan of relief, until the time arrived when I had to hurry back to the town before the portals were closed for the night. They are invariably strongly barricaded.

A new resolution was now firm, and I felt I could say truly—

"I have set my life upon the cast,
And I will stand the hazard of the die."

This place was intended neither for man nor beast. I

myself would go forth to endeavour to unriddle the enigma Sakanii.

The only obstacle was the objections of the men. My feet also were full of torture. I went to John, certainly not for a supply of happy inspiration, but to divulge my resolutions on the subject.

It was long after dark. We sat outside the hut. Our conversation was decidedly melancholy in tone, for it must be remembered that John had returned from an unsuccessful hunt.

"Well, John, what shall we do?"

"My gaut, master," said John, shaking his head, "de sugar is done, and de tea is done, and de rice is done, and everyting is done, and dur is no meat, and us shall die from de hunger!"

"No, John," I answered, "there is one course yet left. I must start myself and try to find Sakanii. I will not return until I do find him. In the morning I will tell the old woman that she must give the boys enough to eat when I am gone."

"She shall give nothing midout de cloth," said John prophetically.

"You know I have gone ahead at different times before this and have not failed. By making long marches I ought to reach the river in three days. Help me to get boys early in the morning, for to-morrow I will go. Goodnight."

Again I confronted the old lady, who this time was sitting at the door of her hut smoking a long cigarette rolled in the dried ear of the corn. More than once she put the lighted end in her mouth, but was so thoroughly dried up that she did not appear to suffer.

Explaining the situation, I said that I wished her to

give me four boys to go to the king, as I could not wait longer; also that my men were very hungry, and that I would bring back cloth and make her a good present if she fed them.

"I will give you boys," she said, "but Sakanii is coming: he will be here *this moon!*"

Then, thought I, there is plenty of time to starve.

"The women are making beer," continued the royal mother; "and see! there are numbers of people gathering from Msenga who bring ivory to sell to him. He must come."

The old lady then told some of her Msenga slave-women to carry down meal to my men. Before the sun was half high I was once more ready to take leave of the party. Umfana came with me, and leaving the rest of the household I quitted Chibinga, evidently much to the astonishment of the inhabitants. A great deal of time had been lost, and all manner of reports had been circulated, some of them no doubt with intent to intimidate, but all of so wild a character as to be beyond description. These reports never found credence in my mind. At any rate they had not the effect of checking my purpose. John informed me that the people had declared that they would kill Karemba and himself if I did not return. He evidently thought that I meditated flight.

I took some boys to accompany me for a few miles, in case I might have the good luck to be able to send some meat back to the party.

About a couple of miles' walk brought us to a small opening which ran for some distance back into the dense forest. Here I could see that the boys had observed something, and taking a rapid survey of the ground, I distinguished, at a distance of about one hundred and eighty yards, a fine boar standing beside a sow. Their colour so closely resembled the little scrub which they were vigorously uprooting that it was by no means easy to get a good "sight" on them, and the difficulty was made greater through the fact of their facing me.

However, as they evidently were startled at something I concluded to have a try, even at that long range. Aiming carefully at the head of the boar, I had the satisfaction of seeing that almost simultaneously with the crack of "C. L. K." down he fell, to the unbounded delight of the boys, but greatly to the sow's discomfort, for she made two or three circles at her highest speed, giving out piercing squeals, and then dashing off into the long grass. At once I was off in hot pursuit; for I had the feeling of a veritable savage, seeing that my camp was hungry, while my own little party had a very small supply of meal.

On I sped as quickly as my legs could bear me. I succeeded in "winging" the sow, but just then down I fell suddenly into a deep hole which was covered with the great folds of forest grass. By the time I got up the sow had too much of a start, and managed to get off.

Returning to the scene of the boar success, I found the boys busily engaged in cutting-up. The bullet had indeed gone straight to the mark, for the beast was shot just between the eyes, an achievement which delighted the boys almost as much as it pleased myself, for shots of this kind were far from being invariably successful. While the cutting-up was proceeding, I struck out to discover what further favours of fortune might be in store; feeling that it would be a great advantage to be able to send plenty of meat back to cheer the heart of the disconsolate John, and fill the hankering voids of himself and his companions.

Hardly had I proceeded a hundred and fifty yards from

the busy butchers when I discovered something moving among the trees at an inconsiderable distance off. Immediately hugging the ground, I crept cautiously up, crocodile fashion, and discovered a herd of those most beautiful animals, the Impala antelopes (*Æpyceros Melampus*); but the cover not being sufficient, my presence was soon detected by the objects of the chase—as sharp of eye and fleet of foot as they are lovely in form—and away they sped fast through the forest. Putting my best foot forward, I was soon pursuing in hot haste; but the thorny creeper tripped me up once or twice, tearing the flesh of my hands in a most unmerciful fashion; but in spite of this I succeeded in wounding a fine specimen, with a good head; and, after a further run, managed to bag him. An extraordinary feature connected with these creatures is their wonderful vitality.

Shouting lustily to the boys they soon appeared, and the reader may believe that it was with a glad heart that I sent back a good supply of meat to the party at Chibinga and proceeded on my journey northwards.

When I departed from the town, I left behind the chances of starvation so far as I was concerned personally. Guineafowl—*Kanga Tore*, as the natives called them—francolins, and turtle-doves abounded in enormous numbers on our line of route. Immense flights of small finches swept swiftly through the air. They would rise and fly with great rapidity in one direction, and then suddenly turn back and sweep past us, making a noise like the gust of a lively gale singing through the rigging of a ship. Many large owls were seen, also grey vultures and storks.

The track during the first part of our journey led us through a dense jungle forest of mimosas, acacias, baobabs, various palms, aloes, and tropical grasses, with sharp needle-like points. The black thorns that were strewn on the ground were constantly sticking in the boys' feet, and it is a curious circumstance that although the people belong to this country, and continually suffer from the painful inconvenience spoken of, they are rarely seen making or possessing a pair of sandals of thick hide, or anything that would afford protection to their lower extremities. While out hunting I have noticed how they would avoid the belts of thorny acacias, for the small twig with its stinging point lies unperceived in the short scrub grass, so that it is impossible for them to avoid it.

Soon we arrived at the Mkumbura river, which may be described as a long winding stretch of sand. It forms a very wide road (broadening in some places to three, four, or six hundred yards) through the vast forest, its shifting sands extending to the union with the Umzengaizi river about twelve miles south of the Zambesi. The fall of the river bed is very gentle, so that the silt is not carried off during the rainy season, which is the only time that there is water to be found in it. Here and there on the banks and out in the centre of the arid silt tall reeds of watercane spring up, also beds of spear-grass, whose bristling prickles are as quick as the point of a cambric needle or sharp as the tsetse fly's stab.

Upon these low and dry sands we saw the spoor of almost every description of wild animal. The whole force of an African menagerie had evidently been out in search of water. There was the great spoor of the elephant; the heavy spoor of the rhinoceros, which left holes dug deep in the sand; the spoor of the hyena with its long claws was clearly imprinted beside the clawless signs of the lion which might be devoid of such weapons, judging from the smooth marks it leaves; then we had smaller animals, such as the jackal, the wild cat, and small wolf; while signs of the leopard were very abundant. The red-legged plover was noticed.

Although we saw the spoor of elephants and rhinoceros these animals in reality were very scarce. Koodoo, impala, eland, wild boar, wart hog and many of the smaller antelopes were plentiful. Reed buck were to be seen in scores.

Speaking of the places where the pools of water lay throughout the dry season, the guide informed me that we should have to go some miles further before we reached them.

It was now late and we had had a very hard day; the first on which I had got a real " benefit " from the tsetse fly. The condition of torment which I thought tiresome before, I would now have welcomed as a state of comparative bliss. The heat had been intense. Bathed in perspiration we walked through the shifting sand, which yielded like soft snow under the feet, while the stifling sultry air was literally alive with the tsetse fly, against whose maddening attacks clothes were no protection, our only safeguard being to beat them off with twigs and small branches of shrubs, giving a by no means pleasant exercise under a torrid heat. For the same purpose the natives generally use the tail of a buffalo mounted on a wooden handle, an implement with which they swisk their naked bodies while travelling through the fly-infested country.

Regarding the fly itself, I cannot remember a more faithful description than that given by the late Mr. Thomas Baines in his admirable book "The Gold Regions of South-Eastern Africa." This author remarks :—

" The tsetse is little more than half an inch long, and rather more slender than a common house-fly. The abdomen is marked with transverse stripes of yellow and dark chesnut fading towards the centre of the back, so as to give the idea of a yellow stripe along it; the belly livid white, the eyes are purplish brown, and the wings, of dusky glassy brown colour, slip one over the other, just as the blades of a pair of scissors when closed—so that the tsetse at rest on man or animal may infallibly be known by this one token.

"No fly which rests with its wings half expanded, like the house-fly, or closed together like a pent-house roof, can be the tsetse; but if one is seen in which the wings exactly overlap—one lying flat upon the other—that is 'the fly.' It has six legs, and tufts of hair over its body; its proboscis of piercing apparatus is about one-sixth of an inch long; its sight and smell seem to be keen; its flight straight and rapid. To speak either of its sting or its bite would convey an erroneous idea. The Dutch colonists say it 'sticks,' and this is certainly more correct, as it first pierces the skin with its lancet, and then injects a fluid (poisonous to oxen, horses, and dogs) to thin the blood before drinking it."

Fortunately at night the flies take a rest; but I have felt them "stick" more than once during nocturnal hours. General experience, however, shows that they do not give much trouble after sundown.

Our guide at length cheered us with the news that the long-looked-for oasis had been reached. The goal of bliss which we had anticipated with so much anxiety was a small pool of water. Near at hand, upon the high bank of the river's sapless bed, stood our old skerm which long before had been used by the natives, but whose deserted circle was now overgrown with thick grass.

I pitched my bed cover a little further into the forest on a small patch of open sandy soil with thicket around, and made a fire directly in front of the little tent.

By this time I lived as the Kaffirs lived. So a little porridge of maize meal and some roasted impala haunch formed an acceptable supper, washed down with the water for which we had thirsted so long. The day had been one of the most fatiguing that I had ever experienced; not on account of the distance, but owing to the nature of the ground, the irritating attacks of flies, the intensity of the heat, and the painfully troublesome condition of my shoes, which were brimming with burning sand. Fatigue was by no means confined to myself, for very soon a chorus of resonant snoring told that the whole company had found grateful rest after the discomforts of the weary day.

I had taken no precaution about making a skerm, contenting myself with telling the boys to keep the fires burning. Tired though I was my sleep was uneasy and interrupted. Occasionally when half awake I could hear the low roaring of a lion, the roar seeming to come from a distance. After listening for a little I rolled over, being anxious to find repose.

A strange noise awoke me. Sitting quickly up with my ears on the alert, I heard a sound like a low purr. What was it? An anxious thrill went through me. Owing to uncertainty or the excitement of the moment, I did exactly what I should not have done; but that I did not know till afterwards. I seized the small rifle which lay close by, and crawled out of the diminutive tent as quickly as possible. Before I could get upon my feet, however, a lion passed by, close in front, and with a low growl disappeared in the bush.

This incident I confess took my breath away for a moment; possibly owing to the noise I heard before it "bolted" me from my calico shelter than the actual sight of the monarch of animals. Had I seen him out at the foot of the tent when I awoke I could easily have shot him, for the moonlight was clear. The lion, however, must have been close to my head when I first heard the purring sound

A NIGHT SURPRISE. MKU'MBU'RA RIVER.

The noise I made in getting out—for crawling was the only means of getting from beneath my covering—had evidently startled my midnight visitor.

The reader may imagine what my feelings were when I looked around and saw that the fires were out and not a Kaffir to be seen! I at once grasped the situation. The wretched creatures had left me, and betaking themselves to the shelter of the old skerm, were at that moment all fast asleep huddled up together in a thicket, and perfectly protected, as they had barricaded it with branches. This discovery gave me not a little annoyance. Certainly I ought to have known better; but I was under the impression on going to rest that the boys would sleep round the fire and keep it blazing, and I was usually careful that it was near the entrance to my shelter.

Next morning on examination we found the lion spoor close to the tent. I followed it with the boys for some distance until it was lost in the thicket. After this startling experience I made up my mind that in future no camp should be formed without a skerm, whatever happened, and no matter how tired the company might be.

How uncomfortable are even my memories of the dawn of those miserable days! Remembering the rising sun I seem yet to feel the scorch of its invincible heat. The early glow invariably proclaimed the advent of terribly oppressive days—days for which it would be impossible to find words to describe the utter misery of their tropical torments.*

---

* Since my return I have been much impressed by the fitness for those times of Mr. Edwin Arnold's powerful lines:—

> "Then breaks fierce Day! The whirling dust is driven
> O'er earth and heaven, until the sun-scorched plain
> Its road scarce shows for dazzling heat to those
> Who, far from home and love, journey in pain,
>   Longing to rest again."

As we proceeded on our way wading through the endless sands of the Mkumbura river, under the blistering heat, the tsetse seemed to stick faster and firmer. Sometimes we came upon small pools of stagnant water, where the sand was damp and walking was not so wearying; but where the sand had drifted dry and fine pedestrian progress was laboured and exhausting. The Kaffirs were constantly sitting down, looking as though their last step on earth had been taken.

I questioned the boys as to the ground we had still to cover. Their reply was that if we could reach a small town called Msenza that night, we should at the rate we were travelling be at Chigurindi on the Zambesi next day at noon. If Sakanii was *en route* we should be sure to meet him, as all his boys used the river road, the forest being too dense to pass through direct.

At five o'clock in the afternoon we reached the junction of the Mkumbura with the Umzengaizi river which we had crossed near to its birthplace, away in the lonesome recesses of the Umvukwe mountains, where it was about the size of a little Scottish burn, although here it coursed as a river of about a hundred yards in width. Shallowness was the chief characteristic of the stream, which at no place exceeded a yard in depth, it being the dry season of the year. The rains would not begin until the end of October or beginning of November, two or three months later. At the junction of the channel the width was about four hundred yards, but the Mkumbura had no running water.

Crossing the Umzengaizi we travelled hard, and long after daylight had departed we halted beside the small town of Msenza. Inquiries were there made whether anything was known of Sakanii, and to my unbounded delight and astonishment I was told that the object of our anxious and weary search was resting in the town with a large party of followers.

I at once sent word that I was near at hand and had come with a view to seeing him. When the boys returned Umfana's (my interpreter) face was aglow with joy at our having encountered the important man we were in search of, and in whose hands our fate might be said to rest. Umfana stated that the king would be glad to see me.

I then made my way to the enclosure, inside of which were numerous huts. At one end of the enclosure beneath the canopy of a sunshade hut I found the all-important Sakanii, whose figure was distinct in the ruddy light of a fire and two candles.

Candles! Here was civilisation absolute! What other luxuries I wondered would be there to fill me with astonishment?

King Sakanii received me most courteously. At a rapid glance I could see that he travelled in as comfortable a way as possible. I had a depressing consciousness that he looked upon my condition as being somewhat dilapidated. He asked me curious questions. Replying to one of them —" How I travelled? "—I clearly astounded him by saying that I had been on foot for months, and that I had arrived from Chibinga in less than two days. Of course I told him that it was impossible for me to bring any animals here for fear of the "fly."

Sakanii then proceeded to tell me of some of his excesses in the way of comfort. He was carried; he only walked a little for the sake of his health. I should see in the morning how nicely his people ran along with him, drumming and singing happily, ever active as long as there was a noise.

"If you are not too tired," he said, "we will start in the

morning. I am going to Chibinga, and have plenty of cloth and beads to buy ivory from the Msenga people."

We could get on fairly well in conversation, but he was a difficult man to understand. He was very dark in complexion, but his features were good. His figure was slight and active. He informed me that he claimed the country we were in, and also had a town called Chigurindi on the Zambesi. The town was situated between Zumbo and the mouth of the Umzengaizi river.

Sakanii's father was named Vicente Rubero de Fonséca, which also was his own name, although the natives called him Sakanii. His mother was the old native lady, my friend at Chibinga, of whom I have already spoken.

Coffee was made, and it seemed to me to be the most refreshing beverage I had ever imbibed; it had the effect of an enlivening tonic, and invigorated my mind with brighter prospects. I felt as though I could reach Chibinga in a day, although the distance was over fifty miles by the course we had taken.

A number of the natives who accompanied Sakanii were of the Wazezurus (of the Banyai family), as they are termed by the Portuguese. They knock out the upper incisors between the eye teeth, the deprivation giving them a singularly hideous appearance.

At Msenza I was within half a day's journey of the Zambesi, this being the second time—the first was at Chuzu's—I was near the great river, although fate decreed that I should see its waters from yet another point. But even if it had not been necessary to return to Chibinga to fulfil my contracts with the boys, I could not have canoed down the river to Tette on account of the Kebrabasa rapids. Step by step I would have to tread the old tracks back to Chibinga—and then? *Nous verrons.*

Early in the morning the beat of the batuka (drum) announced that the time for departure had arrived. A biscuit and a cup of coffee formed our hasty matutinal meal, after which the novel caravan went on its way to Chibinga. After crossing the Umzengaizi river we renewed our acquaintance with the soft yielding sand of the bed of the Mkumbura river. Much to my amazement the men who bore Senhor Rubero de Fonséca in his *machilla*,* ran quickly and almost with gusto through the sand, although it gave way under their feet at every step, and the perspiration in beading streams rolled over their shining ebony skins. Noise was essential in these abnormal efforts of energy. The more the drums were beaten, the greater the spirit displayed by the bearers in quickening their pace. Under such conditions the Kaffirs have very strong staying powers; noise influencing their progress just in the same way as music lightens the feet of dancers. The party progressed under the piercing heat of a fiery sun, which, glaring from a cloudless sky, certainly made the day the hottest I had spent in all my life. The dazzling effect of the glistening white sands was as powerful against the eyes as the blinding reflections of snow-covered regions.

Sakanii's party had a good start, for until I had given myself a good hour's work progress was very slow. But after warming to the task, and in spite of my shoes being full of sand, the pain became less, and I hobbled along like a "six-days-go-as-you-please" man. There was no stopping. To cool off would be ruinous, and would involve much difficulty in getting into swing again. When the *machilla* bearers rested I would pass them, so that on the whole

* The pole was a choice piece of bamboo about four and a half inches through and thirteen feet in length, covered with zebra hide, with wreath-like wrappings of zebra mane at each end of the pole.

we were pretty equal; I making as good time as I could do, for five-and-twenty miles would have to be covered before night, and I was determined to reach our destination simultaneously with the other party.

Bodily pain told that I was a fitter subject for the *machilla* than its occupant, Senhor Rubero.

The tsetse were not so bad as they had been on the previous day. Nevertheless they kept our arms busy all the while. In the afternoon there came towards the banks of the river numerous wart hogs, impala in great numbers, and koodoo. In the bed of the stream I saw a herd of reed buck (*Cervicapra arundinacea*). It is a marvellously beautiful sight to see these animals leaping away in rapid retreat, one after the other bounding high in the air with quickly impulsive and yet remarkably graceful leaps.

Camp-making formed a very lively scene. Compared with my small escort, the sight of a force of eighty picked followers busily at work was quite imposing. When I pitched my small, and, by that time, rather filthy little bed-cover, the contrast between it and Senhor Rubero's sumptuous residential marquee was so marked that the sight occasioned no slight merriment. Laughter rang out on all hands, and I at once had an invitation from the king to share space with him, which I accepted, although I was very well satisfied with my humble but serviceable cover.

Similar experiences and trials were encountered next day, the tsetse being particularly diligent. Evening, however, showed that we had a good record of miles left behind, reducing the distance to Chibinga to ten miles, which we arranged to cover next morning.

My mind had a feeling of airy gladness when I thought that I should now be in a position to satisfy the expectations of my long-suffering men before they set out on their return homewards, and to show that after all there was a possibility of meeting some one foreign to them who would keep his word.

As yet I had not revealed to my new friend Senhor Rubero what my wishes were with regard to the boys; but in the evening, as we sat comfortably imbibing our coffee upon a cane mat and surrounded by numerous camp-fires, which shed a warm and cheerful light upon the scene, I told him where I had come from, and what my intentions were with regard to future movements. I informed him that all my boys were going to leave me here, and that I hoped I could rely upon his assistance in finding men to proceed with me upon my journey. I also asked for some coffee. His reply was that he could give me men, but only a little coffee, as he had brought with him but a small quantity for his own use; such a luxury, as a matter of course, having no sale among the Kaffirs.

Long before daybreak I was up and on the march. I wanted to get a good start of my friend, whose constant relays of *machilleiros* permitted a running pace to be kept up, altogether too fast for me under the circumstances.

The morning air was cool, and I made a good gap between us before Rubero succeeded in striking his tent and getting under way. We crossed fresh spoor of the rhinoceros (black). Something like the excitement of a race inspired the onward movement, but I knew that we should soon be overtaken. I listened with a keen ear, and gradually the faint rumble of drums could be heard in the distance, becoming more audible and swelling louder and louder until the pursuing party came in sight and were upon us.

Now, however, the evenly poled walls of Chibinga were visible in front. In dense masses the inhabitants swarmed out of the town. As they excitedly rushed forward in mad exultation, the *machilleiros* shouted with a new vigour, and drums were beaten with redoubled energy, ceaselessly encouraging the heated throng which moved helter-skelter towards the town. All together we arrived in the plaza of Chibinga just as the hands of my watch touched the hour of nine. Right in front of us was Senhor Rubero's house. We had been away for four days and four hours, and had covered a hundred miles of ground. This statement is given as a fact, not as a feat.

END OF VOLUME I.

LONDON: PRINTED BY WILLIAM CLOWES AND SONS, LIMITED, STAMFORD STREET
AND CHARING CROSS.

www.ingramcontent.com/pod-product-compliance
Lightning Source LLC
Chambersburg PA
CBHW032351230426
43672CB00007B/666